A Meal in a Minute

Annette Wolter

A Meal in a Minute

Nelson

Thomas Nelson and Sons Ltd
36 Park Street London WIY
4DE
PO Box 18123 Nairobi Kenya

Thomas Nelson (Australia) Ltd
597 Little Collins Street
Melbourne 3000

Thomas Nelson and Sons
(Canada) Ltd
81 Curlew Drive Don Mills
Ontario

Thomas Nelson (Nigeria) Ltd
PO Box 336 Apapa Lagos

First published in Great Britain
in 1974

ISBN 0 17 147154 7

Printed by Smeets/Offset,
Weert, Holland.

Contents

Recipes Grouped in Categories

The figure in brackets gives the time (in minutes) it takes to prepare the dish; the figures behind refer to the page on which you find the particular recipe.

Soups

Salads

Snacks

Fish and Shellfish

Recipes Grouped in Categories

Foreword

The less time you have the more important it is to use it to the best possible advantage. This goes as much for cooking as it does for everything else and the purpose of this book is to show all lovers of good food that employing their time in the kitchen most economically need not necessarily lead to a lowering of culinary standards. Given a little streamlining and some confidence in modern methods, the housewife, however hard-pressed she may be for time, can still produce mouth-watering meals. They will, of course, be vastly different from a slap-up five-course dinner, but no less enjoyable for that. Moreover, these modern meals, consisting of no more than one or two dishes and prepared in accordance with present-day standards of dietetics, are not only more nutritious but certainly kinder to the stomachs of your guests than those monster meals of times past. To help you plan your menu according to the time you have available, all cooking times have been clearly indicated throughout the book, while in the Recipe Category index you will find the number of minutes you have to spend in the making of each item. You should thus have no difficulty in composing a menu to your liking without the risk of running out of time.

Suppose you choose as your main dish some fried or grilled meat and a salad or two to go with it, you may have to restrict yourself to either a soup or a dessert, the time factor making it impossible to serve both.

The recipes section is divided into three groups according to the length of time the dishes take to prepare. Thus you may like to choose a soup or dessert from the section containing dishes that take no more than five to ten minutes, having decided to spend most of the time you have available on your main dish. Alternatively, you may wish to spoil your family or guests by putting before them a 25-minute dessert, so you choose a main dish which requires correspondingly less time to get ready.

Next to the recipes you will find three kinds of symbol: they give some idea of the degree of difficulty of the particular recipe, the cost involved in making the dish and whether it is suitable for deep-freezing. For definitions of these symbols see page 16.

Annette Wolter

Helpful Hints

Those with little time to spend on preparing meals must think logically and know how to organise themselves. The time factor should enter into your calculations the moment you start planning your meal, and when it comes to buying the ingredients thinking in terms of time should take precedence over considerations of cost, though don't, of course, neglect commonsense: for instance it's not only cheaper to buy fresh onions and peel and chop them yourself rather than purchase them fully prepared but it takes very little time to do.

There is an ever-growing range of ready foods, such as canned and ready-peeled tomatoes and preserved peppers in a jar, or already cleaned vegetables like carrots which need only be washed quickly under cold running water. Other time-savers are the frozen vegetables, potato chips, mashed potatoes and many others which need only to be cooked. In the cans and jars, even the cooking has been done for you, while salads, too, are nowadays available in jars, ready to be put on the table as they are. Furthermore, making use of sliced bread, sliced sausages and cans of cooked meat saves much precious time.

If, therefore, shortage of time compels you to choose between taking your family to a restaurant and making use of some convenience food you happen to have at home, the second alternative is surely not only cheaper but also preferable from the health point of view.

There's no reason why meals produced in minutes rather than hours should be any less well turned out than meals for gourmets, provided the cook has learned to streamline her work in the kitchen and chosen her equipment and utensils with care — who has, in short, made a hobby of producing meals in minutes as well as a duty.

Useful Tips

The first thing to do when starting work is to determine which part of your meal takes longest to get done. Your calculation must, of course, allow not only for the actual cooking time but possibly also for the time it takes for the cooked dish to cool, and maybe to set. The dish taking the longest time is the first to get under way, so it may well be that you have to start with the dessert. Let's assume you have decided to make a raw vegetable salad. In this case you begin to mixing the dressing. This done, you clean and grate the vegetables, put them straight into the dressing, cover the salad and allow it to marinate. Housewives practising the art of streamlined cookery may find it saves time if they prepare certain parts of the meal well in advance — during the odd moments when they are engaged on some other routine occupation. And why shouldn't potatoes, rice or noodles cook in the morning while the lady of the house is dressing, or at night while she's settling down with some bed-time reading? After all, the 20—25 minutes she can save in this manner count for quite a lot in a tight cooking schedule.

Helpful Hints

A kitchen-timer will remind you when it's time to take your saucepan off the stove, to drain and cool the cooked potatoes, rice or noodles and put them in the refrigerator ready for later use.

It's a good tip, by the way, always to have hot water available; it's invariably needed while cooking is going on, if only to wash your hands, to wash up some utensil or other or for some dish in process of preparation – so if you don't have any running hot, put the kettle on!

If the meal you are planning requires very little time to prepare, it's advisable to pre-heat the electrical equipment you need; this will save you unnecessary waiting.

If the oven is not required it might as well be used at its lowest setting, to warm the plates. But if it is needed the plates should be warmed for at least ten minutes in very hot water.

Before starting work, get all the required ingredients and utensils together. In this way you not only avoid wasting time looking for things but run less risk of forgetting something.

Put some kitchen paper in a convenient place on your working surface for your rubbish, which can then be quickly disposed of when you have finished. Get accustomed to using any spare moment to wash up straightaway any utensils you have done with. This way you will have only the plates, cutlery and glasses to deal with when the party is over (should you be the fortunate possessor of a dishwasher, you can, of course, put any of the used utensils currently into it).

Don't be afraid to make ample use of the deep-frozen food you find at your local shop – though make sure that its deep-freeze chest is kept in good working order! You can tell whether it is by looking at the inside walls of the chest and the outside of the packets stored in it. Both walls and packets should be entirely free of ice-crystals. Nor should the food be stacked above the load line of the chest. The storage temperature should be minus 18°C. One way of checking the temperature

Arrow indicates load-line; nothing must be stored above it!

is by applying the 'ice-cream test': ice-cream becomes soft at the slightest increase in temperature above minus 18°C. All you have to do is take one of the ice-cream packets and press it gently. If it yields to the pressure of your thumb you can be sure that the chest is not cold enough.

Should this be the case, mention it to your retailer, for it's quite possible that he can rectify the fault.

Deep-frozen fish, meat and poultry are suitable for the purposes of rapid cooking only if cut in slices or pieces small enough to thaw quickly during the process of cooking. Whole birds, large fishes or big pieces of meat take a long time first to defrost and subsequently to cook and are therefore usually unsuitable for streamlined cooking. Exceptionally, it may be possible to cook a joint or whole bird a day in advance without loss of time, for, as a rule, the cooking process itself requires no supervision. In such cases the joint or bird need be carved only and re-heated on the day it is served.

Helpful Hints

Labour-Saving Devices

There are nowadays a great many labour-saving devices on the market which will help you to cut down the time you have to spend in the kitchen. It's assumed, of course, that you already have an electric or gas stove with oven, a refrigerator and all those essential pieces of kitchen equipment like saucepans, frying-pans, bowls, sieves and colanders, chopping boards, ladles, scoops and a set of knives.

A deep-freeze is indispensable for cooks in a hurry in that it enables them to keep a generous store not only of industrially-frozen food but also of individually-selected food which may be fresh or already cooked by you.

Among the things you may safely keep in your deep-freeze for later use are: sliced bread, cake, table-ready dishes, soups, vegetables and desserts. Even salads can be stored thus for short periods. Blocks of industrially-produced frozen food can be cut through if only part is required at any given time (this operation is best done with a special, serrated knife).

Frozen fruit for a dessert may be taken out of the deep-freeze the evening before it is needed and transferred, well-covered, to the refrigerator for defrosting. Deep-frozen berries make a delicious sauce for cold puddings or ice-cream. You defrost them in a few minutes by heating a little butter in a saucepan and adding the berries.

Leftovers of rice and pasta keep for months in the deep-freeze. If wanted, you simply thaw them in a sieve over steam. Leftovers from the day before may be kept in the refrigerator for reheating the next day.

The toasting grill (electric spit-roaster) is a valuable aid to rapid cooking. With it, frozen food, whether bought or home-produced, is thawed and heated in next to no time. Bread and rolls can also be easily thawed and at the same time toasted if put under this grill. It's also useful for browning open sandwiches, small sausages, slices of meat and fish and small parts of poultry as well as fruit, all of which are quickly done under the toasting grill. You will soon appreciate how much more useful this type of grill is for producing quick meals than the large electric grill more suitable for the bigger joints and whole birds and which takes too much time to be of much use to a housewife intent on getting her meal done in minutes rather than hours.

The pressure cooker reduces the normal cooking time to a third. Anyone who has a pressure cooker is, therefore, able to include in her repertoire dishes which, if produced in the traditional manner, would take too long. Besides, no nutritive substances get lost in a pressure cooker, which has the additional advantage that

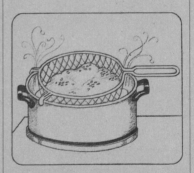

Rice or pasta leftovers are heated in a sieve over steam

you can cook several things in it at the same time. Moreover, the pressure cooker brings out the specific taste of all food better than other methods of cooking and tends to preserve its consistency. All pressure cookers work on the same principle, and manufacturers will supply you with detailed instructions on how to use their make; most of them also let you have a collection of tested recipes.

A deep-fat fryer — and particularly an electric, automatically-functioning one — will also help you to get dishes

Helpful Hints

Grill

done surprisingly quickly.
Thanks to the fact that the
food is totally immersed in hot
fat, the cooking process is
remarkably fast while at the
same time preserving most of
the nutritive substances con-
tained in it. Use, therefore, the
deep-fat fryer not only for the
popular chips but also for fried
potatoes, meat or fish cutlets,
thin steaks and meat balls —
whether breadcrumbed or not
— as well as for chopped vegetables and pastries. For deep-

frying use only vegetable fat
and always sufficient to cover
your fry completely. Its temperature should be between
175 and 200°C (330—350°F).
The frying process completed,
you let the little particles sink
to the bottom, before carefully draining off the still hot
fat from the sediments. The
same fat must not be used
more than six times for deep-
frying; thereafter it can still
be used for shallow frying.
An electric liquidizer makes
work easier in any kitchen, but
especially where the emphasis
is on time-saving. A liquidizer,
provided its motor is strong
enough, is capable of
fragmenting practically everything, starting from cube
sugar, which it turns into
castor sugar, through vegetables for salads and fruit for
desserts to homogenizing
dishes made of curd cheese,
dessert creams, soups, purées
and mixing drinks.

Whether the liquidizer is a
separate piece of equipment or
an attachment to a mixer,
serving various purposes, is
immaterial, but should the
latter be the case you most
probably also have another attachment — a vegetable grater
— which enables you to grate
or slice larger quantities of raw
vegetables, and very useful it is
too.
A hand-mixer, whether part of
an all-purpose mixer or a
separate utensil, is another
indispensable piece of equipment you will need to stir your
cake-mixtures and to whip the
whites of egg or cream.
Another useful utensil is a pair
of multi-purpose scissors.
True, all food packages, of
whatever material they are
made, carry instructions on
how to open them. Frequently, however, something goes
wrong with the opening
mechanism, leaving only
one way out — a strong

Pressure Cooker

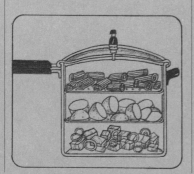

Deep-Fat Fryer

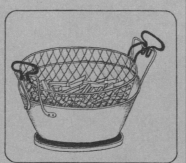

Electric Deep-Fat Fryer

pair of scissors. Such scissors have an additional advantage in that they also serve as bottle-openers and pincers.

Any housewife intent on streamlining her kitchen chores will find it pays to invest in an electric can-opener which should be firmly fixed in an easily accessible spot. Such an electric opener copes with cans of all kinds and is sure to fulfil a useful function in any kitchen, but especially in those where the saving of time is the first consideration. The kitchen-timer, by telling you that what you have on the stove or under the grill is done, not only helps you to keep exactly to the timetable you have laid down for yourself but also enables you to do something useful while you're waiting for the cooking to finish. Whether you stay in the kitchen or go to another room to do some ironing or write a letter, you can always take your 'pinger' with you; it's sure to preserve you from mishaps that are bound to occur in the best-organised kitchens.

You'll find that a measuring beaker comes in handy when it's a question of quickly measuring liquids or smaller quantities of dry ingredients. A small mixing bowl is a useful vessel in which to mix water and flour without producing lumps.

An egg-slicer is better than the sharpest knife in that it cuts a hardboiled egg into neat, even slices in one single operation.

The Herb-Mill chops all fresh herbs quickly, though not as finely as a knife, but this is a minor blemish for which cooks in a hurry may be forgiven. Incidentally, fresh chives are best cut with the

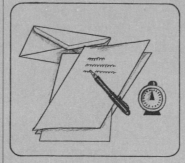

Kitchen-timer

kitchen scissors direct into the salad, the soup or into a cup.

A mandolin or vegetable-grater is not rendered superfluous by the electric vegetable cutter, for it's not worthwhile to assemble the latter if it's merely a question of cutting a small quantity of vegetables or a single fruit.

Good peeling knives, capable of peeling potatoes, cucumbers, carrots or other vegetables, are a 'must' in any kitchen, while small fire-proof dishes or bowls in which to serve individual portions straight from the oven are highly desirable, for they open up many mouth-watering possibilities.

Aluminium foil, film and kitchen-paper are useful aids for cooking, storing and disposing of kitchen waste.

Sensible Buying For Stock

Obviously the greater the variety of convenience foods you have ready to hand, the less restricted you will be in the choice of meals you can offer your guests at a moment's notice. The variety of convenience foods you are able to store in readiness for sudden, unexpected calls on your culinary skills and inventiveness depends, therefore, to a large extent on the available storage capacity and the care with which you utilize that capacity. It's assumed, of course, that being a sensible housewife you carry adequate stocks of such ingredients as flour, rice, sugar, salt, pepper, eggs, some kind of pasta, instant beef and chicken stocks.

You are also more than likely to have laid in some soups, whether canned or in powder

Helpful Hints

form, but maybe you haven't chosen them with quite enough care. Let me illustrate what I mean by an example: ready-prepared tomato soups are available in many different forms — in bags, packets and cans; they are, besides, produced by a multitude of different manufacturers. They all differ in taste: one product may taste deliciously of tomatoes, whereas another brand may have the colour of tomatoes but its flavour is less pronounced. They will probably differ considerably in price. Yet all are bought, which proves that each particular make is fancied by some section of consumers; so before laying in a stock of whatever it is, go in for a little market research and try a number of brands to decide what is the best buy from your point of view.

Nor do two identical labels on a bag of powdered soup necessarily mean their contents are the same. In France, for instance, a well-known brand, produced under the same label in Italy, is considered by some French housewives to be noticeably different and they insist on buying the version marked 'imported from Italy'.

Fortunately, the number of households possessing a home-freezer is rapidly increasing, and this is probably the greatest blessing that modern technology has conferred on busy housewives in recent times. The happy possessor of a deep-freeze will have no difficulty in stocking up for her meals-in-a-minute. For most of the vegetables, fish and meat items she need go no further than her corner shop or local supermarket. Recently-published figures show that freezer-owning homes spend on average three times as much on frozen foods as those without freezers. This trend is likely to accelerate thanks to the growing popularity of specialist freezer-food centres — a field of food retailing which some of the larger retail chains are about to enter in a big way. In these freezer-food centres you can buy what you require in larger quantities at much lower prices. You would, therefore, be well advised to watch out for one of these centres being opened in your vicinity.

There is little point in trying to enumerate the many desirable deep-frozen items you should keep in stock. Flick through the many recipes in these pages and you're sure to get a pretty good idea of what you are likely to need. If you don't yet possess a deep-freeze you'll have to go on depending on cans, jars, bottles and airtight cellophane packets, containing slices of ham or bacon, sliced or grated cheese, ground coffee, instant mashed potatoes and powdered soups — in short, a great many foodstuffs that can be easily stored in any conventional larder.

Finally, a list of what to buy in the way of beverages: beer, mineral water, fruit and vegetable juices; red and white wine, some champagne, German Sekt or other sparkling wine. Instant chocolate and coffee powder, coffee beans, tea, rum, brandy, raspberry brandy or kirsch, some sweet wines and sherry, a few aperitives, a bitter cordial and one or two liqueurs.

The Recipes

The meaning of symbols accompanying the recipes:

All recipes are for four people.

△ The recipe is easy to follow

△△ The recipe is not quite so easy. You should, therefore, strictly adhere to it.

△△△ The recipe assumes your readiness to carry out somewhat more difficult or complicated operations with patience.

○ The suggested dish is not costly to make

○○ The dish is in the medium price range

○○○ The dish is relatively expensive

* The cooked dish keeps fresh for four weeks, if frozen at a temperature of minus 35°C (-31°F) and stored at minus 18°C (0°F)

** The cooked dish in its deep-frozen state will keep for up to three months, if stored at minus 18°C (0°F)

*** The suggested dish, if deep-frozen, keeps for 9—12 months, provided it is stored at minus 18°C (0°F)

Tomato Soup, Cream of Chicken Soup, Cream of Asparagus ▷ Soup, Pea Soup, Potato Soup — recipes on pages 18—20

In 5 to 10 Minutes

Tomato Soup Ursula
△ ○

1 can cream of tomato soup,
containing 4 portions
1 cup diced white bread
1 tablespoon butter
1 generous pinch garlic
powder
1 tablespoon parsley

Heat cream of tomato soup at moderate temperature, according to instructions on the can. Heat butter in a frying-pan. Fry the white bread in it till light brown, turning continually. Dust the 'croutons' — as these small fried bread cubes are called — with garlic powder. The parsley is sprinkled over the soup just before serving.

Illustration on page 17

Recommended Variations of Tomato Soup

Every canned tomato soup can be improved in one of the following ways:

• By putting a small can 140 g (5 ozs) of shrimp or crab meat into it before heating.
• By cutting 100 g (3½ oz) of lean bacon into strips and warming them up in the soup.
• By slicing 2 to 4 pairs of

Vienna sausages and warming them up in the soup.
• By frying diced onions and some sliced Szegedin sausage (or any other heavily-smoked sausage) and adding these to the soup.
• By improving the soup with some soured cream and a generous pinch of paprika.

Cream of Aspargus Soup
△ ○ ○ * *

1 can cream of asparagus
soup, containing 4 por-
tions
1 jar or can artichoke bot-
toms
1 tablespoon butter
1 tablespoon cream

Cover contents of can before heating it at moderate temperature. Put artichoke bottoms into a saucepan, together with 2 tablespoons of liquid; add butter, cover and steam at low heat. When the soup is cooked, stir in cream, pour into cups or individual bowls and add the steamed artichokes with the butter.

Illustration on page 17

Potato Soup 'Chicago'
△ ○ * *

1 can or bag potato soup
(4 portions)
1 onion
1 pepper
1 tablespoon butter
1 can corned beef

Following the instructions on bag or can, cover up soup and heat it over low heat. Peel onion and cut into rings. Wash pepper, remove pips and also cut into rings. Heat butter and lightly fry pepper and onion rings in it. Dice corned beef and heat up in soup. Before serving in individual bowls or plates, garnish with onion and pepper rings.

Illustration on page 17

Suggested Variations of Potato Soup

Any prepared potato soup, whether canned or powdered, can be varied in one of the following ways:
• By adding to it some slices of frying sausage and 2 to 4 tablespoons of cream.
• By enriching with lightly-browned bacon dice and ¼ to ½ cup of canned sweet-corn.

18

In 5 to 10 Minutes

• By heating in it 1 cup frozen peas and adding 100 g (3½ oz) ham, cut in strips.
• By putting into it ½ cup diced carrots (canned or frozen) as well as a few slices of 'Bockwurst' (a continental smoked pork and beef sausage).

Curried Cream of Chicken Soup

1 can cream of chicken soup (4 portions)
300g (11 oz) frozen peas
100g (3½ oz) cream
1–2 teaspoons curry powder (according to taste)

Following instructions on can, cover soup and heat at low temperature. Add frozen peas, replace lid and let cook over low heat for another 5 minutes. Whip cream till stiff, folding curry powder into it. Serve in cups, having garnished each cup with 1 tablespoon of curried cream.

Illustration on page 17

Possible Variations for all Cream Soups

All ready-prepared cream soups, whether of the asparagus, poultry, mushroom, cauliflower or celery variety, can be enriched in one of the following ways:
• By stirring a little cream into the soup and garnishing it with 4 tablespoons of frozen parsley.
• By adding 1 cup of diced boiled chicken meat or veal and a few pepper strips from a jar.
• By adding a small can of asparagus tips, 4 tablespoons of canned tomatoes, cut into slices, and 4 tablespoons white wine.
• By adding 100 g (3½ oz) smoked meat, cut in fine strips and 1 cup of frozen peas.

Cheese Bouillon – recipe above

Cheese Bouillon
△ ○

¾ litre (1½ pt) water
3 level teaspoons instant stock
2 pieces processed cheese
4 tablespoons canned, peeled tomatoes
2 tablespoons frozen chives
2 tablespoons ready-roasted onions from a bag

Bring water to boil, take off the fire and dissolve instant bouillon in it. Flake cheese into it and, while stirring, let cheese dissolve. Cut tomatoes into somewhat smaller pieces and put them, together with the chives, into the soup. Sprinkle roasted onions over it, before serving.

Illustration below

19

In 5 to 10 Minutes

Debreczin Pea Soup
△ ○

1 can creamed pea soup
1 tablespoon cream
1 tablespoon ready-roasted
  onions from a bag
2–4 'Debreczin' sausages
  (small, heavily-smoked – a
  Hungarian speciality)
2 tablespoons frozen chives

Heat creamed pea soup, according to instructions, at low temperature, keeping saucepan covered. Add cream, ready-roasted onions and Debreczin sausages, letting them warm in the soup. When hot, the sausages should be cut up and returned to the soup. Garnish with chives before serving.

Illustration on page 17

Curry Cream Soup
△ ○

¾ litre (1½ pt) instant meat
  stock
1 tablespoon oil
2 level teaspoons flour
2 cups apple purée from a jar
  or can
1 teaspoon butter
2 level teaspoons curry
  powder
100g (3½ oz) cream
2 tablespoons preserved
  peppers

Prepare instant broth according to instructions. Heat oil in a rather large pot, stir in flour and, while continuing to stir, make a roux. Slowly pour instant stock into pot and, while still stirring, let come to boil several times. Add the apple purée to the soup and let it get warm over low heat. Melt butter in a small casserole, heat curry powder in it and add this curry and butter mixture to soup, which is now ready to be rounded off with the cream and taken off the fire. Finally, chop up paprika and use as garnish before serving.

Illustration on Facing page

Consommés with Various Garnishes

Consommés are clear soups the basis of which is in every case the same and which being concerned with rapid results, you can produce by bringing ¾ litre (1½ pt) of water to the boil and dissolving in it 3 level teaspoons of instant meat or chicken stock. You may possibly wish to add a little more instant stock to give the liquor a slightly stronger taste, before proceeding with one of the following garnishes:

Ham and Peas Garnish
△ ○

Cut 100 g (3½ oz) of lean boiled bacon into strips. Put 150 g (5½ oz) of frozen peas into saucepan, cover and cook for 6 minutes. Add consommé liquor and heat in it the ham strips. Enrich with a dash of sherry and sprinkle some parsley over soup before serving.

Egg Thickening
△ ○

2–3 eggs are whisked with a pinch of pepper and salt and stirred into the prepared meat stock. Garnish with chopped parsley or chives.

Tomato Bouillon
△ ○

For this you prepare only 5/8 litre (1¼ pt) of stock. Chop 2 cups canned tomatoes into small pieces and heat up in the prepared liquor. You then add 1/8 litre (¼ pt) cream and sprinkle some chopped parsley over the soup.

Curry Cream Soup – recipe on this page; Corned Beef on ▷ Toast – recipe on page 23

Bouillon with Marrow Dumplings
△ ○ ○

Heat canned marrow dumplings in the prepared stock. Sprinkle chopped parsley or chives over soup before serving.

Herb Bouillon
△ ○

Peel and dice 3 hardboiled eggs and heat them in the prepared stock. Stir into it 1 cup mixed herbs just before serving.

Carrot Bouillon
△ ○

Wash, clean and grate finely 2 large carrots, adding the grated carrots straightaway into the prepared stock. Bring to the boil. Round off with a little cream and pepper.

Bouillon with Rice
△ ○

Add 4 tablespoons of 5-minute rice to the water intended for the bouillon, cook for 5 minutes, before adding your instant stock (instead of the rice, you could use some pre-cooked pasta). You may possibly like to enrich the bouillon with some finely-chopped beef or chicken (leftovers). Garnish with some chopped herbs.

Choux-Paste Pattie Soup
△ ○

Heat up the choux-paste patties (which you can buy ready-prepared) in your consommé.

Egg Bouillon

Prepare the consommé in the usual manner, put 1 egg yolk into each individual soup bowl or cup, pour bouillon over it and garnish with parsley.

Spinach Soup
△ ○

¾ litre (1½ pt) milk
A pinch each of salt and pepper
300–450g (11–16 oz) frozen spinach
2 egg yolks
½ cup cream
A pinch garlic salt
4 tablespoons grated cheese

Put salt and pepper into milk and bring to boil; put block of frozen spinach into it, cover saucepan and cook at moderate heat for 8 minutes. Stir together egg yolks, cream and garlic salt; take soup off the heat, before stirring the egg and cream mixture into it. Serve soup in bowls or cups with grated cheese sprinkled over it.

Bread Rolls with Scrambled Egg – recipe on facing page

In 5 to 10 Minutes

Mock Goulash Soup
△ ○

½ litre (1 pt) instant meat
    stock
1 tablespoon butter or
    margarine
300g (11 oz) minced meat
A pinch each of paprika and
    pepper
1 heaped tablespoon flour
¼ litre (½ pt) canned tomato
    juice
2 level teaspoons ready-
    roasted onions from bag
1 cup cream
2 tablespoons chopped pars-
    ley

Prepare instant meat stock in
usual manner. Heat butter or
margarine in a rather large
saucepan and lightly fry
minced meat in it, turning it
constantly to get it uniformly
brown. Sprinkle paprika,
pepper and flour over the meat
and keep stirring until ingredients are likewise slightly
fried. Fill up slowly with instant stock and, while continuing to stir, bring to boil
several times. Now stir in the
tomato juice, roasted onions
and cream and heat up once
more. Garnish with parsley
before serving.

Rapid Bean Soup
△ ○

400g (14 oz) canned haricot
    beans
250g (9 oz) canned peeled
    tomatoes
½ litre (1 pt) canned tomato
    juice
¼ litre (½ pt) dry white wine
½ teaspoon salt
1 level teaspoon chilli powder

Drain kidney beans. Chop
peeled tomatoes. Mix the
tomato juice with the white
wine, pour mixture into a
saucepan, add beans and
chopped tomatoes, season
with salt and chilli powder,
cover and heat at moderate
temperature.

Bread Rolls with Scrambled Eggs
△ ○

4 teaspoons butter or marga-
    rine
2 eggs
A pinch each of salt and pep-
    per
4 small round bread rolls
4 slices meat sausage
    (Mortadella type)
1–2 tomatoes

Melt half the butter or margarine in a frying-pan; stir together eggs, salt and pepper.

Pour into the hot butter or
margarine, stir gently until
eggs are scrambled. Halve
bread rolls and spread remaining butter or margarine
on them. Now lay meat sausage slices on bottom halves,
cover with some of the
scrambled egg and place upper
halves of rolls on top. Wash
tomatoes, cut them into
eighths and put them around
the rolls.

Illustration on facing page

A good follow-up to *Rapid
Bean Soup* (recipe in adjoin-
ing column). Serve with
Diplomat Salad (recipe on
page 32).

Corned Beef on Toast
△ ○

4 slices toasting bread
2 tablespoons oil
4 slices corned beef
4 eggs
A pinch each of salt and pep-
    per
8 anchovy fillets
1 tablespoon small capers

Lightly toast bread. Heat oil
in a rather large frying-pan
and fry the slices of corned
beef on both sides. Place
corned beef slices on the toast
and keep warm. Fry the eggs,

sprinkle salt and pepper on them, lay one fried egg each on the four slices of corned beef, topping up each piece of toast with anchovy fillets and a few capers.

Illustration on page 21

Serve after *Curry Cream Soup* (recipe on page 20) and together with *Simple Tomato Salad* (recipe on page 32).

Banana Toast Sally
△ ○

4 slices toasting bread
2 bananas
1 teaspoon lemon juice
200g (7 oz) sliced Cervelat sausage (a sausage made of mixed pork, beef and bacon)
3 tablespoons mayonnaise
A pinch each of salt and paprika
½ teaspoon mustard
1 teaspoon tomato ketchup
2 teaspoons chopped parsley

Lightly toast bread slices. Peel and dice bananas and sprinkle lemon juice over them. Cut Cervelat sausage, first into

strips and then into cubes. Mix together mayonnaise, salt, paprika, mustard, tomato ketchup and parsley and add this mixture to the diced bananas and sausage; then distribute it over the 4 slices of toast.

A good follow-up to *Spinach Soup* (recipe on page 22), it goes well with *Chicory Salad* (recipe on page 30).

Sardines on Toast 'Cox'
△ ○

4 sprigs parsley
12 stuffed olives
4 slices toasting bread
1 large apple (Cox Orange)
1 teaspoon lemon juice
4 teaspoons butter or margarine
8 filletted sardines in oil

Wash and drain parsley. Pass olives under cold running water and likewise drain. Lightly toast bread slices. Peel and grate apple, sprinkling lemon juice over it. Spread butter or margarine on toast and sprinkle the coarsely-chopped parsley over it. Cover with the grated apple and lay 2 of the sardine fil-

lets on each slice of toast. Now slice the olives and distribute over the toast.

A good follow-up to *Cheese Bouillon* (recipe on page 19), it goes well with canned vegetable juice.

Toast Tatar
△ ○ ○

4 slices wholemeal bread
2 tablespoons butter or margarine
1 teaspoon anchovy paste
400g (14 oz) Tatar (raw minced steak)
2 egg yolks
¼ teaspoon each of salt, pepper and paprika
A generous dash Worcester sauce
4 anchovies
Some small capers

Lightly toast bread slices. Mix butter or margarine with the anchovy paste and spread mixture on the toast. Mix the Tatar with the egg yolks, salt, pepper, paprika and Worcester sauce and spread on the buttered toast. Garnish each piece of toast with a rolled-up anchovy and a few capers.

24

In 5 to 10 Minutes

Sauerkraut on Toast

△ ○

1 liqueur glass whisky
1 level teaspoon cayenne
4 slices lean uncooked ham
   (of the size of the toast)
4 slices of toasting bread
1 level teaspoon sugar
8–10 tablespoons canned
   sauerkraut
4 slices blue-veined cheese
   (also of the size of the
   toast)
4 cocktail cherries

Heat oven or grill to maximum temperature. Mix whisky with the cayenne, turn ham slices in the liquor and let them marinate for a short while. Lightly toast the bread. Take ham out of the marinade and dab them dry. Now stir marinade together with the sugar and brush the toast slices with that mixture. Place the ham slices on the toast, the sauerkraut on top of the ham and the blue cheese on top of that. Put in oven or under grill until cheese begins to melt. Garnish each toast slice with a cocktail cherry.

Illustration below

To precede, try *Vanilla Ice-Cream with Fruit Sauce* (recipe on page 45).

Sauerkraut on Toast – recipe above

In 5 to 10 Minutes

Festive Scampi
△ ○ ○

1 tablespoon butter or
  margarine
4 eggs
A pinch each of salt and pep-
  per
4 not too small slices of white
  bread
4 slices smoked salmon
12 cooked scampi
½ jar caviar substitute

Melt butter or margarine in
frying-pan. Whisk together
eggs, pepper and salt and
pour mixture into the melted
butter or margarine; turn
gently until set. Distribute
scrambled eggs on the slices
of bread. Turn smoked salmon
into 4 cornets, placing one on
each bread slice. Place scampi
into centre of each open
sandwich, covering each with a
little caviar substitute.

Illustration on facing page

Try as second course to
Marrow Dumpling Soup
(recipe on page 22), and follow with *Nut Mousse*
(recipe on page 44).

Simple Egg on Toast
△ ○

4 nice lettuce leaves
4 slices wholemeal bread
4 teaspoons sandwich spread
4 hardboiled eggs
4 tablespoons curd cheese
  from skimmed milk
1–2 teaspoons grated horse-
  radish
A pinch each of salt and pep-
  per
A few drops Worcester sauce
A little tomato ketchup

Briefly wash lettuce leaves
under cold running water and
drain them. Lightly toast
wholemeal bread slices;
spread sandwich spread over
them. Peel eggs and slice
them with egg slicer.
Place salad leaves on bread
slices and the egg slices
on top of that. Stir to-
gether curd and horseradish,
seasoning to taste with salt
and pepper and a sprinkling
of Worcestor sauce, and pour
this mixture over the egg
slices (you might wish to
cream the curd with a little
milk). Decorate each slice
with a spot of tomato ketchup.

A good Follow-up to *Rapid
Soup* (recipe on page 23), try
it with *Cucumber Salad
Imperial* (recipe on page 30).

Fillet of Smoked
Ham on Toast
△ ○ ○

4 slices wholemeal bread
200g (7 oz) smoked ham
  fillets
4 teaspoons butter or marga-
  rine
1 square Gervais cheese
2 tablespoons canned milk
¼ teaspoon curry powder
1 teaspoon ginger syrup
A generous pinch cayenne
A generous pinch salt
4 small pickled cucumbers

Lightly toast bread slices. Cut
ham into small strips. Spread
butter or margarine on toast.
Stir together the cream
cheese, canned milk, curry
powder, ginger syrup, cayenne
and salt and spread on the 4
slices. Place ham strips on top.
Cut pickled cucumbers fan-
wise, placing one on each
toast.

Following with *Tomato
Bouillon* (recipe on page 20),
try eating it with *Salad Exotica* (recipe on page 31).

In 5 to 10 Minutes

Toast 'Surprise'
△○

400g (14 oz) canned ragoût
   fin (cooked veal)
1 teaspoon butter or margarine
4 slices toasting bread
4 dashes Worcester sauce
2 tablespoons chopped parsley
4 tablespoons breadcrumbs
2 tablespoons grated cheese
2 tablespoons flaked butter

Heat stove to 250°C (450°F
or gas mark 8) or grill to maximum temperature. Heat
ragoût fin together with the
butter or margarine in a small
casserole at moderate temperature for 2 minutes. Lightly
toast bread and lay ragoût fin
on it, sprinkling Worcester
sauce and chopped parsley
over the slices. Mix breadcrumbs with the cheese and
place mixture on top of
ragoût fin. The flaked butter
is put on top of the lot which
is then grilled for 4 minutes in
stove or under grill.

It goes well with *Simple Tomato Salad* (recipe on page
32); as dessert serve *Yoghurt
Cream 'pour vous'* (recipe on
page 45).

Roast Pork
Sandwich △○○

8 thin slices white bread
4 teaspoons butter or margarine
8 thin slices roast pork
2 slices canned pineapple
1 tablespoon mayonnaise
1 teaspoon grated horseradish
½ teaspoon chilli powder
1 teaspoon tomato ketchup

Thinly butter white bread
slices before putting pork slice
on each. Halve pineapple
slices by cutting them through
horizontally and distribute
them over the four sand-
wiches. Mix mayonnaise with
the horseradish, chilli powder
and tomato ketchup and fill
this mixture into the centre
of the pineapple rings; cover
the sandwiches with the remaining bread slices.

A good follow-up to *Carrot
Bouillon* (recipe on page 22),
serve with spiced tomato
juice.

Hawaii Toast
△○

4 large lettuce leaves
4 slices toasting bread
4 teaspoons butter
2 teaspoons grated horse-
   radish
6 tablespoons shredded pineapples
2 tablespoons mayonnaise
1 teaspoon mango chutney
5 tablespoons curd cheese
2 level teaspoons paprika
8 slices ham, large enough to
   cover the toast

Wash and dry lettuce leaves.
Lightly toast the bread. Mix
butter with horseradish and
spread on the toast. Mix 4
teaspoons of the grated pineapples with the mayonnaise,
mango chutney, curd cheese
and paprika. Now lay on each
bread slice 1 lettuce leaf and
then 1 slice of ham; spread
the mayonnaise-curd cheese
mixture on the ham and put
another ham slice, on which
you have distributed the remaining pineapple, on top of
that.

A good follow-up to *Herb
Bouillon* (recipe on page 22),
serve with green salad.

In 5 to 10 Minutes

Colourful Bread Rolls △○

8 Vienna sausages
4 fresh bread rolls
8 thin slices of cheese
About 4 tablespoons pickled
  red peppers in strips
8 nice lettuce leaves
1 tube remoulade sauce

Place sausages in boiling water and leave them to simmer for 5 minutes. Preheat oven to 250°C (450°F or gas mark 8) or grill to maximum temperature. Cut open bread rolls. Lift sausages out of the hot water, drain them a little and cut them in half. Place 2 sausage halves on one half of each roll, covering with a slice of cheese. Garnish with the red pepper strips and bake in oven or under grill till cheese begins to melt. Wash and dry lettuce leaves before placing the toasted sandwiches on them. Garnish each roll with a dot of remoulade sauce.

Illustration on this page

Serve with spiced tomato juice and follow with *Wine and Lemon Mousse* (recipe on page 43).

Rapid Rarebits △○

4 teaspoons butter or marga-
  rine
4 slices toasting bread
250g (9 oz) grated cheese
4 tablespoons light ale
2 teaspoons mild mustard
1 teaspoon Worcester sauce

Preheat oven to 250°C (450°F, gas mark 8) or grill to maximum temperature. Heat butter or margarine in a frying pan and fry the 4 bread slices in it, but on one side only. Mix cheese with the beer, mustard and Worcester sauce and spread the resulting mixture on the 4 slices, which you grill for 5 minutes.

To follow: *Mock Goulash Soup* (recipe on page 23).

Colourful Bread Roll – recipe on this page

Springtime Toast △○

4 large lettuce leaves
4 slices wholemeal or black
  bread
4 teaspoons butter or marga-
  rine
1 teaspoon anchovy paste
2 large tomatoes
150 g (5½ oz) table-ready
  cottage cheese with herbs

Wash and dry lettuce leaves. Lightly toast bread slices. Knead butter or margarine together with anchovy paste and spread on the toast. Wash, dry and slice the tomatoes and put on the toast. Place the cottage cheese on top of the tomatoes.

Serve with celery salad. Recommended first course: *Ham and Peas Bouillon* (recipe on page 20).

In 5 to 10 Minutes

Green Salad with Mayonnaise Sauce
△ ○

1 head of lettuce
2 tablespoons mayonnaise
2 tablespoons canned milk or cream
2 tablespoons wine vinegar
¼ teaspoon sugar
¼ teaspoon salt
½ teaspoon paprika

Separate lettuce leaves, remove imperfect leaves and larger ribs and tear remaining leaves into small pieces. Wash several times and dry. Mix mayonnaise with the milk or cream, the vinegar, sugar, salt and paprika and stir gently into the lettuce.

Green Salad Variations

Instead of the mayonnaise you may like to use lemon juice, salt, sugar and orange or pineapple juice as salad dressing. Alternatively, you may prefer a dressing, made up of some 80 g (3 oz) Danish Blue cheese, mixed together with ½ cup cream, 1 teaspoon lemon juice and a generous dash of pepper.

Cucumber Salad
△ ○

1 small fresh cucumber
1 beaker yoghurt
Salt and pepper to taste

Wash and finely slice cucumber unpeeled on a mandolin. Mix with the yoghurt, season to taste, serve immediately.

Emmental Cheese Salad
△ ○

100g (3½ oz) canned luncheon meat
200g (7 oz) Emmental cheese in a piece
2 hardboiled eggs
4 tablespoons yoghurt
2 tablespoons mayonnaise
A generous pinch each of sugar, salt and paprika
2 teaspoons lemon juice
1 teaspoon mild mustard
2 tablespoons chopped chives

Cut luncheon meat and cheese into dice or strips of equal size. Peel eggs and dice likewise. Mix yoghurt with mayonnaise, sugar, salt, paprika, lemon juice and mustard and stir this dressing gently together with the salad ingredients. Sprinkle chopped chives over salad.

Chicory Salad
△ ○

200g (7 oz) chicory
2 bunches radishes
½ fresh cucumber
1 tablespoon oil
1 tablespoon wine vinegar
1 tablespoon apple juice
1 tablespoon orange juice
½ teaspoon salt
¼ teaspoon pepper
2 tablespoons chopped parsley

Cut off hard stalks of the chicory, halve the larger heads and wash several times, then drain. Cut into slices. Clean radishes, wash and slice them. Wash and slice cucumber unpeeled. Mix oil with the vinegar, apple and orange juice, the salt and pepper and stir together with salad ingredients. Sprinkle over the chopped parsley and then lightly toss the salad once more.

In 5 to 10 Minutes

Salad Exotica
△ ○

1 head of lettuce
2 tomatoes
1 banana
2 teaspoons lemon juice
1 cup grated celeriac from can
    or jar
3 slices canned pineapple
2 tablespoons oil
2 tablespoons canned pine-
    apple juice
2 tablespoons grated nuts
½ teaspoon salt
1 tablespoon chopped parsley
½ walnut kernel

Separate lettuce leaves, cutting out any hard bits. Pluck
leaves into small pieces and
wash them several times before drying them thoroughly.
The tomatoes are then washed, dried and cut into eighths.
Peel and slice banana and
sprinkle lemon juice over it.
Mix the lettuce with the tomato eighths, the banana and
the grated celeriac. Cut pineapple slices horizontally,
keeping back one of the

slices. The remaining slices are
then cut into small pieces and
mixed under the other salad
ingredients. Mix oil with the
pineapple juice, grated nuts,
salt and chopped parsley and
gently mix with the salad.
The remaining pineapple slice
is placed in the centre of the
salad bowl and the walnut
kernel half in the middle of
the pineapple slice.

Illustration below.

Salad Exotica – recipe above

In 5 to 10 Minutes

Shrimp Salad Yalta
△ ○ ○

*4 large lettuce leaves in
perfect condition
250g (9 oz) canned or deep-
frozen shrimps
2 hardboiled eggs
1 slice canned pineapple
½ teaspoon lemon juice
1 tablespoon canned milk or
cream
A pinch sugar
4 tablespoons French dressing
(a ready-prepared spicy
sauce)*

Wash and dry lettuce leaves.
Separate the shrimps, briefly
wash them under cold running
water and drain. Peel and dice
eggs. Dice pineapple slice likewise. Stir together lemon
juice, cream or milk, sugar as
well as the French dressing
and add the mixture to the
salad ingredients. Place the
lettuce leaves on 4 plates and
arrange the shrimp salad on
them.

Serve with toast; a good follow-up to *Cream of Curry
Soup* (recipe on page 20).

Simple Tomato Salad
△ ○

*4 large tomatoes
1 onion
¼ teaspoon each of pepper
and salt
1 tablespoon oil
1 teaspoon lemon juice*

The tomatoes are washed,
dried and cut into thin slices,
and the onion peeled and
finely diced. Arrange the tomato slices on a plate and
sprinkle salt, pepper and diced
onion over them. Mix oil and
vinegar and pour over salad.

Diplomat Salad
△ ○

*8 tablespoons canned shred-
ded pineapples
8 tablespoons grated celeriac
from a jar
4 tablespoons mayonnaise
2 tablespoons canned pineapple juice
¼ teaspoon each of salt and
white pepper
2 tablespoons coarsely-
chopped walnuts*

Mix pineapple with the celeriac and the mayonnaise
with the pineapple juice, salt
and pepper. Gently mix the
two together. Sprinkle the
walnuts over the salad.

Bean Salad as Appetizer
△ ○

*1 cup canned haricot beans
½ cup pickled peppers
½ cup grated celeriac from jar
100g (3½ oz) thin slices of
cheddar cheese
4 tablespoons mayonnaise
1 teaspoon wine vinegar
½ teaspoon mustard
A dash Worcester sauce
¼ teaspoon salt*

Drain canned haricot beans.
Chop up peppers. Drain celeriac. Cut cheddar slices first
into strips and then into dice.
Stir together mayonnaise,
vinegar, mustard, Worcester
sauce and salt. Add dressing
to the salad and mix well.

Serve with wholemeal bread;
a good second course to *Egg
Bouillon* (recipe on page 22).

In 5 to 10 Minutes

Macédoine Salad
△ ○

400g (14 oz) canned macé-
  doine of vegetables
200g (7 oz) meat sausage
½ beaker yoghurt made of
  skimmed milk
3 tablespoons mayonnaise
1 teaspoon lemon juice
¼ teaspoon sugar
½ teaspoon salt
¼ teaspoon white pepper
A dash tabasco sauce
2 tablespoons chopped parsley

Drain macédoine in a sieve.
Cut sausage into cubes of
even size. Stir together the
mayonnaise with the yoghurt,
lemon juice, sugar, salt and
pepper, the tabasco and the
chopped parsley, and gently
stir this dressing into the meat
and vegetable ingredients.

It goes well with *Rapid Rarebits* (recipe on page 29) or
Simple Egg on Toast (recipe
on page 27).

Tatar with Pickled Delicacies
△ ○ ○ ○

400–600g (14–22 oz) Tatar
  (raw minced steak)
Some small capers
1 jar mixed pickles
4–8 cornichons from a jar
4–8 tiny, slightly soured,
  corn-cobs
4 teaspoons caraway seeds
4 teaspoons chopped parsley
  or chives
Salt and pepper to taste

Tatar with Pickled Delicacies — recipe above

In 5 to 10 Minutes

Arrange Tatar on 4 individual plates and around it in small heaps the capers, mixed pickles, cornichons, mini corn-cobs and caraway seeds, as well as the chopped parsley or chives. Serve salt and pepper separately. Everyone can thus season his Tatar to his own taste and choose from among the various garnishes the ones he likes best.

Illustration on page 33

Serve with wholemeal or farmhouse bread; a good follow-up to *Choux-Paste Pattie Soup* (recipe on page 22).

Coconut Ham
△ ○ ○

4 slices boiled ham, weighing 100g (3½ oz) each
2 tablespoons butter
4 teaspoons canned shredded pineapples
4 teaspoons grated cheese
4 teaspoons grated coconut

The ham slices should be heated on both sides for 2 minutes in the butter at moderate temperature in a frying-pan with a lid on. Distribute the shredded pineapples over the ham and then sprinkle the cheese and grated coconut over the pineapple layer. Replace the lid and fry the ham slices for a further 5 minutes without turning them.

Serve, possibly as a second course to *Debreczin Soup* (recipe on page 20), with

'Spirited' Skewers — recipe on facing page

In 5 to 10 Minutes

French bread and lettuce salad.

'Spirited' Skewers
△ ○ ○

4 skewers with pieces of fillet
*   of beef already stuck on*
1 tablespoon dripping
1 level teaspoon curry powder
½ teaspoon paprika
A generous pinch each of salt
*   and pepper*
2 tablespoons soya sauce
1 tablespoon kirsch
1 tablespoon sherry
1–2 tablespoons tomato
*   ketchup*

Heat dripping and fry the skewered meat at high temperature for 1 minute, turning constantly. Season with the curry powder, paprika, salt and pepper and continue frying process as well as the turning for a short time longer. Pour 1–2 tablespoons hot water on the meat juice in the frying-pan and stir to loosen any sediment. Now stir soya sauce, the kirsch and sherry into it and allow to get hot. Finally, add tomato ketchup and keep stirring until sauce thickens. Arrange skewers on a platter, serving sauce separately.

Illustration on facing page

It goes well with either *Lettuce Salad with Mayonnaise* (recipe on page 30) or *Simple Tomato Salad* (recipe on page 32).

Cocktail Skewers
△ ○

16 canned cocktail sausages
100g (3½ oz) streaky bacon
*   rashers*
24 pearl onions from jar
4 cocktail cherries
2 tablespoons oil
2 level teaspoons paprika

Preheat oven to 250°C (450°F or gas mark 8) or grill to maximum temperature. Cut cocktail sausages in half. Put on each of the skewers in turn: half a sausage, a rolled-up bacon rasher and a pearl onion, repeating the process till there is only room on the skewers for a cocktail cherry. Stick that on. Now brush with oil and sprinkle the paprika over the skewers. Place them on the upper sliding tray in the oven or put them under the grill and cook them on all sides for 5 minutes.

Serve with *Chicory Salad* (recipe on page 30) and sticks of French bread.

Breadcrumbed Sausage Slices
△ ○

4 slices meat sausage, weigh-
*   ing about 80g (3 oz each)*
1 heaped tablespoon flour
1 egg
4 tablespoons breadcrumbs
2 tablespoons dripping

Turn the sausage slices first in the flour, then in the whisked egg and lastly in the breadcrumbs. Heat fat in a frying-pan and cook the sausage slices on both sides for three minutes.

It goes well with *Horseradish Purée* (recipe on page 68) and *Chicory Salad* (recipe on page 30).

Garnished Vienna Sausages
△ ○

8 Vienna sausages
4 thin slices of cheese
8 thin but long bacon rashers
1 tablespoon oil
Tomato ketchup to taste

Cut the Vienna sausages half open lengthways. Halve the cheese slices, fold each half and put into the openings of the sausages. Wrap each sausage in a bacon rasher, fastening it with a wooden toothpick. Heat oil and fry the sausages at fierce heat on all sides, turning them constantly until they are crisp and brown. Offer tomato ketchup separately so that anyone who wants it can help himself.

It goes well with *Quick Potato Salad* (see page 66) or bought potato salad or beetroot from a jar.

Recommended dessert: *Apple Snow with Kiss* (recipe on page 44).

Black Pudding with Egg
△ ○

300g (11 oz) black pudding
2 tablespoons oil
4 eggs
2 tablespoons ready-roasted onions from a bag
A pinch each of salt and pepper per egg

Slice black pudding and fry in half the oil on both sides till crisp. Heat roasted onions together with the black pudding in the liquor. Use remaining oil to fry eggs and season them with salt and pepper. Arrange the black pudding together with the roasted onions

either on a platter or on individual plates, placing a fried egg on top.

Serve with wholemeal bread and bought vegetable salad, and as dessert try *Pears with a 'Kick'* (recipe on page 44).

Fillet of Veal with Tomatoes
△ ○ ○

1 tablespoon oil
4 rounds of filleted veal, each weighing 75g (2½ oz)
½ teaspoon salt
A generous pinch pepper
4 tomatoes

Heat oil in a frying-pan and fry the veal fillets on one side only for 4 minutes. Mix salt and pepper; wash and dry tomatoes and cut them in half. Sprinkle some of the salt and pepper over the veal rounds, then turn them and let them cook for a further 4 minutes. Put some salt and pepper on the tomato halves and fry them for 4 minutes with the veal rounds. Put what is left of the salt and pepper on the fillets before serving.

Serve with toast and frozen peas. A suitable dessert would be canned stewed apricots.

Filled Roast Beef Rolls
△ ○ ○ ○

1 jar mixed pickles
½ jar sweet-sour cucumbers
½ cup pickled peppers
500g (18 oz) roast beef in slices

Part of the mixed pickles, the sweet-sour cucumbers and the pickled peppers are chopped and placed on the roast beef slices which are then rolled up. The remainder of the pickled vegetables are served separately.

Illustration on facing page

A suitable follow-up to *Bouillon with Rice* (recipe on page 22); serve with sticks of French bread or wholemeal bread.

36

Filled Roast Beef Rolls – recipe on facing page 37 ▷

In 5 to 10 Minutes

Mexican Meat Balls
△ ○

4 meat balls (bought ready-
   prepared)
1 tablespoon oil
2 tablespoons butter or margarine
6 tablespoons mini corn-cobs
   from can or jar
4 tablespoons pickled peppers
2 tablespoons cream or canned
   milk
1 level teaspoon paprika
A pinch each of salt and pepper
1 tablespoon tomato ketchup

Heat meat balls in the oil at
moderate temperature for 8
minutes, turning them frequently. Heat butter or margarine in a small casserole;
add the mini corn-cobs with a
little of their liquid and heat
them likewise, stirring gently.
Chop the pickled peppers
coarsely and mix them under
the corn cobs. Stir together
the cream or canned milk with
the paprika, salt, pepper and
tomato ketchup; add these to
the corn-cobs and heat the lot
right through. Arrange the
meat balls on a preheated
platter or on individual plates
and cover with the corn-cobs.

Serve with *Rapid Potato Salad*
(recipe on page 68) or wholemeal bread. A suitable dessert:
*Vanilla Ice-cream with Fruit
Sauce* (recipe on page 45).

Smoked Pork Chops in Apple Sauce
△ ○ ○

4 smoked pork chops (already
   cooked), each weighing
   100–120g (3½ –4 oz)
2 tablespoons butter or margarine
½ cup instant meat stock
1 cup canned apple-purée
4 tablespoons cream or canned
   milk
A pinch each of salt, pepper
   and ground ginger
A dash Worcester sauce

Smoked pork chops are a
German speciality which you
may be able to buy ready-
cooked in a delicatessen shop.
They consist of pickled and
slightly-smoked pork chops
and are a delicacy worth trying.
Heat pork chops in the butter
or margarine on both sides at
medium temperature; take
them out and keep warm. Stir
together the instant meat
stock with the apple purée,
cream or canned milk, the
salt, pepper, ground ginger
and Worcester sauce, add to
the fat in the frying-pan and
stir until well-heated. Serve
the chops in the sauce on a
preheated platter.

Goes well with instant mashed
potato (made of powder) and

Cucumber Salad (recipe on
page 30); For a suitable
dessert try a fruit yoghurt.

Orange Liver
△ ○ ○

3 oranges
500g (18 oz) calf's or chick-
   en liver
1 tablespoon herb mustard
About 2 tablespoons flour
1 tablespoon oil
2 tablespoons butter
1 liqueur glass bitter orange
   liqueur
½ teaspoon salt

Halve oranges and squeeze
out juice. Slice liver and
thinly spread herb mustard
all over; turn the slices in the
flour, shaking off superfluous
flour. Heat oil in frying-pan
and fry liver slices on both
sides for at most 6 min-
utes. Take liver out of frying-
pan and keep warm. Add
orange juice, butter and
liqueur to the fat left in the
pan, stir and allow to thicken
a little. Salt liver slices and
serve with the sauce poured
over them.

Goes well with instant potato
purée and green salad. A
suitable dessert is ice-cream
from the deep-freeze.

Paprika Chicken (bottom of page), Ravioli with Vegetables ▷
(top) – recipes on page 41

In 5 to 10 Minutes

Sausage Goulash 'Lyon' △○

*500g (18 oz) 'Lyon' sausage
(any other meat sausage,
particularly Mortadella,
will do)
1 onion
1 jar mixed pickles
2 tablespoons oil
10 tablespoons tomato ketchup
A dash vinegar
A pinch each of salt, sugar,
pepper and dried marjoram*

Skin and dice sausage. Peel and dice onion. Drain and coarsely chop mixed pickles. Heat oil in a saucepan and lightly fry onion cubes and mixed pickles in it. Add to the onions and mixed pickles the tomato ketchup, vinegar, salt, sugar, pepper, dried marjoram and the diced sausage, stirring well. Cover the sausage goulash and heat at moderate temperature for a further few minutes.

Goes well with instant mashed potatoes or sticks of French bread; a suitable dessert: ready-bought curd cheese dessert.

40   Sausage Goulash 'Lyon' — recipe above

In 5 to 10 Minutes

Paprika Chicken
△ ○ ○

1 onion
2 tablespoons butter or margarine
2 level tablespoons flour
400g (14 oz) canned peeled tomatoes
2 cups pickled peppers
1 cup deep-frozen peas
1 canned chicken
¼ teaspoon salt
A generous pinch each of pepper and paprika
$^1/_8$ litre (¼ pt) soured cream

Peel and chop onion. Heat butter or margarine in a rather large pot; lightly fry onion in it. Dust flour over onions and while stirring lightly fry it also. Pour the peeled tomatoes and their liquid into the pot, mix well and heat. Add peppers and frozen peas, cover and cook at moderate temperature. Cut chicken into individual portions and warm it up in the sauce. Mix salt, pepper, paprika together with soured cream and stir into the sauce at the last moment.

Illustration page 39

Goes well with instant potato purée or boiled potatoes. Recommended dessert: instant cold pudding with canned stewed berries.

Ravioli with Mixed Vegetables
△ ○

1 large can ravioli in tomato sauce
400g (14 oz) canned macédoine of vegetables
$^1/_8$ litre (¼ pint) soured cream
100g (3½ oz) grated cheese
2 tablespoons chopped parsley
2 tablespoons flaked butter

Preheat oven to 250°C (450°F; gas mark 8). Fill oven-proof dish with a layer of ravioli, then a layer of vegetables and, finally, another layer of ravioli. Pour soured cream over it. The grated cheese comes next. The parsley is then sprinkled over, and the flaked butter is finally distributed over the surface. Put ravioli into oven for ten minutes or till cheese is golden brown.

Illustration on page 39

Best eaten with *Salad Exotica* (recipe on page 31) or bought celeriac salad. Recommended dessert: *Orange Surprise* (recipe on page 44).

Chicken Liver Ragoût △ ○

2 cups canned peeled tomatoes
200g (7 oz) canned button mushrooms
4 tablespoons butter
2 tablespoons ready-roasted onions
500g (18 oz) chicken liver
1 level teaspoon cornflour
½ teaspoon salt
¼ teaspoon pepper
½ cup cream or canned milk
3 tablespoons chopped parsley

The tomatoes and the button mushrooms are drained in a sieve. The liquor from both cans is mixed with water to make up ½ litre (1 pt). Heat butter and warm roasted onions in it; add chicken liver and, while constantly turning, let it fry on all sides at medium heat for 4 minutes. Mix the cornflour with a little of the liquor, the salt and the pepper. Add the rest of the liquor, the tomatoes, the mushrooms and the cornflour to the liver, mix well and bring to the boil several times, while stirring. Take ragoût off the stove and round off with the cream or canned milk and the chopped parsley.

In 5 to 10 Minutes

Serve with sticks of French bread or five-minute rice or *Simple Tomato Salad* (recipe on page 32). As dessert serve fresh fruit according to season or *Apple Snow with Kiss* (recipe on page 44).

Fried Eggs on Bacon
△ ○

1 tablespoon oil
8 rashers bacon
8 eggs
½ teaspoon salt
¼ teaspoon pepper
4 slices wholemeal bread (optional)

Heat oil in frying-pan; fry rashers in it till crisp. Break egg into a cup and let it slip onto the bacon in the pan; repeat process 8 times. Season them with pepper and salt and let them fry until the white has become firm. Arrange the slices of wholemeal bread on 4 plates and transfer 2 fried eggs with the bacon underneath to each of the bread slices.

A possible variation: in place of the bacon you may like to fry some diced ham, on which you pour the beaten eggs for scrambling. In this case, garnish with some chopped parsley.

Goes well with ready-prepared carrot salad or *Emmental Cheese Salad* (recipe on page 30). Recommended dessert: instant chocolate pudding.

Tomato Pancake
△ ○

400g (14 oz) canned peeled tomatoes
100g (3½ oz) streaky bacon in rashers
4 eggs
4 level tablespoons flour
4 tablespoons milk
½ teaspoon salt
1 tablespoon butter or margarine
¼ teaspoon pepper
1 tablespoon ready-roasted onions
2 tablespoons chopped parsley

Drain tomatoes in a sieve. Coarsely chop bacon and render down at low heat in a covered pan. Stir eggs together with the flour, milk and salt to a thick running batter (you may possibly have to add a little water). This pancake mixture is now poured over the crispy bacon and allowed to set for a few minutes. The drained tomatoes are distributed over the still runny pancake mixture, seasoned with

the pepper and garnished with the roasted onions and the chopped parsley. Replace the lid and cook the lot at low heat for a further 5 minutes. Serve on a preheated dish.

Goes well with black or white bread and *Macédoine Salad* (recipe on page 33). As dessert: fruit yoghurt or curd cheese from the deep-freeze.

Quick Paprika Goulash
△ ○

400g (14 oz) canned goulash
200g (7 oz) sliced tongue
4 large potatoes cooked in their jackets
1 cup pickled peppers
2 tablespoons ready-roasted onions
1 level teaspoon paprika
4 tablespoons cream or canned milk
2 tablespoons chopped parsley

Put the goulash into a rather large pot, cover and heat up over low heat. Cut the slices of tongue first in strips and then in dice. Peel potatoes and cut them in small slices. Stir diced tongue, potato slices, peppers and roasted onions into the goulash, replace lid and allow to get hot.

Stir the paprika and chopped parsley into the cream or canned milk and mix with the goulash before serving.

Goes well with *Salad Exotica* (recipe on page 31) or *Cucumber Salad* (recipe on page 30). May be followed by *Peach Curd* (recipe on page 48).

Wine and Lemon Cream
△ ○ ○

$^1/_8$ litre (¼ pt) white wine
$^1/_8$ litre (¼ pt) water
1 small packet lemon-flavoured pudding powder

1 beaker skimmed-milk yoghurt
$^1/_8$ litre (¼ pt) whipped cream (optional)
½ lemon
1 tablespoon chopped pistachio nuts

Mix white wine and water (both should be at room temperature) and pour mixture into a bowl. Pour pudding powder all at once into the liquid and stir vigorously for 1 minute with a whisk. Add the lemon essence (which you find in a separate capsule in the pudding packet) as well as the yoghurt. Pour the wine and lemon cream into 4 glasses. Garnish with whipped cream, stick some very thin slices of lemon into the cream and sprinkle the grated pistachio nuts over it. This cream becomes stiffer the longer it is allowed to set; it tastes best when still in a semi-soft state.

Illustration below

A tip: When you have children among your guests replace the white wine with water. For any weight-watcher the whipped cream had better be replaced by canned berries.

Wine and Lemon Cream — recipe on this page

In 5 to 10 Minutes

Apple Snow with Kiss
△ ○

Juice of ½ lemon
3 egg whites
2 level tablespoons glucose
1½ cups canned apple purée
2–3 teaspoons preserved
    cranberries

Whisk egg whites into a stiff snow before strongly stirring glucose into it. Mix apple purée with lemon juice and fold under the snow. Fill four glasses or bowls with the apple snow and garnish each portion with a dab of cranberries.

Fruit Cocktail with a Kick
△ ○

2 cups canned fruit cocktail
½ teaspoon lemon juice
4 sponge fingers
3 liqueur glasses cherry
    brandy
1 tablespoon grated almonds

Mix fruit cocktail with the lemon juice and fill into four glasses or small bowls. Crumble the sponge fingers and sprinkle the cherry brandy over the biscuit crumbs. Put these on the four portions of fruit cocktail, topping them up with the grated almonds.

A tip: Should there be children among your guests, use raspberry juice instead of cherry brandy.

Pears with a Kick
△ ○

4 canned pear halves
4 tablespoons preserved cran-
    berries
1 tablespoon lemon juice
3 tablespoons pear brandy
2 tablespoons grated coconut

Arrange the pear halves on four individual plates. Stir together cranberries, lemon juice and pear brandy. Pour mixture over the pears and garnish with the grated coconut.

A tip: For children leave out the pear brandy.

Orange Surprise
△ ○

2 oranges
4 level teaspoons glucose
4 tablespoons egg liqueur
1 level teaspoon coffee pow-
    der

Peel orange, removing all the pith. Divide into wedges and dice them, removing all pips. Distribute oranges over four plates and dust them with the glucose. Mix egg liqueur with coffee powder and sprinkle over the oranges.

A tip: For children mix the coffee powder with cream, rather than egg liqueur.

Nut Mousse
△ ○

3 eggs
4 level teaspoons icing sugar
5 heaped tablespoons grated
    nuts
20 maraschino cherries from
    a jar
A generous dash cherry
    brandy

Separate egg yolks from whites. Whisk whites till stiff. Beat yolks with the icing sugar till frothy and add nuts to the yolks. Chop maraschino cherries into small pieces and fold them, together with the egg whites, under the egg yolk mixture. Fill into four glasses and let them get cold in the refrigerator before serving.

In 5 to 10 Minutes

Vanilla-Ice with Fruit-Sauce △ ○ ○

2 tablespoons butter
2 cups preserved morello-
cherries or deep-frozen
raspberries
4 beakers or one block vanilla
ice-cream
2 liqueur glasses raspberry
brandy or kirsch

Melt butter in a saucepan
over low heat and heat cherries or raspberries in it. Fill
ice-cream into four glass
bowls. Add the raspberry
brandy or kirsch to the warm
fruit in the saucepan, stir

well and pour the hot fruit
sauce over the ice-cream.

A hint: Leave out the
alcoholic ingredient in the
case of children being
present.

Illustration below

Yoghurt Cream 'pour vous' △ ○

2 eggs
2 beakers yoghurt from
skimmed milk
4 tablespoons crushed
linseed
2 level tablespoons glucose

1 cup stoned morello
cherries from a jar
4 tablespoons cherry
brandy

Separate egg yolks from
whites. Mix together yolks,
yoghurt, linseed, glucose
and morello cherries. Whisk
egg whites till stiff and fold
under the yoghurt mixture.
Fill the resulting cream into
four glasses and pour 1 tablespoon of cherry brandy
each into the glasses.

A hint: In the event of children being present, use raspberry syrup instead of the
liqueur.

Vanilla-Ice with Fruit Sauce —
recipe on this page

In 5 to 10 Minutes

Müsli

Müsli, meaning something like 'pap', originated in Switzerland. It is a health food which has by now become very popular in many countries. There are various ways of preparing 'Müslis' of which the following are some of the better-known ones:

Apple and Orange Müsli
△ ○

2 apples
2 oranges
1 tablespoon lemon juice
2 tablespoons milk
100g (3½ oz) curd cheese
*   from skimmed milk*
4 tablespoons honey
2 tablespoons grated hazel-
*   nuts from a bag*
6 tablespoons cornflakes

Peel, quarter and dice apples. Peel oranges, separate into wedges and dice them as well. Stir together the lemon juice, milk, curd cheese and honey. Mix apples and oranges and place this mixture into four bowls and pour the honey-curd cheese mixture over them. Sprinkle the grated hazel-nuts over that and top up with the cornflakes.

Illustration on facing page

A good follow-up to *Mock Goulash Soup* (recipe on page 23) or *Colourful Bread Rolls* (recipe on page 29).

Yoghurt Müsli
△ ○

4 canned peach halves
1 tablespoon lemon juice
2 beakers yoghurt from
*   skimmed milk*
1 egg yolk
2 tablespoons honey

Dice peach halves. Mix together lemon juice, yoghurt, egg yolk and honey. Add peach dice to the mixture. Put into four individual bowls.

Illustration on facing page.

A suitable dessert after either *Spinach Soup* (recipe on page 22) or *Sauerkraut on Toast* (recipe on page 25).

Fruit Müsli
△ ○

½ cup canned shredded pine-
*   apples*
½ cup tangerine wedges from
*   a can*
1 cup canned apple purée
2 beakers yoghurt from
*   skimmed milk*
3 tablespoons honey
3 tablespoons grated nuts
*   from a bag*

Coarsely chop shredded pineapples and tangerine wedges, mix them with the apple purée and put the mixture into four individual bowls. Stir together yoghurt and honey, pour into the four bowls and garnish with the grated nuts.

Illustration on facing page

A suitable dessert to follow either *Rapid Bean Soup* (recipe on page 23) or *Shrimp Yalta* (recipe on page 32).

Banana Müsli
△ ○

1 tablespoon lemon juice
3 tablespoons orange juice
3 bananas
2 beakers yoghurt from
*   skimmed milk*
4 level teaspoons sugar
4 tablespoons porridge oats

Mix the lemon with the orange juice. Peal bananas, cut into thin slices and put them into four individual bowls. Pour the juice over. Stir sugar into yoghurt and add to the sliced bananas. Lightly fry porridge oats in a saucepan and sprinkle them over the yoghurt.

Illustration on facing page

Yoghurt Müsli (top left), Fruit Müsli (bottom right), Banana Müsli (bottom left), Apple and Orange Müsli (top right) — recipes on this page

In 5 to 10 Minutes

A suitable dessert to follow: either *Tomato Soup Ursula* (recipe on page 18) or *Rapid Rarebits* (recipe on page 29).

Variations of Curd Cheese Desserts
△ ○

The basic ingredient for all the recipes in this section is the same – 200g (7 oz) of curd cheese, made of skimmed milk. We have chosen curd cheese from skimmed milk because it is rich in proteins, while containing few calories. You are, of course, free to use curd cheese made of whole milk instead, if you don't mind the higher calorie-content.

Banana Curd Cheese
△ ○ * *

Mix the curd cheese with 1 level tablespoon glucose, 1 tablespoon milk, 1 teaspoon honey and 2 beaten egg whites. Slice 1 banana, sprinkle 1 teaspoon lemon juice over it and fold gently under the curd.

A possible variation to the above: The taste of Banana Curd Cheese can be enhanced by the addition of a little stewed rhubarb. In winter,

you may like to try adding a few grated and roasted nuts. You can also use some very ripe bananas (with spotty skin). These you mash with a fork before sprinkling the lemon juice over it and mixing it with the curd cheese.

Peach Curd Cheese
△ ○ * *

You mix the curd cheese with 3 chopped peach halves from a can or with 2 fresh peaches, 1 tablespoon honey, 2 tablespoons cream and 1 teaspoon lemon juice.

Instead of the peaches, you may prefer apricots, (yellow) mirabelle plums or Zwetschen (a superior kind of damson).

Berry Curd Cheese
△ ○ * *

Pick over and wash 150g (5½ oz) berries. Mix these with the curd cheese, 4 tablespoons cream, 1 level tablespoon sugar and 1 teaspoon lemon juice. Should the berries turn out to be rather sour, add some honey to taste. Instead of the berries you could use blackcurrant syrup.

Chocolate Curd Cheese
△ ○ * *

Mix the curd cheese with 1–2 tablespoons instant chocolate powder, 6 tablespoons cream, adding sugar to taste. You may also use some flaked almonds as garnish. For special occasions you may want to mix in some whipped cream instead of the liquid cream.

Orange Curd Cheese
△ ○ * *

For orange curd cheese the mixture consists of: the curd cheese, 1 large diced orange, 1 teaspoon lemon juice, 1 level tablespoon sugar and 2 tablespoons cream.

For those liking their dessert rather creamy, you fold under 1–2 egg whites, whisked stiff. If your guests are not concerned about calories, you can use whipped cream in the place of the egg whites.

Melon Curd Cheese
△ ○ * *

Mix the curd cheese with 1 egg yolk, 2 tablespoons cream, 1 teaspoon lemon juice, 1 teaspoon honey and 1 cup melon cubes.

If the mixing is done in the liquidizer you may use deep-frozen melon cubes; if the mixing is done in other ways, frozen melon cubes are too soft.

Various Yoghurt Desserts
△ ○

The basic ingredient for all yoghurt desserts is the same — 2 beakers of yoghurt made of skimmed milk. We've purposely chosen skimmed-milk yoghurt because it is rich in proteins, but contains relatively few calories. We suggest you try the recipes at least once as this may help to dispel any prejudice you have in regard to skimmed-milk yoghurt. Remember that it's perfectly possible to make up for the calories you save by generously replacing them with other exquisitely-flavoured ingredients.

Don't forget: Neither yoghurt or any yoghurt mixtures are suitable for deep-freezing, for this changes the consistency of the yoghurt in an un-pleasant manner.

Hazelnut Yoghurt
△ ○ ○

1 beaker of yoghurt made of skimmed milk is mixed in the mixer together with: 200 g (7 oz) grated hazelnuts from a bag, 2 egg yolks and 2 level tablespoons glucose. Then add the second beaker of yoghurt and mix once again thoroughly.

Serve in individual bowls.

Pineapple Yoghurt
△ ○ ○

Mix in the mixer: 200 g (7 oz) canned shredded pineapples, together with their juice from the can, 1 tablespoon lemon juice, 1 tablespoon honey and 2 beakers skimmed-milk yoghurt. Crumble 4 sponge fingers and place them in the 4 bowls before pouring the mixture into the bowls.

Apple Yoghurt
△ ○

Mix thoroughly in the mixer: 1 cup canned apple purée, 2 beakers skimmed-milk yoghurt and 2 tablespoons blackcurrant syrup. Whisk 2 egg whites till stiff, stir in 1 level tablespoon icing sugar and mix the beaten egg whites with the apple yoghurt which is served in individual portions.
Optional garnish: small macaroons.

If time permits you may use, instead of the canned apple purée, 2 fresh apples which have, of course, to be peeled and grated.

Ready-Prepared Desserts

This chapter would not be complete without at least a brief mention of the many kinds of curd-cheese desserts, complete with fruit, which have begun to appear in the deep-freeze chests of the better-class shops. These re-quire no preparation, but they have, of course, to be taken out of the freezer for a few hours before they are ready to be served.
Excellent also are the many prepared yoghurt mixtures which are now obtainable in most shops. They are all time-saving, nutritious and easy on the stomach — in short, ideal sweets to round off *A Meal in a Minute.*

In 10 to 15 Minutes

Vegetable Soup Summer Day △○○

1 scarce litre (1¾ pt) water
*450g (16 oz) deep-frozen
    mixed vegetables*
4 veal sausages
*4 level teaspoons instant
    chicken stock*
*2 tablespoons chopped
    parsley*

Bring water to the boil, put the frozen vegetables into it, cover and cook for 12 minutes over low heat. In a second saucepan, bring a little water to the boil. Remove skin from sausages, form small balls out of the sausage meat, put them into the boiling water and let them simmer for 5 minutes. When the vegetables are done, add to them the instant stock to taste. Pour soup into 4 soup plates, add the meat balls and garnish with the parsley.

Vegetable Soup Variations

● Having cooked the vegetables as in the previous recipe and having added instant chicken stock to taste, you heat some sausage slices in it, instead of the meat balls.
● 5 minutes before the vegetables are completely done, add 2 tablespoons of 5-minute rice and let it cook for the remaining 5 minutes
● Thicken soup with 2 beaten eggs.
● Serve Parmesan cheese with the soup.

Goulash Soup Piroshka △○

(Hungarian for 'Red Riding Hood')

*1 four-portion can goulash
    soup*
2 peppers
*1 tablespoon butter or
    margarine*
1 level teaspoon paprika
¼ cup cream

Pour goulash soup into a pot, stir an equal quantity of water into it, cover and let get hot over low heat. Halve peppers, remove pips, wash and dab dry and cut them into strips. Fry the pepper strips in the butter or margarine for 5 minutes, stirring constantly. Add them to the soup together with the fat. Add also the paprika. Now take soup off the stove to stir the cream in.

Goulash Soup Variations

Canned goulash, ox tongue or Pushta soup can be refined in the following ways:
1) By stirring in: 4 tablespoons yoghurt, 2 tablespoons tomato purée and 2 tablespoons of deep-frozen herbs.
2) By adding some diced fried onion or bacon.
3) By adding some diced leftovers from a roast or slices of sausage, ½ cup red wine and 2 tablespoons chopped parsley.

Crayfish Soup Cognac △○○○

1 can cream of crayfish soup
*150g (5½ oz) canned cray-
    fish meat*
1 hardboiled egg
4 tablespoons cream
1 tablespoon brandy

Prepare canned crayfish soup according to instructions on the can. Rinse crayfish meat briefly under cold running water, shred slightly and heat in the soup. Peel and finely dice egg. Mix cream with brandy. Take soup off the stove and stir in the brandy and cream mixture. Serve in individual soup bowls. Garnish with the chopped egg. Toast goes well with it.

In 10 to 15 Minutes

Gratinated Onion Soup △△○

1 four-portion can onion soup
6 tablespoons white wine
4 small slices white bread
1 pinch garlic powder per
*   bread slice*
4 tablespoons grated cheese
2 teaspoons butter

Preheat oven to 250°C
(450°F; gas mark 8) or grill
to maximum temperature.
Heat onion soup according to
instructions on can and stir
wine into it. Halve bread
slices and sprinkle garlic over
them. Pour soup into 4 oven-
proof bowls, put 2 pieces of
bread on each portion, flake
the butter and place the
flakes on top of the bread.
Bake in oven until cheese begins to brown.

Illustration on this page

Lettuce Soup △○

2 small lettuce
¾ litre (1½ pt) water
4 level teaspoons instant
*   chicken stock*
2 egg yolks
½ cup cream
1 dash Worcester sauce

Remove outer lettuce leaves
and any hard bits, cut the remaining lettuce into strips,
toss these in cold water and
put them into a saucepan.

Pour water into saucepan,
cover and cook over low heat
for 5 minutes. Take off fire
and season liquor to taste with
instant chicken stock. Whisk
egg yolks and Worcester sauce
together and thicken soup
with this mixture.

Gratinated Onion Soup —
recipe on this page

In 10 to 15 Minutes

Zuppa Pavese
△ ○

¾ litre (1½ pt) water
3 level teaspoons instant beef
    stock
4 slices toasting bread
4 egg yolks
2 tablespoons chopped pars-
    ley
4 tablespoons grated Parmesan
    cheese

Bring water to the boil. Take
it off the heat and dissolve
the instant beef stock in it.
Toast the bread slices and put
one each in a soup plate. Lay
1 egg yolk on each slice of
toast and sprinkle the parsley
over the yolks. Now pour the
beef stock into the plates and
sprinkle the Parmesan cheese
over the soup.

Noodle Soup
△ ○

¾ litre (1½ pt) water
3 level teaspoons instant
    chicken stock
½ cup small noodles or pasta
    shapes
1–2 packets deep-frozen or
    dried soup vegetables
4 tablespoons grated
    Parmesan cheese

Bring water to the boil, take
off the heat to dissolve instant chicken stock in it. Put

back on heat, add soup vegetables and pasta and let them
cook in the soup. Garnish
with grated Parmesan cheese.

Cucumber 'Kaltschale'
△ ○

'Kaltschale' is the German
name of a group of dishes,
comprising mainly fruit soups
and desserts, which are eaten
not cooked, but liquidized.
They are much appreciated
for their appetizing and diges-
tive qualities. The following
recipe is an example of this
type of dish.

1 fresh cucumber
½ cup pickled peppers
¼ teaspoon salt
1 pinch each of celery salt
    and garlic powder
A dash Worcester sauce
1 level tablespoon paprika
3 beakers yoghurt
4 tablespoons chopped pars-
    ley

The cucumber is peeled and
cut into large pieces. These
are then put into the liquidizer together with the
pickled peppers, the salt, the
celery salt, the garlic powder,
the paprika and between ½
and 1 beaker yoghurt. After
liquidizing this mixture at
medium speed, the remaining
yoghurt is added and also the

parsley. All is thoroughly
stirred and served in 4 soup
plates.

Delicate Tuna Sandwiches
△ ○ ○

4 large lettuce leaves in
    perfect condition
4 small sprigs dill
250g (9 oz) artichoke hearts
    from a jar
150g (5½ oz) canned tuna in
    oil
150g (5½ oz) canned shrimps
½ shallot
1 green pepper
2 teaspoons butter
1 teaspoon anchovy paste
4 slices wholemeal bread

Briefly rinse lettuce leaves
and dill under cold running
water and dry. Drain tuna.
Rinse and drain shrimps,
separating them from one another. Peel shallot and cut
into rings. Halve pepper, remove pips and cut likewise
into rings. Wash these
briefly under running water
and dab dry. Mix together
butter and anchovy paste and
spread this mixture on the 4
bread slices. Place lettuce
leaves on the buttered bread,
distribute on the tuna pieces
and the artichoke hearts and
arrange on top of that the
pepper rings and the shrimps.

Garnish each sandwich with a sprig of dill.

Illustration below

Goes well following *Tomato Soup Ursula* (recipe on page 18) or *Vegetable Soup Summerday* (recipe on page 50). Suggested sweets:*Iced Cream with Fruit* (recipe on page 81) or *Peach Meringues* (recipe on page 82).

Melon Sandwich
△ ○ ○

4 large lettuce leaves in
  perfect condition
4 slices wholemeal bread
2 teaspoons butter
8 slices smoked fillet of ham
½ honeydew melon
12 canned mandarin segments

Briefly rinse and dry lettuce leaves. Butter bread slices. Place on them the lettuce leaves and on them 2 slices each of the smoked fillets of ham. Remove pips from the honeydew melon, quarter it, peel and slice each quarter and put them on top of the ham. Garnish each sandwich with 3 mandarin segments.

Illustration below

Goes well with *Vegetable Soup Summerday* (recipe on page 50); as a sweet try *Strawberry Omelette* (recipe on page 80) or *Vanilla-Ice with Chocolate Sauce* (recipe on page 79).

Delicate Tuna Sandwiches and Melon Sandwich — recipes on facing page and above

In 10 to 15 Minutes

Toast 'Ahoi'
△ ○

4 slices toasting bread
2 teaspoons butter or margarine
2 apples
3 teaspoons grated horseradish
1 teaspoon lemon juice
½ teaspoon salt
200g (7 oz) any kind of smoked fish
4 thin slices cheese
2 level teaspoons paprika

Preheat oven to 250°C (450°F; gas mark 8) or grill to maximum temperature. Toast the bread slices and butter them. Peel and grate apples, mix them with the lemon juice, salt and horseradish and spread the mixture on the toast. Cut the smoked fish into smaller pieces and also put on the toast. The cheese slices are now laid on top of everything before the slices of toast are baked or grilled for 5 minutes. Sprinkle the paprika over before serving.

A suitable first course is *Gratinated Onion Soup* (recipe on page 31); and as a sweet: *Ice-Cream with Fruit* (recipe on page 81).

Fried Sausage on Toast △ ○ *

4 slices toasting bread
6–8 veal frying sausages (depending on size)
1 tablespoon butter or margarine
½ onion
2 tomatoes
4 slices cheese
½ teaspoon paprika

Preheat oven to 250°C (450°F; gas mark 8) or grill to maximum temperature. Toast bread slices. Press frying sausages out of their skins and spread thickly on the toast. Heat butter or margarine in a saucepan and fry the toast in it with the sausage meat at bottom. Peel onion and cut into rings. Wash, dry and slice tomatoes. Remove the fried sandwiches from the saucepan. Put the onion rings and the tomato slices into the fat, fry them briefly and arrange them on the toast. Cover with the cheese slices and bake for five minutes. Garnish with the paprika before serving.

Illustration on facing page

For first course try *Salad Soup* (recipe on page 51); a suitable dessert is *Vanilla-Ice with Chocolate Sauce* (recipe on page 80).

Mussels on Toast △○○

4 slices toasting bread
2 glass jars of preserved mussels in brine or frozen mussels
1 cup canned peeled tomatoes
2 teaspoons butter or margarine
1 pinch each of salt and pepper per bread slice
4 thin slices Cheddar cheese

Preheat oven to 250°C (450°F; gas mark 8) or grill to maximum temperature. Lightly toast bread on both sides. If you use canned mussels, drain them in a sieve or, if the mussels are frozen, rinse them under cold running water. Butter toast. Put on it the mussels and on top of these the peeled tomatoes, seasoning them with the salt and pepper. Place the cheese slices on top of the tomatoes and bake the sandwiches for five minutes in the oven or under the grill.

Suitable first course: *Marrow Dumpling Soup* (recipe on page 22) or *Carrot Bouillon* (recipe on page 22).

◁ Fried Sausage on Toast — recipe on this page

In 10 to 15 Minutes

Mussel Salad on Toast
△ ○ ○

2 hardboiled eggs
1 teaspoon lemon juice
2 teaspoons chilli sauce
2 teaspoons gin
1 tablespoon oil
1 generous pinch each of salt,
    pepper, garlic powder and
    sugar
6 tablespoons canned peeled
    tomatoes
2 cans mussels in brine or
    deep-frozen
4 slices toasting bread
2 tablespoons mayonnaise

Peel eggs, chop whites and
squash yolks with a fork. Mix
the yolks with the lemon
juice, chilli sauce, gin, oil, salt,
pepper, garlic powder, sugar
and egg whites. Lightly drain
tomatoes and cut them into
small pieces. Drain or defrost
mussels. Toast bread slices on
both sides. Mix tomatoes and
mussels with the egg sauce.
Spread the mayonnaise on the
toast, putting the salad on
top.

Tarvisio Toast
△ ○

4 slices toasting bread
1 clove garlic
2 teaspoons butter or mar-
    garine
150g (5½ oz) canned tunny
    fish
100g (3½ oz) French beans
    pickled in vinegar
½ cup pickled peppers
12 stuffed green olives
8 pickled pearl onions
12 mini corn-cobs from a jar
4 slices Cheddar cheese

Preheat oven to 250°C
(450°F; gas mark 8) or grill
to maximum temperature.
Lightly toast bread slices, rub
them over thoroughly with
garlic clove and butter them.
Drain tunny fish, but keep
the oil from the can. Drain
likewise the beans, peppers,
olives, pearl onions and corn-
cobs. Lay the beans on the
toast, then the peppers, pearl
onions, olive halves and corn-
cobs. Shred the tuna with a
fork (usually included with
can). Put the cheese slices on
top. Now bake the sandwiches
for 5 minutes in the hot oven
or under the grill.

Illustration on facing page

Goes well with *Goulash Soup
Piroschka* (recipe on page 50)
or *Cucumber 'Kaltschale'*
(recipe on page 52).

Haricot Bean Salad
△ ○

200g (7 oz) canned haricot
    beans
1 cup canned peeled toma-
    toes
½ cup sliced celeriac from a
    jar
1 large apple
1 tablespoon wine vinegar
2 tablespoons oil
A generous pinch each of
    salt, garlic salt and pepper
A few drops Worcester sauce
2 tablespoons chopped pars-
    ley

Drain beans. Drain tomatoes
and celeriac slices also and
chop them. Peel apple, halve,
core and dice it. Mix the vinegar with the oil, salt, garlic
salt, pepper and Worcester
sauce and gently stir into the

In 10 to 15 Minutes

salad ingredients. Put salad into a bowl and sprinkle parsley over it. You may prefer to add a medium-sized onion instead of the Worcester sauce which makes the salad more savoury.

Radish and Apple Salad △ ○

1 small radish
2 small apples
2 teaspoons lemon juice
1 level teaspoon sugar
A generous pinch each of salt and pepper
1 tablespoon wine vinegar
1 tablespoon oil
½ teaspoon mustard
2 tablespoons chopped parsley

Wash and grate radish. Peel and grate the apples. Mix both together with the lemon juice, sugar, salt, pepper, vinegar, oil and mustard. Put salad in bowl and sprinkle chopped parsley over it.

An alternative: If you like your salads a little stronger in taste, use half a fresh cucumber instead of the radish, go easy with the lemon juice and leave out the sugar altogether.

Tarvisio Toast — recipe on facing page

In 10 to 15 Minutes

Filled Peach Halves
△ ○ ○

4 large lettuce leaves in
perfect condition
4 canned peach halves
1 teaspoon lemon juice
200g (7 oz) canned prawns
1 pickled cucumber
2 tablespoons mayonnaise
2 tablespoons cream
2 teaspoons sherry
2 teaspoons tomato paste
1 pinch each of salt, pepper
and sugar per portion
A few small sprigs of dill

Wash and dry lettuce leaves.
Drain peach halves and arrange
on the lettuce leaves. Sprinkle
lemon juice over them. Rinse,
drain and shred prawns and
arrange them on top of the
peach halves. Dice pickled cucumber. Mix mayonnaise with
the cream, sherry, cucumber
dice, tomato paste, salt and
sugar and pour over the
prawns. Garnish with the dill
sprigs.

Possible alternatives: Instead
of the peach halves, you may
like to use canned pineapple
slices or some plums preserved
in Armagnac brandy.

Goes well with toast.

Delicate South Sea Salad
△ ○ ○

1 grapefruit
200g (7 oz) canned shrimps
4 canned pineapple slices
1 banana
½ fresh cucumber
220g (8 oz) canned artichoke
bottoms
½ cup cream
1 teaspoon grated horseradish
1 tablespoon tomato ketchup
A generous pinch each of salt
and pepper
1 level teaspoon paprika

The grapefruit is peeled, divided into wedges, then diced
after the pips have been removed. Rinse shrimps under
cold running water and separate them. Drain pineapple
slices and cut into pieces. Peel
and slice banana. Peel cucumber, cut it into halves lengthways, remove seeds and slice
the halves. Briefly rinse artichoke bottoms, drain and cut
them in half. Stir together the
cream with the grated horseradish, tomato ketchup, salt,
pepper and paprika. Toss all
the salad ingredients gently
together, put them into 4
individual glass bowls, pouring
the dressing over them.

Illustration on facing page

Mushroom and Tongue Salad
△ ○

200g (7 oz) canned button
mushrooms
100g (3½ oz) sliced tongue
2 tablespoons mayonnaise
2 tablespoons soured cream
2 tablespoons wine vinegar
4 perfect lettuce leaves
2 tablespoons chopped dill

Drain the mushrooms. Cut
tongue first in strips and then
in dice. Stir together mayonnaise, soured cream and vinegar. Wash and dry lettuce
leaves. Mix mushrooms with
the diced tongue, salad
dressing and chopped dill and
arrange on the lettuce leaves.

Delicate South Sea Salad – recipe on this page ▷

In 10 to 15 Minutes

Herring Salad
△ ○

4 marinated herrings
150g (5½ oz) canned tunny
*   fish*
1 small lettuce
6 tomatoes
3 hardboiled eggs
½ cup buttermilk
A dash wine vinegar
½ teaspoon sugar
A generous pinch each of salt,
*   pepper and dried chervil*

Soak marinated herring for a short while in cold water. Shred tunny fish into small pieces and drain through a sieve, retaining the oil. Pick over lettuce leaves, tearing the larger leaves in half and cutting out the hard bits. Wash and dry them. Wash and dry tomatoes and cut them into eighths. Peel and chop eggs. Whisk together the buttermilk, vinegar, sugar, salt, pepper, chervil and the oil from the tunny fish. Lightly toss

all the salad ingredients and pour dressing over them.

Illustration below

Serve with potatoes in their jackets or *Quick Potato Salad* (recipe on page 68).

Goes well following *Gratinated Onion Soup* (recipe on page 51) or *Zuppa Pavese* (recipe on page 52); for sweet try *Iced Cream with Fruit* (recipe on page 81).

Herring Salad — recipe above

In 10 to 15 Minutes

A Richly-Laden Salad Platter

△ ○ ○

1 small lettuce
50g (2 oz) canned asparagus tips
50g (2 oz) canned beans
50g (2 oz) canned wax beans
50g (2 oz) canned button mushrooms
50g (2 oz) celeriac slices from a jar
50g (2 oz) pickled peppers
1 onion

10 stuffed green olives
2 tomatoes
50g (2 oz) smoked raw ham
50g (2 oz) canned salmon slices
2 hardboiled eggs
2 tablespoons oil
2 tablespoons wine vinegar
1 teaspoon salt
A pinch each of pepper and celery salt
2 tablespoons mayonnaise
1 tablespoon cream
2 tablespoons chopped parsley

Pick over lettuce and tear larger leaves into somewhat smaller pieces. Wash the leaves under cold running water and dry them. Drain the canned vegetables. Peel the onion, dice one half and cut other half into rings. Briefly rinse olives under cold running water and halve them. Wash, dry and slice tomatoes. Cut ham into broad strips. Roll up salmon slices. Peel and halve eggs. Arrange lettuce leaves on a large flat

A Richly-Laden Salad Platter — recipe above

61

dish, putting on each some of the asparagus tips, mushrooms, pickled peppers, beans, celeriac slices, wax beans, ham strips and tomato slices.

Garnish the beans with the onion rings and the tomato slices with the diced onions. Distribute the olive halves over the whole platter. Stick the salmon rolls into the salad. Place the egg halves in the middle of the salad dish. Stir together the oil, vinegar, salt, pepper and celery salt and sprinkle this dressing over the salad. Mix the mayon-

naise with the cream and chopped parsley and pour this mixture over the egg halves.

Illustration on page 61

Refreshing Corn Salad — recipe on this page

Refreshing Corn Salad △○

1 large carrot
2 apples
1 can sweet-corn
2 teaspoons lemon juice
½ teaspoon sugar
½ cup red pepper strips from a jar
½ beaker yoghurt
1 tablespoon oil
½ teaspoon salt
¼ teaspoon paprika

Scrape and wash carrot, peel apples and coarsely grate both carrot and apples. Drain sweet-corn. Mix the grated apples and carrot with the lemon juice, sweet-corn and sugar. Chop the pepper strips and mix them with the yoghurt, oil, salt and paprika and fold under the salad.

Illustration on facing page.

Goes well with *Fried Fishfingers* (recipe on page 68) or *A Classic Steak* (recipe on page 73). Alternatively, you can serve *Corn Salad* in individual portions, each on a lettuce leaf or together with the fishfingers.

In 10 to 15 Minutes

Serbian Salad
△ ○

200g (7 oz) cucumbers
    pickled in mustard
    marinate
2 apples
2 bananas
2 teaspoons lemon juice
1 small lettuce
2 tomatoes
4 tablespoons curd cheese
2 tablespoons mayonnaise
1 tablespoon grated hazel-
    nuts

Dice cucumbers. Peel apples
and bananas and dice them
also. Sprinkle the lemon juice
over all the diced fruit. Pick
over lettuce, separate, wash
and dry leaves and cut them
into strips. Wash, dry and dice
tomatoes. Mix curd cheese
with mayonnaise, gently stir
dressing into salad and
sprinkle grated hazel-nuts
over it.

Scampi Bouchées
△ ○ ○

2 slices Edam cheese
4 ready-bought puff pastry
    cases
200g (7 oz) canned scampi
200g (7 oz) canned mussels
    in their natural juice or
    deep-frozen
1 cup cooked diced carrots
    from a can
Juice of half a lemon
1 jar caviar substitute for
    garnishing

Preheat oven to 250°C
(450°F; gas mark 8) or grill
to maximum temperature.
Quarter cheese slices and put
one quarter each at the
bottom of the 4
bouchée cases. Put these into
the oven or under the grill.
Briefly rinse scampi under
cold running water, separate
and drain them, retaining 8
particularly good ones. Drain
canned mussels and carrots.
Sprinkle lemon juice over
scampi, mussels and carrots.
Cut the remaining cheese
slices into strips. Now put the
scampi-mussel-carrot filling
into the warm bouchée cases,
topping them up with the
sliced cheese, and put them
back into the oven or under
the grill for five minutes.
Garnish with caviar substitute and the retained scampi
before serving.

Illustration on page 65

Bouchées à la Sophia △ ○

4 ready-prepared bouchée
    cases
200g (7 oz) canned ragoût
    fin or cream chicken
100g (3½ oz) roast fillet of
    veal
4 tablespoons canned aspa-
    ragus tips
2 tablespoons cream
1 tablespoon dry white wine
4 lemon wedges
Worcester sauce to taste

Preheat oven to 220°C
(425°F; gas mark 7) or grill
to maximum temperature.
Warm bouchée cases. Heat
canned ragoût fin (or substitute) in a saucepan. Cut
fillet of veal into narrow
strips and add these to ragoût
fin in the saucepan. Add also
asparagus tips and stir cream
and white wine into the mixture. When thoroughly heated
through fill into the hot
bouchée cases and garnish
with the lemon wedges. Serve
Worcester sauce separately.

In 10 to 15 Minutes

A Crash Course on Rice

Meals in Minutes are normally prepared with 5-minute rice which is precooked and should be treated as prescribed on the packet. So remember:
• It is always worthwhile cooking a whole bag of 5-minute rice at a time, even if only a few spoonfuls are required.
• Rice, if covered, keeps for several days in the refrigerator.
• Rice kept in the refrigerator can be used in soups, in salads or as a side-dish.
• The reheating of rice is best done in a sieve over steam; in this way the properties of the individual rice grains are most effectively preserved.
• Those who dislike 5-minute rice should use the long-grained variety. Long-grained rice is put into fast-boiling water and cooked for 12 minutes (and so just qualifying for inclusion in the chapter on *Meals in 10–15 Minutes*).
• As a side dish you allow 60 g (2 oz) of rice per person, which when cooked represents about 1 cupful.

Various Rice Side-Dishes

4 cups of cooked rice can be turned into the following side-dishes:

Rice with Mushrooms

Thinly slice 1 cup of canned mushrooms and lightly fry them in 1–2 tablespoons of butter or margarine. Add rice, cover and let rice get hot. Before serving stir in 1 tablespoon chopped parsley.

Curried Rice

Heat rice over steam. Melt 1 tablespoon butter or margarine in a saucepan, turn the hot rice in the fat together with 1–2 teaspoons curry powder. You may like to add also some canned red peppers; these ought to be chopped first.

Risi Pisi

This is an Italian rice dish. Reheat rice over steam. Melt butter or margarine in a saucepan; add 8 tablespoons frozen peas, cover and allow these to cook over low heat for 6 minutes. Finally mix rice with peas.

Tomato Rice

Heat rice over steam. Melt butter or margarine in a saucepan. Dissolve 3–4 tablespoons of tomato purée in the fat and add rice.

Finally, to conclude the section on salads and appetizers, a recipe for a salad with cooked rice:

Colourful Rice Salad
△ ○ *

2 small pickled cucumbers
1 banana
½ cup canned mandarin wedges
280g (10 oz) canned prawns
3 cups cooked rice
1 beaker yoghurt from skimmed milk
2 tablespoons mayonnaise
2 tablespoons mandarin juice from the can
½ teaspoon salt
1 level teaspoon curry powder
1 generous pinch sugar
A few drops lemon juice

Dice pickled cucumbers. Peel banana and dice likewise. Drain and chop mandarin wedges. Briefly rinse prawns under cold running water, chop them and add them to the cucumbers, banana and mandarins as well as the cooked rice. Mix well. Stir yoghurt together with the mayonnaise, mandarin juice, lemon juice, salt, curry powder and sugar and gently fold under the salad ingredients.

Rice Dish 'Jardinière'
△○

1 tablespoon oil
300g (11 oz) mixed minced meat
2 tablespoons pre-roasted onions from a bag
½ cup instant meat stock
4 cups cooked rice
2 cups canned peeled tomatoes
1 small can asparagus tips
1 small can button mushrooms
A pinch each of pepper and paprika
2 tablespoons chopped parsley

Heat oil in a rather large pot. Add minced meat and lightly fry on all sides, stirring constantly. Add the roast onions. Gradually pour in the made-up instant meat stock. Add rice and the tomatoes with their juice; mix well. Drain asparagus tips and mushrooms and gently stir into the rice mixture. Add salt, pepper and paprika to taste, heat right through. Garnish with parsley before serving.

An acceptable dessert to follow: fruit yoghurt or cold chocolate pudding.

Scampi Bouchées — recipe on page 63

In 10 to 15 Minutes

Paprika Rice
△ ○

3 green peppers
2 tablespoons oil
400g (14 oz) mixed minced
*   meat*
2 tablespoons ready-roasted
*   onions*
½ cup instant meat stock
4 cups cooked rice
4 tablespoons grated cheese
½ teaspoon salt
½ teaspoon paprika

Halve peppers, remove pips, wash and cut into strips. Heat oil in a saucepan and fry the pepper strips for five minutes, stirring all the while. Stir in minced meat and ready-roasted onions. Pour dissolved instant meat stock into the mixture. Now add the rice and paprika, cover and allow to simmer at medium heat for five minutes.

Illustration on facing page

Suitable desserts include *Yoghurt Müsli* (recipe on page 46) and *Vanilla-Ice with Fruit Sauce* (recipe on page 45).

Some Tips on Potatoes

• For *A Meal in a Minute* it's advisable to use precooked potatoes which can be bought in tins or vacuum-packed.
• Warm them up, according to instructions, over low heat before serving them either in a sauce or tossed in butter, or as plain boiled potatoes with some chopped parsley sprinkled over them.
• People who love potatoes should perhaps try the taste of pre-cooked potatoes first to find out whether they really like the flavour. They may come to the conclusion that freshly-cooked potatoes are worth spending the time it takes to prepare them.
• Boiled potatoes, freshly-cooked, take 20–25 minutes to get done and potatoes in their jackets 25 minutes.
• Those who have absolutely no time to spare use processed potatoes from a packet, such as potato purée, potato pancakes or deep-frozen chips.
• The preparation of potato products should always be done strictly in accordance with the manufacturer's instructions.
• Any leftover mashed potato may be heated up in a frying-pan on the following day with the addition of various ingredients.

Various Ways of Serving Ready-Cooked Potato Purée

We assume you have time to prepare the purée according to instructions.

Potato Purée with Bacon

50–100g (2–3½ oz) of diced bacon and 1 diced onion are lightly fried in a frying-pan before the purée is added and smoothed. After a few minutes, the mixture is turned with a palette knife.

Sauerkraut and Mashed

Coarsely cut 10 tablespoons sauerkraut and mix it, together with 2–3 tablespoons apple juice, into the potato purée. Heat a little fat in a saucepan and warm the purée over low heat, turning occasionally.

Horseradish Purée

Peel and grate 1 large apple. Mix it with 2–3 tablespoons of grated horseradish (depending on the strength of the horseradish). Now stir the mixture together with the mashed potatoes and heat it all up in a little fat.

Paprika Rice (Top) — recipe on this page, Sweet-Sour Potato ▷
Salad (centre), Fried Fishfingers (below) — recipes on page 68

In 10 to 15 Minutes

Various Ways of Serving Pre-Cooked Whole Potatoes

As a side-dish for 4 persons you require between 500 and 600g (18–22 oz) of potatoes. This works out at 6 large or 8 small potatoes.

Fried Potatoes

Heat 1–2 tablespoons of fat; dice a medium-sized onion and lightly fry it in the fat. Slice potatoes, salt them to taste and fry over low heat, turning them from time to time.

Sautéed Potatoes

Heat 3 tablespoons butter fat in a frying-pan; slice potatoes, salt and pepper them and fry them in the fat until golden brown. As you turn the slices while they are getting done you progressively break them up so that in the end you have a nearly homogeneous substance.

Bacon Potatoes

Prepare potatoes as for *Fried Potatoes* (see above), but fry them with 100g (3½ oz) diced bacon. You may like to en-

rich your bacon potatoes by stirring into them 1–2 eggs which you have seasoned with a few caraway steeds.

Quick Potato Salad

Slice the potatoes and pour over them ¾ cup of hot dissolved instant meat stock. You now stir in 2 tablespoons chopped parsley, 1 tablespoon vinegar, 2 tablespoons oil as well as a good pinch of salt and pepper. If you like you may also add some sliced Vienna sausages, some diced meat sausage of the Mortadella type or some ham cut into strips, or the remains of a roast, cut into cubes.

Quick Herring Salad

Slice potatoes and season them with salt and pepper. Add 1 cup of chopped beetroot from a jar and 300g (11 oz) of bought herring salad; mix well.

Sweet-Sour Potato Salad

Slice potatoes and season them with salt and pepper. Dice 1 apple, 1 pickled cucumber and 1 onion; mix these with the potatoes. Mix

together 1 tablespoon wine vinegar, 6 tablespoons mayonnaise, ½ teaspoon sugar, a generous pinch of marjoram and, according to taste, a few drops of lemon juice and stir into the salad.

Illustration on page 67

Any of the recipes given in this section can be quickly converted into a main dish by adding to the salads either a slice of black pudding (cold or fried), a can of meat balls of chopped veal or a slice of cold roast meat.

Fried Fishfingers
△ ○

600g (22 oz) deep-frozen fishfingers
2 tablespoons dripping

Heat dripping in a saucepan and fry in it the fishfingers, according to instructions on the packet, on all sides over low heat for 8–10 minutes.

Illustration on page 67

Goes well with *Sweet-Sour Potato Salad* (recipe on page 68) and green salad.

An Alternative: Instead of potato salad you may like to

serve the fishfingers with a home-made curd cheese remoulade dressing. You make it by dicing 1 pickled cucumber and stirring together 6 tablespoons curd cheese, 2 tablespoons mayonnaise, 2 tablespoons apple purée, 2 tablespoons chopped parsley, some salt, pepper and garlic powder and a few drops of Worcester sauce. Serve dressing separately.

Artichoke-Fry
△ ○ ○

*220g (8 oz) canned artichoke
    bottoms*
2 tomatoes
2 tablespoons oil
½ teaspoon salt
¼ teaspoon pepper
4 eggs
2 tablespoons cream
2 tablespoons tomato purée
2 tablespoons chopped parsley

Drain artichoke bottoms, retaining the liquor. Wash, dry and slice tomatoes. Heat oil in a frying-pan to fry in it the artichoke bottoms and the sliced tomatoes on both sides over low heat. Mix salt and pepper, using half of it to season the tomato slices. Break eggs over tomatoes for fried eggs, sprinkling the remaining pepper and salt over them. Now mix the cream with 1 tablespoon of the liquor

Artichoke-Fry — recipe above

In 10 to 15 Minutes

from the artichokes, the tomato purée and the chopped parsley and pour this mixture over the eggs shortly before serving.

Illustration on page 69

Goes well with French bread or deep-frozen chips; for dessert try *Strawberry Omelette* (recipe on page 79).

Tortas de Papas
△ ○

1 packet potato croquettes
½ litre (1 pt) water
4 tablespoons Parmesan cheese
8 small rashers streaky bacon
2 tablespoons dripping
1 onion
1 cup canned peeled tomatoes
2 tablespoons chopped parsley
½ teaspoon salt
¼ teaspoon pepper
1 tablespoon oil
1 tablespoon wine vinegar
4 tablespoons cottage cheese

Stir potato croquettes into the cold water with a whisk, mix in Parmesan cheese and let mixture stand for five minutes. Fry bacon rashers until they are a crispy brown. Take them out of the frying-pan and use it to heat up

dripping. Knead the potato dough briefly and form 8 potato cakes from it. Fry these in the dripping on both sides over low heat until crispy brown. Peel and dice onion. Cut tomatoes into small pieces. Mix the diced onions with the tomatoes, parsley, salt and pepper, the oil, vinegar and cottage cheese to serve separately as sauce. Cover each fried torta with a rasher of bacon and arrange the tortas on one platter.

Illustration on facing page

Suitable dessert: *Apple Snow with Kiss* (recipe on page 44) or fresh fruit according to season.

Ravioli Soufflé
△ ○

1 large can egg ravioli in tomato sauce
450g (16 oz) frozen peas
400g (14 oz) cooked ham
4 tablespoons breadcrumbs
6 tablespoons grated cheese
2 tablespoons flaked butter

Preheat oven to 250°C (450°F; gas mark 8). Open ravioli can, leaving lid lying loosely on top. Stand can in boiling water to heat up. Put frozen peas into a saucepan, cover with 2 tablespoons salted water and let them cook for 3 minutes over low heat. Dice ham. Grease oven-proof form, put into it half the ravioli, the peas and the diced ham and fill up with the remaining ravioli. Mix breadcrumbs with the cheese and distribute over the ravioli. Arrange the flakes of butter on top of the cheese and bake in the oven or under the grill for 10 minutes.

Goes well with *Refreshing Corn Salad* (recipe on page 62) or *Radish and Apple Salad* (recipe on page 57).

70

Tortas de Papas — recipe on this page ▷

In 10 to 15 Minutes

Tips on Frying Meat

Fried meat dishes, whether breadcrumbed or not, can be produced in 15 minutes. But if you like to serve the fried meat with some delicate sauce or some side-dish which takes more time to prepare, you will find suitable suggestions in the section dealing with *15–25 minute meals.*

Now for a few general hints:
• All slices of meat should be briefly rinsed under cold running water and dried with kitchen-paper.
• Meat slices which are not breadcrumbed should not be salted until *after* frying.
• Breadcrumbed meat slices should be salted first, then breadcrumbed and fried immediately.
• Cutlets require beating. Several incisions should be made into the fat surrounding them. They can be turned in a little flour or egg — and breadcrumbed prior to frying.
• Escalopes, whether fried 'nature' or breadcrumbed should be beaten or pressed flat.
• Beef steaks are not beaten; they are fried without being breadcrumbed.
• Meat slices weighing about 150g (5½ oz) and of a thickness of 1½ cm (about $^5/_8''$) take 4–7 minutes per side to fry; they take 2 minutes longer if breadcrumbed.
• Beef steaks, weighing 200g (7 oz), take 2–6 minutes per side to fry, depending on whether you want them

72

Classic Steak — recipe on facing page

underdone, medium-done or well-done. (See page 73).

• All meat slices should first be fried over fierce heat, but the cooking process should be completed over medium heat.

• Use only pure fats for frying, such as oil, lard or pure vegetable fat.

Entrecôte Garni

△ ○

2 tablespoons oil
4 entrecôtes, each weighing 200g (7 oz)
1 tablespoon butter
4 eggs
A pinch each of pepper and salt for entrecôte and egg
4 teaspoons caviar substitute as garnish
4 slices cooked lean ham

Heat oil. Gently press steaks with the ball of your thumb, put them into the hot fat and fry them for 4 minutes on either side. Heat butter in second pan to fry the eggs, lightly seasoning them with salt and pepper. Season the steaks likewise after they are done, put them on preheated plates, spread the caviar on them and lay the fried eggs on top. Garnish each entrecôte with a slice of ham.

Goes well with French bread and *Delicate South Sea Salad*

(recipe on page 58). A suitable dessert to follow is *Strawberries Romanoff* (recipe on page 80).

Classic Steak

△ ○ ○

4 steaks of 200g (7 oz) each
2–3 tablespoons oil
½ teaspoon salt
¼ teaspoon pepper

Rinse steaks briefly under cold running water and thoroughly dry them with some kitchen paper. Heat oil in frying-pan over fierce heat and fry the steaks on either side for anything between 2 and 5 minutes, depending on how you like your steaks. Finally season with salt and pepper and any other seasoning of your choice.

Frying Times for Steaks of about 200g (7 oz)

• Nearly raw: Fry each side for 1 minute over fierce heat, simply to seal so that the juices cannot escape; very thin outer crust, but inside raw.

• Rare or under-done: Fry for 2 minutes on either side over fierce heat till crust has formed, but before the inside gets cooked.

• Medium-done: Fry for three minutes on either side over medium heat. This will leave the inside slightly pink.

• Well-done: Fry for 4–5 minutes on either side over medium heat. This suffices to cook the meat right through.

Illustration on facing page

A few tips: A proper steak should never be too thin, for it would be cooked right through in no time and that is regarded by steak lovers as sacrilege. Meat intended for steaks must hang a long time. So don't insist on rump steak when buying your meat. Always ask your butcher first what kind of steak meat he recommends and follow his advice. Classic steaks may be: fillet, rump or sirloin.

Classic steaks may be garnished with herb butter (maître d'hôtel as shown on the cover illustration). They are normally served with peas from the freezer and fried tomatoes.

In 10 to 15 Minutes

Hunter's Steak
△△○○

2 tablespoons oil
4 fillet steaks of 180g (6½ oz)
    each
½ teaspoon salt
½ teaspoon pepper
1 small can chanterelles
4 canned artichoke bottoms
4 eggs
2 tablespoons chopped pars-
    ley

Heat oil and fry the steaks in
it, for 5 minutes on either
side. Season with half the
pepper and salt and keep
warm. Drain chanterelles and
artichoke bottoms. Whisk
together the eggs, parsley, the
remaining pepper and salt.
Heat chanterelles in the fat
left in the frying-pan, pour
the egg mixture over them,
put the artichoke bottoms
around the edge of the frying-
pan to heat them up.

To serve: Place on the steaks
first the artichoke bottoms
and then cover them with the
egg and chanterelle mixture.

Illustration on facing page

Goes well with green salad
and French bread.

Steak 'au poivre' – Paris Fashion
△○○

4 tablespoons white pepper-
    corns
4 fillets of steak weighing
    200g (7 oz) each
2 tablespoons oil
A pinch each of salt and
    celery salt per steak
2 tablespoons butter
3 liqueur glasses brandy

Coarsely crush peppercorns
with the blade of a knife and
gently press the steaks into
the pepper so that it sticks to
both sides. Heat oil in saucepan and fry the steaks on
both sides, cooking time
depending on how you like
them (see page 73). Frying
finished, you season the
steaks with the salt and the
celery salt. Pour away oil, but
retain steaks in pan; melt butter in the frying-pan, pour
brandy into a ladle, carefully
set it alight and pour the
flaming brandy over the
steaks After one minute turn
the steaks over, which should
extinguish the flame.

Goes well with French bread
or chips from the freezer and
fried tomatoes garnished with
parsley or lettuce salad with
Mayonnaise Dressing (recipe
on page 30). Recommended
dessert is *Vanilla-Ice with Hot
Chocolate Sauce* (recipe on
page 80).

Russian Beefsteak
△○○

4 beefsteaks of 200g (7 oz)
    each
2 tablespoons oil
A generous pinch each of salt
    and pepper
1 tablespoon butter
4 eggs
4 tablespoons cream
1 teaspoon anchovy paste

Fry steaks in very hot oil for
one minute on either side,
then change to moderate heat
and continue frying process
for another 6 minutes – 3
minutes for either side. Season with salt and pepper and
keep warm. Melt butter in the
remaining oil and fry eggs.
Arrange eggs on top of the
steaks and salt slightly. Heat
cream in the fat, stir in anchovy paste and pour mixture
around the steaks.

Goes well with French bread
and *Simple Tomato Salad*
(recipe on page 32). Recommended dessert: *Grapefruit
Cocktail* (recipe on page 82).

◁ Hunter's Steak – recipe on this page

In 10 to 15 Minutes

Steak Quebec
△△○○

*4 fillet steaks of 150g (5½ oz)
  each
3 tablespoons oil
½ teaspoon salt
¼ teaspoon paprika
A pinch garlic powder
1 small can tomato purée
1 cup canned peeled toma-
  toes
1 large pickled cucumber
A pinch dried basil
A pinch each of salt and
  sugar
4 lemon segments*

Brush steaks with oil; heat
the remaining oil and fry the
steaks in it for 4 minutes on
either side. Mix salt, paprika
and garlic powder and sprinkle
over both sides of steaks. Stir
the tomato purée with an
equal quantity of water and
heat up. Cut tomatoes and cucumber into strips and add to
the tomato sauce. Now season this sauce with the basil,
salt and sugar. Serve the
steaks on a dish with the juice
and pour the sauce over them.
Garnish each steak with a
segment of lemon.

Illustration on facing page

Goes well with plain boiled
rice or chips from the deep-
freeze.

Fried Liver Royal – recipe
on this page

Fried Liver Royal
△△○○

*2 slices canned pineapples
1 banana
1 teaspoon lemon juice
4 slices calf's liver at 150g
  (5½ oz) each
1 tablespoon oil
A pinch each of salt and pepper per liver slice
4 teaspoons butter
A few lettuce leaves
Some parsley
2 teaspoons preserved cranberries*

Drain pineapple slices and cut
them through horizontally.
Peel banana, halve it lengthways and crosswise, sprinkling
lemon juice over it. Wash liver
and dry thoroughly. Heat oil,
fry liver slices in it for a total
of 8 minutes, turning them
repeatedly. Take them out
and keep warm. Add butter
to oil and fry in it the pineapple and banana slices on
both sides. Wash and dry
lettuce leaves and arrange
them on 4 plates. Put the liver
slices on the lettuce leaves
and garnish them with the
pineapple and banana slices
and a sprig of parsley each.
Fill the hole in the pineapple
slices with the cranberries.
(If calf's liver is not available,
use chicken liver instead).

Illustration on page76

Steak Quebec – recipe on this ▷
page

Goes well with French bread or mashed potatoes. Recommended dessert: *Vanilla-Ice with Hot Chocolate Sauce* (recipe on page 80).

Veal Steak Maryland
△ ○ ○

4 veal steaks at 150g (5½ oz) each
2 tablespoons oil
A generous pinch each of salt, pepper and paprika
1 cup canned sweet-corn
4 tablespoons cream or canned milk

Fry steaks in hot oil for 4 minutes on either side, season them with salt, pepper and paprika and keep warm. Heat sweet-corn together with the cream or canned milk in the same fat as the steaks, at low heat. Sprinkle some salt and paprika over the corn and cover the steaks with them.

Goes well with *Horseradish Purée* (recipe on page 66). Recommended dessert: *Flamed Rum Cherries* (recipe on page 82).

Herb Curd Cheese
△ ○

300–400g (11–14 oz) curd cheese from skimmed milk
6–8 tablespoons milk or cream
½ teaspoon salt
¼ teaspoon pepper
1 cup deep-frozen mixed herbs
1 onion

Mix together the curd cheese, milk or cream, salt, pepper and herbs. Peel and dice onion and gently stir into curd.

Goes well with wholemeal, rye or crisp bread.

A hint: Instead of the deep-frozen herbs, you could use about 3 tablespoons dried herbs. But if you do, you'd better mix the curd cheese with fresh cress.

Curd Cheese Variations

Curd Cheese with Cucumbers

Mix the curd cheese with the juice of 1 lemon, ½ unpeeled fresh cucumber, a bunch of finely-chopped dill and salt and celery salt to taste. Garnish, if you like, with pumpernickel crumbs.

Tomato Curd Cheese

Mix the curd cheese with 2 cups of canned, peeled and finely-chopped tomatoes (or fresh tomatoes), 1 diced onion, as well as salt and pepper to taste.

Horseradish Curd Cheese

Mix curd cheese with 4–6 tablespoons finely-grated horseradish, 1 teaspoon mustard and some salt, pepper and lemon juice to taste; stir in 4 tablespoons cream or milk as well as 1 large grated apple.

Paprika Curd Cheese

Mix the curd cheese with some diced red and green peppers, diced onions, paprika, salt and chopped chives.

Ham Curd Cheese

Mix the curd cheese with 6–8 tablespoons milk or cream, 200g (7 oz) finely-chopped ham as well as parsley and salt to taste. Lastly add 6 finely-chopped pearl onions.

Strawberry Omelette
△ ○ ○

450g (16 oz) frozen straw-
*   berries*
4 tablespoons butter
6–8 eggs
A pinch salt

Put the deep-frozen strawberries together with 1 tablespoon butter into a frying-
pan, cover and heat up at low
heat. Whisk eggs together
with the salt. Melt the remainder of the butter in another frying-pan and make
successively 4 omelettes from
the whisked eggs. Allow the
underside of each omelette
to set, before gently moving
the pan backwards and for-
wards. Slip each omelette
onto a plate, fill one half with
a quarter of the warm strawberries and fold the other half
over.

Illustration below

Possible alternatives: 'Omelette nature', which is just
the whisked eggs, or the
eggs mixed with some herbs
(aux fines herbes) or with
grated cheese (au fromage),
may be preferable on occasions when something more
savoury is wanted.

Any kind of salad goes well
with savoury omelettes.

Strawberry Omelette – recipe above

In 10 to 15 Minutes

Spinach Pancakes
△ ○

300–450g (11–16 oz) deep-
    frozen creamed spinach
4 eggs
1/8 litre (1/4 pt) milk or water
A generous pinch of salt
8 level tablespoons flour
2 tablespoons dripping

Heat up the creamed spinach
according to the instructions
on the packet. Whisk to-
gether the eggs, milk or water,
and salt. Stir in flour by the
spoonful. Heat dripping in a
frying-pan and successively
bake in it 4 pancakes. These
are then placed on 4 preheated
plates and filled with the
creamed spinach.

Possible alternatives:
• You may like to make the
pancakes with rendered down
and chopped bacon slices.
That way they are more
savoury and go extremely
well with green salad.
• Stewed mushrooms or
chanterelles from a can provide excellent fillings for pancakes. Other recommended
fillings would be canned ragoût fin or fried chicken liver.
• Pancakes can also be prepared as a dessert or as a main
dish. In that case they are
served with apple purée or
with jam thinly spread on
them or sprinkled over with a
mixture of cinnamon and
sugar.

• For apple pancakes you
bake 1–2 finely-sliced apples
with the pancake mixture.
You can also make pancakes
with slices of banana, pears or
peaches.
• To make pancakes with a
filling of berries you can also
proceed in the following,
more sophisticated, manner:
you separate the eggs, whisk
the whites till stiff and fold
them under the dough. The
berries, whether from a can, a
jar or the deep-freeze, are
heated with a little butter, before being used as filling.
• You can, of course, serve
the berries separately, in the
form of stewed fruit, as
accompaniment to the pan-
cakes.

Vanilla-Ice with Hot Chocolate Sauce
△ ○

4 portions frozen vanilla ice-
    cream
1 can ready-made chocolate
    cream
2 tablespoons cream
2 tablespoons diced ginger
    from a jar
2 tablespoons preserved
    ginger syrup

Put the vanilla ice-cream into
4 glasses, which are then kept
in the refrigerator. Heat the
chocolate cream in a *bain
marie,* mixing it with the
cream, ginger and ginger syrup.
This hot sauce is then poured
over the ice-cream.

Strawberries Romanoff
△ ○ ○

400g (14 oz) fresh straw-
    berries
2 level tablespoons sugar
8 tablespoons deep-frozen
    raspberries or 200 g (7 oz)
    fresh raspberries
1/4 litre (1/2 pt) cream
1 level teaspoon icing sugar
2 liqueur glasses maraschino
    liqueur

Wash and pick over straw-
berries, put them into a bowl
and sprinkle the sugar over

them. Purée raspberries in liquidizer together with 2 tablespoons of the cream. Whisk the remaining cream till stiff, mix with the raspberry purée and the icing sugar and gently stir in the maraschino liqueur. Pour the raspberry cream sauce over the strawberries.

Iced Cream with Fruit
△ ○

1 packet deep-frozen vanilla
ice-cream
4 canned peach halves
4 slices canned pineapple
slices
$^1/_8$ litre (¼ pt) cream
½ cup cherries from a jar
8 tablespoons egg liqueur

Cut vanilla ice-cream into cubes and put these into a bowl. Cut the peach halves into thin slices and the 2 pineapple slices into cubes. Whisk cream till stiff and fill it into a piping bag. Drain cherries. Put the vanilla ice cubes in the liquidizer and turn them into a smooth substance. Stir egg liqueur into it. Now the 'half-frozen' cream — the German description of this type of dessert — is filled into a bowl — always one layer of

cream, one layer of fruit and so on, finishing with a layer of cream. Pipe the cream on top, arrange the 2 pineapple slices over the cream, placing the cherries in the centre of the pineapple slices.

Raspberry Curd Cheese Beaker
△ ○

2 eggs
1 packet vanilla sugar
200g (7 oz) curd cheese
4 tablespoons icing sugar
2 tablespoons lemon juice
4 tablespoons canned orange
juice
4 tablespoons raspberry jam

Separate eggs. Whisk whites till stiff; stir vanilla sugar into it. Mix together the curd cheese, egg yolks, icing sugar and lemon juice and fold the egg whites into this mixture. Mix orange juice with the raspberry jam. Fill the curd cheese cream into 4 glasses and cover it with the raspberry sauce.

Illustration on this page

Raspberry Curd Cheese
Beaker — recipe on this page

In 10 to 15 Minutes

Grapefruit Cocktail
△ ○

2 grapefruit
1 cup canned mandarin seg-
*   ments*
1 banana
2 teaspoons lemon juice
10 cocktail cherries
2 tablespoons mandarin juice
*   from the can*
2 level tablespoons icing sugar
2 tablespoons raspberry
*   brandy*
2 tablespoons Cointreau

Halve grapefruit, take out
and dice fruit flesh, removing
pips and pith. Halve mandarin
segments. Peel and dice banana
and sprinkle lemon juice
over it. Halve cherries and
mix with all the other fruit.
Now fill the fruit mixture
into the hollowed-out grapefruit halves. Mix together
mandarin juice, icing sugar,
raspberry brandy and
Cointreau. Pour the sauce
over the fruit cocktail, but
allow to infuse for a short
while before serving.

Flamed Rum Cherries
△ ○ ○

2 cups stoned morello cherries
*   from a jar*
2 tablespoons butter
2 tablespoons Campari
4 level tablespoons sugar
6 liqueur glasses rum
6 tablespoons cream
6 tablespoons cherry juice
*   from the morello jar*
1 cup coarsely-crumbled
*   sponge fingers*

Drain cherries in a sieve,
keeping the juice. Melt butter
in a saucepan and mix it with
the Campari and sugar. Add
cherries and heat up for five
minutes, shaking the pan all
the while. Pour rum over the
cherries, set it alight and let it
burn for about half a minute.
Extinguish flame with the
cream and the cherry juice;
keep on fire for another
minute to complete warming
process. Distribute the sponge
finger crumbs between 4 individual glass bowls and pour
the hot cherries with their
sauce over the sponge fingers.

Peach Meringues
△ △ ○

8 canned peach halves
2 teaspoons lemon juice
2 tablespoons raspberry jam
3 egg whites
1 teaspoon finely-grated
*   lemon peel*
6 level tablespoons icing sugar

Preheat oven to 250°C
(450°F; gas mark 8) or grill
to maximum temperature.
Drain peach halves. Stir together lemon juice and raspberry jam and fill the peach
halves with this mixture.
Whisk egg whites till stiff,
folding under the grated lemon
peel and the icing sugar. Put a
little mound of whisked egg
white on each peach half, put
them into an oven-proof dish
and bake them until the
meringue caps begin to brown.

Illustration on facing page

Alternatives to the above:
Instead of the canned peach
halves, you can use: fresh
peach halves, pineapple slices,
apricot halves, peeled orange
or apple slices, pear halves or
fresh ripe berries. In the event
of the fruit being rather too
sour, mix the raspberries, not
with lemon juice, but with
egg liqueur.

Peach Meringues — recipe above ▷

In 15 to 25 Minutes

Savoury Pea Salad
△ ○

1 cup water
A generous pinch salt
300g (11 oz) deep-frozen
  peas
100g (3½ oz) cooked ham
2 hardboiled eggs
Some lemon balm, if
  available
1 tablespoon lemon juice
1 level teaspoon sugar
A pinch white pepper
1 beaker yoghurt from
  skimmed milk
2 tablespoons chopped
parsley

Bring water with the salt to
the boil, pour the frozen peas
into it, cover and let cook for
6 minutes over low heat. Cut
ham into strips, peel eggs and
cut them into eighths (wash
and chop lemon balm, if
available). Drain cooked peas
in a sieve. Mix lemon juice,
sugar, pepper and yoghurt together and stir gently into
salad ingredients. Garnish
with chopped parsley and
lemon balm (if available).

Goes well with toast. As a
first course try *Mock Goulash
Soup* (recipe on page 23).

Smoked Fish Salad
△ ○

1 green pepper
1 apple
1 cup of celeriac slices from a
  jar
1 pickled cucumber
200g (7 oz) canned smoked
  fish
6 tablespoons tomato ketchup
½ teaspoon curry powder

Halve pepper, remove pips,
wash and cut into thin strips.
Peel and quarter apple, core
it and cut also into strips.
Chop celeriac slices, dice cucumber, celeriac slices and
fish. Mix tomato ketchup
with the curry powder and
stir gently into salad.

Serve with sticks of French
bread. Try *Spinach Soup* (recipe on page 22) as first course.

Transylvanian
Bean Salad △ ○

1 cup water
450g (16 oz) deep-frozen
  sliced green beans
50g (2 oz) smoked bacon
1 cup pickled red peppers
1 onion
¼ teaspoon salt
¼ teaspoon pepper
A pinch garlic powder
1 tablespoon wine vinegar

Bring water to the boil, put
frozen beans into it, cover
and slimmer over low heat for
12 minutes. Dice bacon and
render down in a frying-pan.
Cut peppers into strips. Peel
and dice onion. Drain beans
in a sieve, rinse them briefly
under cold running water,
drain and mix them with the
fat of the rendered-down
bacon, bacon dice, pepper
strips, diced onion, salt, pepper, garlic powder and vinegar.

Prawn Toast 'au gratin' △○○

280g (10 oz) canned prawns
2 tablespoons butter
4 slices toasting bread
200g (7 oz) canned asparagus tips
2 egg yolks
6 tablespoons cream or canned milk
6 tablespoons grated cheese
½ teaspoon salt
A generous pinch pepper

Preheat oven to 250°C (450°F; gas mark 8) or grill to maximum temperature. Briefly rinse prawns under cold water and drain. Melt 1 tablespoon butter in a frying pan, fry the slices of toasting bread in it (one side only), take them out and transfer them to an oven-proof dish. Now put the prawns and the remainder of the butter into the pan and heat them up for 1 minute, stirring all the time. Drain asparagus tips, keeping the liquor. Add the asparagus to the prawns and heat up briefly. Stir together egg yolks, cream or milk, cheese, salt and pepper, adding a little of the asparagus liquor. Distribute prawns and asparagus tips over toast slices and pour the sauce over. Bake the toast in the oven or under the grill for 8—10 minutes.

Illustration below.

Goes well with celeriac salad from a jar, mixed with apple and tomato slices, or *Salad Peasant Girl* (recipe on page 86). For dessert try stewed plums from a jar or *Peach Curd Cheese* (recipe on page 48).

Rice Curry with Ham and Bananas △○

4 firm bananas
1 bag 5-minute rice
2 tablespoons dripping
1 level teaspoon paprika
4 slices cooked ham, each weighing 50g (2 oz)
4 tablespoons curry paste

Bring water for rice to the boil. Peel bananas and cut them through lengthwise. Preheat oven to 250° C (450° F; gas mark 8). Cook 5-minute rice in the bag in the boiling water, according to instructions. Heat dripping in a frying-pan and place banana halves into it. Sprinkle paprika over them and let bananas fry over low heat for 1 minute. Now take 2 banana

Prawn Toast 'au gratin' — recipe on this page

halves at a time and wrap them in 1 slice of ham. Drain and briefly rinse cooked rice in a sieve. Stir curry paste into dripping, add rice, turning it over until it has completely blended with the curry fat. Put the curried rice into an oven-proof dish, place the banana-ham rolls on top and let the whole soak through in the oven or under the grill for another 5 minutes.

Goes well with *Simple Tomato Salad* (recipe on page 32) or *Lettuce Salad with Mayonnaise Dressing* (recipe on page 30). Suitable desserts include stewed apricots from a can or *Orange Surprise* (recipe on page 44).

A Tip: These banana-filled ham rolls may also be served as appetizers, without rice, but with toast. Incidentally, there is another way of preparing banana-filled ham rolls: cut the bananas into slices of about 4 cm (1½″), wrap ham around each slice, fastening it with a wooden toothpick; dip rolls into a thick-running batter and then deep-fry till golden brown.

Lobster Bread Rolls
△ ○ ○

1 cucumber pickled in mustard marinate
A bunch of parsley or dill
2 tomatoes
2 bread rolls
2 tablespoons butter
2 tablespoons mayonnaise
2 tablespoons tomato ketchup
4 tablespoons curd cheese from skimmed milk
200g (7 oz) canned lobster or crayfish meat
½ lemon

Preheat oven to 250°C (450°F; gas mark 8) or grill to maximum temperature. Dice cucumber; wash and chop parsley or dill. Wash tomatoes and cut them into slices. Cut open bread rolls, hollow out the halves, thinly butter the insides and toast them with the opening pointing upwards in the oven or under the grill. Stir together mayonnaise, tomato ketchup, curd cheese and diced cucumber. Shred the lobster or crayfish meat, briefly rinse it under cold water, drain and fold it under the mayonnaise mixture. Fill the warmed hollowed-out bread roll halves with the lobster mayonnaise, garnish with parsley or dill and serve with a slice of lemon per portion.

Goes well with *Savoury Pea Salad* (recipe on page 84). As a dessert try *Vanilla-Ice with Fruit Sauce* (recipe on page 45).

Salad Peasant Girl
△ ○

A bunch of fresh mixed herbs
2 small heads of lettuce
80g (3 oz) Roquefort Cheese
1 cup cream
1 teaspoon lemon juice
A generous pinch pepper

Wash and chop herbs. Separate lettuce leaves, removing the outer ones, wash and drain the rest and shred them. Squash the Roquefort with a fork and mix it with the cream, lemon juice, pepper and herbs. Now gently stir the dressing into the lettuce leaves.

Paprika Toast

△ ○

4 slices toasting bread
2 small green peppers
12 stuffed green olives
200g (7 oz) garlic sausage
100g (3½ oz) Jarlsberg
   cheese

Preheat oven to 250°C
(450°F; gas mark 8) or grill to
maximum temperature.
Slightly toast bread slices.
Clean and wash peppers and
cut them into rings. Briefly
rinse olives under cold
running water, drain and cut
them into thin slices. Slice
sausage and cover the toast
with it. The pepper rings are
placed on top of the sausage
slices and the cheese, coarsely-
grated, straight over the peppers. The little olive slices
are arranged on top of the
cheese. The toast is finally
put in the oven or under the
grill until cheese begins to
melt.

Illustration below

Follows well *Zuppa Pavese*
(recipe on page 52). As dessert try *Strawberry Omelette*
(recipe on page 79).

A Tip: The cooking time is so
short that the pepper rings remain nearly raw. Those who
prefer them completely
cooked may like to scald them
in boiling water for a few minutes.

Paprika Toast — recipe above

In 15 to 25 Minutes

Tuna Patties
△ ○ ○

4 puff pastry cases (bought
  ready for use)
½ onion
½ cup pickled peppers
1 can tunny fish in oil
4 hardboiled eggs
A pinch each of salt, pepper,
  paprika and garlic salt
1 small can shrimps
A bunch of parsley

Preheat oven to 250°C (450°F; gas mark 8). Heat patties in oven. Peel and chop onion. Chop peppers as well, but keeping 4 strips back. Shred tunny fish into small pieces; peel and chop hard-boiled eggs. Season the diced onions, chopped peppers, tunny fish and chopped eggs with salt, pepper, paprika and the garlic powder, fill the patties with this mixture and heat once again in the oven. Separate shrimps, briefly

rinse them under cold water and drain. Wash and dry parsley and divide into 4 smaller bunches. The patties done, garnish them with the shrimps, pepper strips and parsley.

Illustration below

Serve after *Lettuce Soup* (recipe on page 51).

Tuna Patties — recipe above

In 15 to 25 Minutes

Egg Salad on Toast
△○

2 tomatoes
4 hardboiled eggs
1 pickled cucumber
1 apple
100g (3½ oz) meat sausage
    of the Mortadella type
1 tablespoon lemon juice
½ teaspoon salt
A generous pinch pepper
4 tablespoons curd cheese
    from skimmed milk
2 tablespoons cream
½ teaspoon mild mustard
A generous pinch horseradish
1 level teaspoon sugar
4 slices toasting bread
2 tablespoons chopped pars-
    ley

Bring to the boil about 1 cup
water. Make a few incisions
into the bottom end of the
tomatoes, pour some boiling
water over them and let them
lie in it for a few minutes.
Peel and dice eggs. Also dice
cucumber. Peel and core apple
and cut it into small cubes.
Remove skin from sausage
and dice it. Skin tomatoes,
cut them into small pieces
and mix them with the eggs,
cucumber, apple and sausage.
Add lemon juice and season
with salt and pepper. Stir together the curd cheese, cream,
mustard, grated horseradish
and sugar and gently mix
with the salad ingredients.
Toast bread slices. Heap salad
on the toast, sprinkling it
with parsley.

Goes well with beetroot from
a jar or *Transylvanian Bean
Salad* (recipe on page 84).
Suitable desserts include curd
cheese from the freezer or
Banana Curd Cheese (recipe
on page 48).

A Hint: The above egg salad
also makes an excellent
evening main course, but
you'd have to double the
quantities and serve the toast
separately, unless you prefer
potato croquettes or a green
salad as a side-dish. If you
prepare the egg salad the day
before, keeping it covered in
the refrigerator, it is sure to
dry out a little as the eggs
soak up some of the liquid.
You would be well advised,
therefore, to mix into it a
little milk before putting it
on the table.

Fish Fillets 'au gratin' △○

600g (22 oz) fish fillets, fresh
    or deep-frozen
1 tablespoon lemon juice
1 teaspoon salt
4 tablespoons water
300g (11 oz) canned button
    mushrooms
2 tablespoons chopped pars-
    ley
4 tablespoons grated cheese
1 tablespoon butter

Preheat oven to 250°C
(450°F; gas mark 8) or grill
to maximum temperature.
Sprinkle lemon juice over fish
fillets, season with salt and
put them in a fish kettle to
steam for 10 minutes (keep
the lid on). Drain button
mushrooms in a sieve. Put
the fish fillets with the liquor
in an oven-proof dish, add
mushrooms, parsley and
grated cheese, flake butter
and sprinkle flakes over fish.
Bake in oven for 8 minutes.

Serve with either 5-minute
rice or boiled potatoes and
green salad. Suitable desserts
include either canned stewed
pears or stewed rhubarb.

Fish Fillets in White Wine Sauce
△ ○

1/8 litre (1/4 pt) water
1/2 teaspoon salt
1 tablespoon lemon juice
600g (20 oz) frozen fish
   fillets
1/8 litre (1/4 pt) white wine
A bunch of fresh dill
2 egg yolks
6 tablespoons cream
A generous pinch sugar

Bring to the boil the water with the salt and lemon juice, place the frozen fish fillets into the water, cover and let simmer for 12 minutes over low heat. Pour wine into it and allow to get warm. Wash, dry and chop dill. Whisk eggs together with cream and sugar, add a little of the fish liquor. Thicken the remaining fish liquor, with the egg yolk-cream mixture. Take the pot off the fire immediately. Sprinkle dill over the fillets in their sauce before serving.

Goes well with *Rice and Mushrooms* (recipe on page 64) and green salad. For dessert try *Orange Curd Cheese* (recipe on page 48).

Cod with Creamed Horseradish Sauce
△ ○ ○

600g (22 oz) cod fillets
2 teaspoons lemon juice
1/2 teaspoon salt
1/2 litre (1 pt) water
2 slices lemon
A bunch of herbs
1 apple
75g (2 1/2 oz) grated horse-
   radish from a jar
A pinch each of salt and
   sugar
1/8 litre (1/4 pt) cream

Wash and dry fillets, rub salt into them and sprinkle lemon juice over them. Bring to the boil the water, cider, lemon slices and herbs, put the fish fillets into the liquor and let them simmer over low heat for 15 minutes. Peel and grate apple. Mix the grated apple with the horseradish, salt and sugar. Whisk cream till stiff and fold under the apple-and-horseradish mixture.

Illustration on facing page

Goes well with parsley potatoes or French bread. A suitable dessert is instant cold chocolate pudding.

Mussel Ragoût
△ ○ ○

200g (7 oz) noodles in the
   shape of shells
1 level teaspoon salt
1 onion
400g (14 oz) mussels canned
   in their natural juice
2 tablespoons oil
2 cups canned peeled tom-
   atoes
A generous pinch each of
   salt, pepper and garlic
   powder

Pour noodles into fiercely-boiling salt water and cook for 15 minutes. Peel and dice onion. Drain mussels, keeping back liquor from the can. Heat oil; lightly fry diced onion; add tomatoes, mussels and some of the liquor from the mussels, cover and warm the lot over low heat for ten minutes. Drain the cooked noodles, stir under the mussels and season to taste with salt, pepper and garlic powder.

For dessert: ready-to-serve fruit yoghurt.

In 15 to 25 Minutes

Some Tips on Pasta

The various kinds of pasta — like uncooked rice and raw potatoes — only just make the grade as admissible ingredients in a kitchen where the emphasis is on speedy results. But as pasta takes between 12 and 16 minutes to produce, it can still be useful when preparing tasty dishes falling into the 20–25 minute category.

Whatever pasta you use, whether it be spaghetti, spaghettini (the very thin type of spaghetti), macaroni, flat noodles (Lasagnes) or one or the other of the various pasta shapes, it's important that you follow the manufacturer's cooking instructions strictly.

• Don't bother if the cooking time is a little longer than you'd wish, for in the meantime you'll be able to prepare a tasty sauce or some side-dish you'd like to serve with your pasta.
• If your intention is to serve pasta as the main course you must reckon on between 75 and 100g (2½–3½ oz) per person.
• Cook all pasta in plenty of salt water, rinse briefly under cold running water and drain, before you do anything else with it.

• There are now on the market ready-prepared pasta dishes complete with sauce.

Various Pasta Dishes

In the following recipes the cooking time for the pasta is about 15 minutes.

Italian Noodles

Drain the cooked spaghetti or macaroni and serve it with generous helpings of browned butter and grated Parmesan cheese.

Ham Noodles

Briefly rinse the cooked noodles under cold running water, then drain them. Heat 1–2 tablespoons butter in a frying-pan and in it fry a chopped onion and 200g (7 oz) of ham, cut in strips. Heat noodles in this ham and onion mixture. If you like you can also whisk together ½ cup of soured cream and 1 egg, pour it over the hot noodles and allow to set.

Serve with a green salad.

Noodles in Tomato Sauce

Take a packet of instant tomato sauce, prepare it according to instructions and enrich it by adding at the last minute a tablespoon of tomato purée, 2 tablespoons of tomato ketchup and 4 tablespoons of cream. Garnish with some chopped parsley. Serve with the cooked noodles. If you like you can also lightly fry 200–300g (7–11 oz) of minced meat together with some diced onions and mix this in with the sauce.

Serve with a green salad.

Spaghetti with Meat Sauce – recipe on page 94 ▷

In 15 to 25 Minutes

Spaghetti with Meat Sauce
△ ○

3 litre (6 pt) water
1½ teaspoons salt
300g (11 oz) spaghetti
3 tablespoons olive oil
2 tablespoons tomato purée
1 cup canned peeled toma-
toes
400g (14 oz) mixed minced
meat
2 tablespoons ready-roasted
onions
¼ teaspoon pepper
1 level teaspoon paprika
2 cups white wine
1 cup grated Parmesan cheese

Bring the water, to which you have added 1 teaspoon of salt, to the boil and cook the spaghetti over fierce heat for 14 minutes. Heat the oil in a casserole, stir the tomato purée and the peeled toma-toes into it until hot; add the minced meat and lightly fry it, while continuing to stir. Now add the roasted onions, the remainder of the salt, the pepper, paprika and white wine; mix well, cover and let simmer for 10 minutes. Drain spaghetti in a sieve, fill it into a dish and pour the meat sauce over it. Garnish with the Parmesan cheese.

Illustration on page 93

Goes well with green salad or chicory salad.

Yugoslav Chicken Fry △ ○

200g (7 oz) spaghetti
1 level teaspoon salt
1 chicken from a can
1 onion
1 clove garlic
1 cup pickled peppers
1 cup canned peeled toma-
toes
2 tablespoons oil
¹/8 litre (¼ pt) red wine
2 tablespoons chopped pars-
ley

Cook spaghetti in a lot of boiling salted water over medium heat for 14 minutes. Take chicken from can, separate meat from bones and skin and cut meat into small pieces. Peel and dice onion. Peel garlic clove, dice it and squash the dice thoroughly. Drain pickled peppers and the canned tomatoes, cutting both into somewhat smaller pieces. Heat oil in a rather large pot and in it lightly fry the diced onion and the squashed garlic, stirring all the while. While continuing to stir, add pickled peppers and tomatoes and lightly fry these as well. Add the chicken meat and red wine and heat them up over low heat. The cooked spaghetti is drained, rinsed briefly under cold running water, before being mixed with the chicken sauce and allowed once more to get properly hot. Garnish with

chopped parsley before serving.

Illustration on facing page

Suitable sweets to follow include *Rustic Strawberry Dessert* (recipe on page 110) and *Cold Apricot Dessert* (recipe on page 107).

A few hints: If, instead of canned chicken, you try some ready-grilled spring chicken, you may be able to keep back, say, 2 cups of chopped chicken meat for the follow-ing day when it will come in handy to enrich a *Curried Cream of Chicken Soup* (rec-ipe on page 19) or *Vegetable Soup Summerday* (recipe on page 50).

In 15 to 25 Minutes

Spring Chicken Mignon △ ○ ○

4 deep-frozen filleted spring chicken breasts
2 teaspoons lemon juice
2 tablespoons oil
12 pickled pearl onions
200g (7 oz) canned button mushrooms
1 cup canned peeled tomatoes
A generous pinch each of salt and pepper
4 tablespoons tomato ketchup

Sprinkle the lemon juice over the frozen chicken breasts. Heat oil and in it fry the pearl onions till they are brown. Add the chicken fillets and fry them over low heat on both sides — 6–7 minutes on either side. Distribute the mushrooms and tomatoes evenly over the fillets, cover and allow to heat through. Stir together salt, pepper and tomato ketchup and pour over the chicken dish.

Goes well with potato purée and *Richly-Laden Salad Platter* (recipe on page 61). For dessert try *Fruit Salad Simone* (recipe on page 110).

A Tip: If really pressed for time you can prepare the above dish still more simply by using a ready-fried spring chicken. This you merely keep warm while you concentrate on preparing the sauce.

Yugoslav Chicken Fry — recipe on facing page

In 15 to 25 Minutes

Curly Kale with Meat Balls

△ ○

450g (16 oz) canned curly kale
1 teaspoon salt
1 tablespoon oil
4 canned meat balls (generally known as 'Frikadellen')
1 tablespoon butter or margarine

Heat the curly kale in a little salted water over low heat.

Heat oil in a frying-pan and in it heat the meat balls. Before serving the curly kale pour 1 tablespoon of melted butter or margarine over it.

Illustration below

Goes well with potato purée (made from powder). A suitable sweet is *Rustic Strawberry Dessert* (recipe on page 110).

Pancakes with Sauerkraut △ ○

250g (9 oz) canned sauerkraut
200g (7 oz) smoked pork chops (cooked)
1 tablespoon lard
1 tablespoon ready-roasted onions
4 eggs
1 teaspoon salt
1 liqueur glass whisky
¼ litre (½ pt) water
8 level tablespoons flour

Curly Kale with Meat Balls — recipe above

In 15 to 25 Minutes

2 tablespoons dripping
¼ litre (½ pt) hot water
2 heaped teaspoons instant
white sauce
4 tablespoons tomato purée
2 tablespoons grated cheese

Tease sauerkraut apart with two forks. Dice the pork chops. Melt the lard in a fairly large saucepan into which you put the pickled cabbage, the meat and roasted onions; stir well, cover and cook for 15 minutes. Whisk

together the eggs, salt and whisky, add the water and slowly stir in the flour so that you end up with a thick running batter. Melt the dripping in a frying pan and in it make four pancakes from the batter. Keep these warm. Put the hot water into a saucepan, in it dissolve the instant white sauce; stir into it the tomato purée and the grated cheese and allow everything to get thoroughly hot.

You serve the pancakes by placing them on 4 individual plates, filling them with the sauerkraut and pouring a little of the cheese sauce over each.

Illustration below

As dessert serve table-ready curd cheese from the freezer.

Pancakes with Sauerkraut — recipe on facing page

In 15 to 25 Minutes

Minced Beef Steaks in Cucumber Sauce
△ ○ ○

1 onion
8 canned anchovy fillets
2 pickled cucumbers
400g (14 oz) minced beef
1 teaspoon salt
¼ teaspoon pepper
A pinch grated nutmeg
2 egg yolks
2 tablespoons dripping
4 tablespoons cream or
   canned milk

Peel and dice onion. Chop anchovy fillets. Dice pickled cucumbers. Season the minced meat with the salt, pepper and nutmeg and knead together thoroughly with the diced onion, chopped anchovies and egg yolks. Now you form with wet hands even-sized flat meat cakes; heat the dripping in a frying-pan and fry the meat cakes for 5 minutes on each side. Transfer the meat cakes from the pan to a serving dish which you keep warm in the oven. Add the diced cucumbers and the cream or canned milk to the dripping and heat them for 2 minutes, stirring constantly. The cucumber sauce is finally poured over the meat cakes.

Goes well with either *Quick Potato Salad* (recipe on page 68) or *Salad Country Girl* (recipe on page 86). Suitable sweets include ice-cream from the freezer and *Apple Snow with Kiss* (recipe on page 44).

Veal Steak in Soya Sauce
△ ○ ○

4 veal steaks at 120g (4½ oz)
   each
2 tablespoons oil
A pinch of salt per steak
1 beaker yoghurt
1 level teaspoon coarsely-
   milled pepper
2 teaspoons soya sauce
1 tablespoon chopped parsley

Briefly rinse veal steaks under cold running water and dry. Heat oil in frying-pan and fry steaks in it for 5—6 minutes on either side. Salt steaks and keep warm. Now mix into the fat the yoghurt, pepper, soya sauce and parsley and when hot pour sauce over the steaks.

Illustration on page 107

Goes well with white bread or potato chips from the freezer. For a suitable dessert try *Cold Apricot 'Kaltschale'* (recipe on page 107).

Pork Cutlets 'Extra'
△ ○ ○

4 pork cutlets, each weighing
   120g (4½ oz)
½ teaspoon salt
¼ teaspoon pepper
About 1 tablespoon flour
1 egg
6 tablespoons breadcrumbs
2 tablespoons oil
1 small can mushrooms
4 tablespoons any spicy sauce
2 tomatoes
4 slices toasting bread
4 thin slices Edam cheese

Preheat oven to 250°C (450°F; gas mark 8) or grill to maximum temperature. Lightly salt and pepper the pork cutlets and turn them first in the flour, then in the beaten egg and finally in the breadcrumbs. Heat oil in a frying-pan and fry the cutlets on both sides for about 6 minutes until crisp and brown. In the meantime, drain and slice mushrooms and heat them in the spicy sauce. Wash tomatoes and cut them in slices. 1 tomato slice is now placed on each cutlet and a slice of cheese on top of that. Toast the bread, put the cutlets on the toast and bake the lot in the oven or under the grill until the cheese begins to melt. Finally, pour the sauce over the cooked cutlets.

Goes well with *Lettuce with Mayonnaise Dressing* (recipe on page 30).

A Tip: The cutlets may also be served without toast in which case you serve fried potatoes instead.

Illustration below

Fillet Steak with Parsley Potatoes
△ ○ ○

250g (9 oz) potatoes cooked
*   in their jackets*
1 tablespoon dripping
1 level teaspoon salt
1 tablespoon chopped parsley
4 fillets of beef, each weighing
*   150g (5½ oz)*
1 tablespoon oil
½ teaspoon paprika
4 tomatoes
1 tablespoon butter
A pinch of pepper per tomato

Peel tomatoes, cutting larger ones into halves or quarters, but leaving the smaller ones whole. Heat dripping in a frying-pan, toss the potatoes in it, salt them, cover the pan, and over low heat allow them to warm right through, stirring repeatedly and mixing the parsley under the potatoes. Briefly rinse fillet steaks under cold running water and dry them well with kitchen paper. Heat the oil in another frying-pan and fry the fillets for 6 minutes on each side.

Pork Cutlets 'Extra' – recipe on facing page

In 15 to 25 Minutes

Then season them with the remaining salt and the paprika and keep them warm on a preheated dish. Wash tomatoes, making a few incisions at the bottom ends. Add the butter to the fat left from frying the meat, place in it the tomatoes, season them with a little pepper, cover and allow them to warm through over medium heat for a few minutes. Serve steaks and tomatoes on one dish and the parsley potatoes separately.

Goes well with *Lettuce Salad with Mayonnaise Dressing* (recipe on page 30). A suitable dessert is *Pears with a Kick* (recipe on page 44).

Rosemary Cutlets
△ ○ ○

¹/8 litre (¼ pt) water
4 tomatoes
300g (11 oz) frozen peas
1 teaspoon salt
1 tablespoon butter

4 veal cutlets of 150g (5½ oz) each
2 tablespoons oil
A pinch of pepper per cutlet
4 small sprigs of fresh rosemary or some dried rosemary

Bring water to the boil. Make some incisions into the bottom end of the tomatoes, pour the boiling water over them and leave them for 3 minutes in the hot water. Put the frozen peas into a saucepan together with a pinch of

Rosemary Cutlet – recipe above

In 15 to 25 Minutes

salt and 2 tablespoons of water, cover and cook them for 6 minutes over low heat. Peel the tomatoes, cut off the upper third and carefully hollow out the rest. Melt the butter, place the tomatoes in it, cover and let them simmer for 5 minutes. Briefly rinse the cutlets under cold running water, dab them dry and fry them in hot oil on each side for about 6 minutes. Season them with what remains of the salt and pepper. Arrange the cutlets on a preheated dish, garnishing them with the sprigs of rosemary (alternatively, sprinkle the dried rosemary over them). Drain peas, fill the hollowed-out tomatoes with them and arrange the tomatoes around the cutlets.

Illustration on facing page

Goes well with parsley potatoes; for dessert try *Orange Curd Cheese* (recipe on page 48).

Some possible variations:
• If you coat the cutlets with egg and breadcrumbs, – turn them first in flour, then in a beaten egg and finally in a mixture of breadcrumbs and parmesan cheese – the very acceptable result is 'Côtelette Milanese'.
• If, before serving your egg and breadcrumbed cutlets, you garnish them with some herb butter (called 'maître d'hôtel') you will produce 'London Cutlets'.

Spanish Fried Eggs – recipe on page 102

In 15 to 25 Minutes

● If, finally, you serve with your egg and breadcrumbed cutlets peas tossed in butter and mixed with strips of ham, your guests will be eating 'Côtelettes Bardoux'.

Spanish Fried Eggs
△ ○ ○

100g (3½ oz) streaky bacon
1 onion
1 clove garlic
1 green pepper
4 tomatoes
2 tablespoons chopped pars-
*   ley*
A few drops tabasco sauce
A pinch each of dried oregano
*   and salt*
280g (10 oz) canned prawns
4 eggs

Dice bacon. Peel and dice onion. Peel and dice garlic and crush thoroughly. Halve pepper, remove pips, wash the halves and cut them into strips. Wash and dry tomatoes and cut them into eighths. Render down bacon in a frying-pan, add sliced onion and crushed garlic and lightly fry mixture, stirring all the while. You then add the pepper strips, tomato eighths and chopped parsley, cover and allow to simmer for 10 minutes. Mix in tabasco, oregano and a pinch of salt, as well as the prawns. Finally break 4 eggs over the vegetables and

cook over fairly strong heat till done.

Illustration on page 101

Goes well with rye or wholemeal bread; for a suitable dessert try yoghurt müsli (bought table-ready).

Eggs in Mustard Sauce
△ ○

8 eggs
½ litre (1 pt) hot water
4 level tablespoons instant
*   white sauce*
1–2 teaspoons mustard to
*   taste*
½ teaspoon sugar
1 tablespoon wine vinegar
1 teaspoon grated horseradish
2 tablespoons chopped pars-
*   ley*

Put eggs in boiling water, leave them to boil for 6 minutes, then rinse them in cold water and peel them. Dissolve the instant sauce in the hot water, adding the mustard, sugar, wine vinegar and horseradish. Place eggs in the sauce which is then thoroughly heated up over low heat. Cut them in half and garnish with the parsley before serving.

Illustration on facing page

Goes well with instant mashed potatoes.

Possible variations: You may like to replace the mustard sauce with a savoury tomato sauce, which you prepare in the following manner:
Melt 2 tablespoons of butter or margarine and into it stir 1 tablespoon of flour to make a roux; to this you add 1 small can of tomato purée and finally 1 cup of water, stirring constantly. Season to taste with some salt, pepper and paprika. Stir in 1 cup canned tomato juice and ½ cup of tomato ketchup. Heat up eggs in this sauce.

Illustration on facing page

For another variation, try eggs in curry sauce:
Melt 2 tablespoons butter, stir in 1½ tablespoons flour to make a roux. Add 2–3 teaspoons of curry powder and fill up with 1½ cups of instant meat stock. Add 1 tablespoon of ready-roasted onions, season to taste with salt and pepper; finally, mix in 1 cup of cream. Reheat eggs in the sauce before serving.

Illustration on facing page

Eggs in Mustard, Tomato and Curry Sauce (bottom left, ▷ top right, bottom right) – recipes on this page

In 15 to 25 Minutes

Egg 'en cocotte'
△ ○ ○

4 tablespoons butter
150g (5½ oz) smoked fillet
   of ham
100g (3½ oz) Edam cheese
   in a piece
4 eggs
A generous pinch of salt and
   pepper per egg
4 tablespoons cream
4 level teaspoons paprika

Grease 4 small oven-proof
forms with butter. Dice ham
and cheese before putting

them into the forms. Break
1 egg into each of the forms
and season it with pepper and
salt. Beat cream with a fork
until half stiff, mix in paprika
and distribute over the eggs.
Cover forms with foil, stand
them in a hot-water bath,
normally called 'bain marie'
for 15 minutes, to allow the
eggs to get done.

Goes well with tomato ketchup, or any other sharp
sauce, and toast; as a dessert:
Wine and Lemon Cream (recipe on page 44).

Ham Ragoût 'California' — recipe on this page

Ham Ragoût 'California' △ ○ ○

2 cups water
½ teaspoon salt
450g (16 oz) deep-frozen
   macedoine of vegetables
300g (11 oz) cooked ham in
   a piece
4 canned peach halves
4 tablespoons peach juice
6 tablespoons white wine
2 level tablespoons flour
2 tablespoons Shashlik sauce
A generous pinch paprika
A few drops of a spicy sauce

Salt water and bring to boil,
pour vegetables into it, cover
and allow to cook over low
heat for 12 minutes. Dice ham
and peach halves. After 5
minutes add diced ham to
vegetables. Stir together
peach juice, white wine and
flour. Add this mixture to the
vegetables and bring once
more to the boil. Now season
to taste with the Shashlik
sauce, the paprika and the
other spicy sauce you have
chosen. Finally, gently stir in
the diced peaches.

Illustration on this page

Goes well with plain boiled
rice. For dessert try caramel
yoghurt (bought table-ready).

In 15 to 25 Minutes

Rapid Ragoût Sacha
△ ○ ○ * *

1 pickled cucumber
*4 tablespoons pickled beet-
   root*
*4 tablespoons canned mush-
   rooms*
Some capers
250g (9 oz) fillet of beef
200g (7 oz) lean pork
2 tablespoons butter
1 tablespoon oil
½ teaspoon salt
¼ teaspoon pepper
½ teaspoon paprika
4 tablespoons cream
1 glass Madeira wine

Cut cucumber and beetroots into thin strips. Drain mushrooms and cut into slices. Drain capers. Remove gristle and skin from beef and pork and cut meat into small even-sized strips. Heat butter and oil in a frying-pan, gradually add the meat strips, tossing them about until they are all brown; season them with the salt, pepper and paprika. Now add the cucumber, beetroot, mushrooms and capers, mix thoroughly and allow to cook over low heat for a further 10 minutes. The ragoût is then ready to be taken off the fire and rounded off with the cream and the Madeira wine.

Goes well with white bread and *Salad 'Country Girl'* (recipe on page 86). For a suitable sweet: *Nut Mousse Dessert* (recipe on page 44).

A Hint: If the ragoût is to be deep-frozen, postpone putting the wine and the cream in until after you've defrosted it.

Breakfast – Country Style
△ ○

*500g (18 oz) potatoes cooked
   in the jackets*
1 onion
*200g (7 oz) roast or boiled
   meat*
4 Vienna sausages
4 eggs
*A pinch each of salt, pepper
   and paprika*
2 tablespoons dripping
*1 level teaspoon caraway
   seeds*
*2 tablespoons chopped pars-
   ley or chives*

Peel and slice potatoes. Peel and dice onion. Dice meat as well. Slice Vienna sausages. Beat together the eggs, salt, pepper and paprika. Melt dripping in a frying-pan, lightly fry the diced onion in it, stirring all the while; add the potatoes, meat, sausage and caraway seeds, heating it all up, while turning it over several times. Now pour the beaten and seasoned eggs over, allowing the eggs to set. Garnish with the parsley or chives before serving.

Illustration on page 106

Goes well with either *Simple Tomato Salad* (recipe on page 32), or *Green Salad with Mayonnaise Dressing* (recipe on page 30). For dessert try *Banana Soufflé* (recipe on page 107).

In 15 to 25 Minutes

Apricot 'Kaltschale'
△ ○

*500g (18 oz) canned apricot
    halves*
¹/₈ litre (¼ pt) white wine
5 tablespoons curd cheese
5 tablespoons cream
*4 tablespoons grated coco-
    nut*

Mash the apricots with their
juice and the white wine in
the liquidizer. Add the curd
cheese and cream and mix
well the apricot purée. Fill
into 4 individual bowls and
garnish with the grated coconut.

Illustration below

Banana Souffle
△ ○

6 bananas
1 tablespoon lemon juice
1 tablespoon honey
1 cup flaked rice
4 teaspoons butter

2 tablespoons icing sugar
1 tablespoon vanilla sugar

Preheat oven to 250°C
(450°F; gas mark 8) or grill
to maximum temperature.
Peel bananas and squash them
with a fork. Mix them with
the lemon juice and honey
and gently stir in the flaked
rice. Grease 4 oven-proof
forms with the butter and
distribute the soufflé mixture
into them. Mix the icing sugar
with the vanilla sugar and
sprinkle this mixture on top

◁ Veal Steak in Soya Sauce – recipe on page 98 Apricot 'Kaltschale'
  – recipe above
Breakfast – Country Style – recipe on page 105

In 15 to 25 Minutes

of the 4 forms. The forms are now placed in the oven or under the grill and left there until they begin to brown on the surface.

Morello Cherry Meringue

△ △ ○

¼ litre (½ pt) milk
½ vanilla pod
4 cups cooked rice
4 egg whites

6 level tablespoons sugar
500g (18 oz) morello cherries from a jar
2 tablespoons butter or margarine

Preheat oven to 250°C (450°F; gas mark 8) or grill to highest temperature. Heat milk with the vanilla pod in it, add rice and warm right through for several minutes over low heat. Whisk egg whites till stiff, folding sugar under it at the last moment.

Drain morello cherries. Thoroughly grease an oven-proof form with the butter or margarine and fill morello cherries into it. Mix the stiff egg whites with the rice pudding and heap it in the form of a mound onto the cherries. The dessert is now left in the oven or under the grill until the points of the meringue begin to get brown.

Illustration on facing page

Fruit Salad Simone – recipe on page 110
Morello Cherry Meringue – recipe above

In 15 to 25 Minutes

A suitable sweet after *Mock Goulash Soup* (recipe on page 23) or *Pea Soup Debreczin* (recipe on page 20).

Rustic Strawberry Dessert △○

*400g (14 oz) fresh straw-
    berries
1 tablespoon honey
2 tablespoons canned orange
    juice*

*200g (7 oz) cottage cheese
2 tablespoons milk
1 level tablespoon sugar
4 tablespoons chopped
    pistachio nuts*

Wash and pick over the strawberries. Halve 12 especially good strawberries and keep them on one side. Mash the others in the liquidizer together with the orange juice and honey. Mix the cottage cheese with the milk and sugar. Now cursorily and for a moment only mix cottage cheese with the liquidized strawberries, before filling the lot into individual dessert bowls or glasses. Garnish with the strawberry halves you have kept on one side and decorate the rims of the glasses or bowls with the pistachio nuts.

Illustration below

Fruit Salad Simone △○○

*1 honey-dew melon
2 oranges
200g (7 oz) black grapes
Juice of 1 lemon
A pinch ground ginger
1 level tablespoon sugar*

Halve melon, scrape out pips with a spoon, cut out the fruit flesh and dice it. Peel oranges, separate into segments and cut these into dice, removing pips. Wash and drain grapes. Now mix the diced melon, orange pieces and grapes with the lemon juice, ginger and sugar and fill it all into one of the hollowed-out melon halves to serve.

Illustration on page 109

Rustic Strawberry
Dessert — recipe above

In 15 to 25 Minutes

Bilberry Ice-Bowl
△ △ ○ ○

*400g (14 oz) bilberries
(called 'blueberries' in the
USA)
200g (7 oz) sugar
¼ litre (½ pt) cream
2 liqueur glasses blackberry
liqueur
4 liqueur glasses egg liqueur
4 wafers*

Carefully pick over bilberries,
before washing them several
times and pressing them
through a fine-meshed sieve.
The resulting bilberry purée is
then mixed with the sugar.
2/3 of the cream should now
be whisked stiff and gently
stirred into the bilberry purée
together with the blackberry
liqueur. Now fill the purée
into an ice-cube tray and leave
overnight in the freezing
compartment of the refrigerator. Before serving whisk the
remainder of the cream till
stiff, and cut the ice cream
into 4 portions which you fill
into 4 bowls. Pour a little egg
liqueur over each portion.
With a piping bag squirt a
spiral of whipped cream on
top of each portion. Garnish
with a wafer into each.

Illustration on page 112

A Hint: It takes 25 minutes
altogether to prepare this
dessert but it's advisable to
get the bilberry purée ready
the evening before leaving it
in the freezing compartment
overnight to get stiff.

Flamed Bananas
△ △ ○

*4 bananas
2 tablespoons butter
1 tablespoon vermouth
1 level tablespoon sugar
6 tablespoons white rum
4 sponge fingers
4 tablespoons banana liqueur*

Peel bananas and cut them
into slices of even thickness.
Melt butter in a frying-pan
over low heat. Stir vermouth
and sugar into it to warm
right through. Add bananas
and leave them to simmer for
5 minutes during which time
you turn them over repeatedly. Pour the rum into a
ladle and warm it over a
candle before pouring it over
the bananas and lighting it.
After 1 minute, extinguish
flame by turning the bananas over. Coarsely crumble
sponge fingers, dividing the
crumbs between 4 individual
bowls. The banana liqueur is
poured over the sponge
fingers, before the banana
mixture is filled into the
bowls.

Mocha Mousse
△ ○

*4 eggs
200g (7 oz) icing sugar
2 level teaspoons instant
coffee powder
1 level tablespoon instant
chocolate powder*

Separate egg yolks from
whites. The whites are
whisked stiff and the yolks
mixed with the icing sugar,
instant coffee and instant
chocolate powder. This mixture is then heated over very
low heat in a bain marie and
constantly stirred until it
turns creamy. It is then taken
off the fire, the stiff egg
whites are folded into it; the
mocha mouse is now filled
into 4 dessert bowls which
are put into the refrigerator
until it is time to serve them.

111

Ready-to-Serve Dishes

A complete list of ready-to-serve dishes on sale today would take up more space than the whole of this book. Besides, such a catalogue would be largely a waste of time — the very commodity our modern housewife is particularly short of. For modern housewives-in-a-hurry it's quite sufficient to know that, as far as food is concerned, practically everything is nowadays available in the form of made-up dishes. No housewife has to stray very far from home to find on the shelves of the supermarkets and in her local shop round the corner a varied choice of all kinds of convenience foods — complete meat and poultry dishes in cans or in deep-frozen form; canned sausages; fish and fish specialties, likewise canned or deep-frozen. The vegetable section, too, offers a wide range: in the supermarket freezing cabinets is a bewildering array of items all taking only a few minutes to cook. In competition with these are the innumerable cans containing vegetables already cooked. Then there are the specialties in cans and packets such as soups and soup garnishes, ready-to-serve pasta and rice dishes, sauces and desserts, in addition to the innumerable ready-prepared ingredients which, if used properly, will not only help you to save time, but will make the meal itself more varied and enjoyable. There are, however, a few general hints which you'd be well advised to heed:

- Follow strictly the instructions printed on the packets of deep-frozen food as far as length of storage time and method of preparation are concerned.
- When buying cans, packets or air-tight packs, choose for preference those date-stamped.
- Scorn blown or dented cans and damaged packets as well as all products whose manufacturer is not clearly named.
- Keep your own stock of food, whether deep-frozen or canned, *at most* only as long as the date stamp tells you — *never* longer.

Possible Refinements

Completely made-up dishes have, as a rule, a characteristic taste — a special taste which long experience has shown to be popular with large sections of the consuming public. To try and improve on these dishes is a risky undertaking. The situation is very different when it comes to individual processed food items. Here you have practically unlimited scope to adapt them to your own personal taste — not that table-ready dishes may not, on occasions, benefit from a few carefully-applied finishing touches. For instance you may, without doing irreparable damage, add a little water, milk, cream or fruit juice to soften the taste. At times, a dish may be made to taste just a shade more pleasant by the addition of no more than a pinch of sugar. Conversely, a dish may be made to taste a little more piquant by the addition of a little acidity in the form of a few drops of vinegar, wine, lemon juice or spicy sauce. But the main field in which you can show your inventiveness is in the use of processed food items, for these, after all, are just natural products which, though prepared for the kitchen or even for the table, have not yet been given a definitive taste. The following is a list of the products in most general use, to which have been added some tips on how to improve on them.

Spinach, deep-frozen, cooking time 3—6 minutes.
As vegetable with:
    fried eggs
    poached eggs
    fried sausages
    meat rissoles
As soufflé with:
    slices of potato and 'au gratin' (with an egg, cheese and cream crust)

◁ Bilberry Ice-Bowl — recipe on page 111

Ready-to-Serve Dishes

As filling for:
  egg pancakes
  omelettes
As soup:
Especially good with a
  little garlic powder improved with a piece of
  butter or a little cream

Peas, deep-frozen, cooking
time 6 minutes, or already
cooked from a can.
As vegetable with:
  fried meat
  fried pork sausages
  fried liver
  rice
As ingredient in:
  vegetable salad
  egg salad
  rice salad
  sausage salad
  chicken salad
  chicken fricassée
  ragoût fin
As filling for:
  omelettes
  tomatoes
As soup garnish.
Especially to be recom-
mended, if improved with:
  a piece of butter
  sprinkled over with
  chopped fresh dill or mint
  or
  seasoned with dried oregano
  cooked together with
  some lettuce leaves

Beans, French, deep-frozen,
cooking time 3–5 minutes, or
cooked from a can.

As vegetable with:
  boiled beef
  meat rissoles
  mutton chops
  egg-and-breadcrumbed
  fried black pudding
As salad with:
  ham or bacon
  onions and tomatoes
As ingredient in:
  vegetable salad
  potato salad
  hot-pots
As soup garnish.
Especially to be recom-
mended, if improved with:
  a pat of butter
  cooked with savory
  sprinkled over with fresh
  chopped dill or parsley
  seasoned with cayenne,
  ground ginger or dried
  marjoram

Mixed Peas and Carrots, deep-
frozen, cooking time 5–8
minutes, or canned and already cooked.
As vegetable with:
  meat rissoles
  fried meat
  fried sausage
  fried fish fingers
As ingredient in:
  vegetable salad
  sausage salad
  egg salad
  chicken, sausage or meat
  hot-pot
As filling for:
  omelettes
  egg pancakes
  tomatoes

Especially to be recom-
mended, if improved with:
  a piece of butter
  sprinkled over with
  chopped parsley or dill
  cooked with some canned
  morel (an edible fungus) or
  some canned asparagus tips

Broad Beans, deep-frozen,
cooking time 10–20 minutes
or already cooked from a can.
As vegetable with:
  boiled beef
  mutton cutlets
  meat rissoles
As salad with:
  ham or bacon
  tomatoes and onions
  corned beef
As ingredient in:
  various meat and sausage
  hot-pots
Especially to be recom-
mended, if sprinkled over
with:
  fresh chopped parsley
  mixed with rendered-down
  bacon dice
  seasoned with garlic
  powder

Brussels Sprouts, deep-frozen,
cooking time 10–12 minutes.
As vegetable with:
  quick-fried meat or game
  boiled beef
  meat rissoles
  fried poultry
As ingredient in:
  vegetable stews
As soup garnish.
Especially to be recom-

mended, if prepared with:
  onions
  seasoned with grated
  nutmeg or dried sage
  cooked with diced ham

Asparagus, canned and already cooked.
As vegetable with:
  ham and ready-bought
  Sauce Hollandaise
  quick-fried meat
  scrambled eggs
As salad with:
  sauce vinaigrette
  chopped hardboiled eggs
  mayonnaise sauce
As ingredient in:
  vegetable salad
  egg salad
  poultry salad
  fricassée
  prawn or shrimp dishes
As filling for:
  omelettes
  tomatoes
As garnish for:
  steaks
  appetizers
Especially to be recommended, if served with:
  melted brown butter
  chopped hardboiled eggs
  cooked or heated up in
  saffron
  served with creamed horseradish as ham roll filling

Mushrooms, canned and already cooked.
As vegetable in cream sauces for:
  rice dishes

quick-fried meat
steamed fish
As garnish in:
  soups and sauces
As ingredient in:
  rice salad
  poultry salad
  meat salad
  egg salad
  fricassées
As filling for:
  omelettes
  tomatoes
  bouchées
Especially to be recommended, if sprinkled over with:
  chopped chives, fresh rosemary or fresh dill
  seasoned with garlic powder
  mixed with chopped eggs

Red Cabbage, pre-cooked from a can, cooking-time 15 minutes.
As vegetable with:
  poultry
  pork
  game
  rissoles
  fried sausages
As salad with:
  grated apples
  diced onions
  grated nuts
As ingredient in:
  stews
Especially to be recommended, if cooked with:
  diced apples
  canned edible chestnuts

sweetened with redcurrant jelly
seasoned with basil, caraway seeds
cooked with cloves or juniper berries

Sauerkraut, pre-cooked in cans, cooking-time 20 minutes, or fully-cooked in cans.
As vegetable with:
  pork cutlets
  fried pork sausages
  pickled and lightly-smoked pork chops
  Vienna sausages
As salad with:
  diced apples
  shredded pineapples
  diced onions
  cranberry preserves
  peppers
As ingredient in:
  goulash
  potato purée (mixed)
Especially tasty, if:
  cooked in lard
  prepared with diced apples
  prepared with pineapple juice and diced pineapples
  champagne or Sekt is poured over it
  seasoned with paprika, caraway seed
  cooked with bay leaf
  cooked with cloves
  cooked with fresh peppers
  cooked with juniper berries

Lentils, canned, cooking-time 10—20 minutes.
As vegetable with:
  pickled and lightly-smoked pork chops

115

Ready-to-Serve Dishes

belly of pork
fried sausages
As stew with:
    diced potatoes
    pieces of smoked sausages
    pieces of pork
    soup vegetables
Especially to be recom-
mended, if:
    cooked with smoked
    bacon rind
    seasoned with tarragon or
    marjoram or thyme

Beetroot, pre-cooked from a
jar.
As salad, particularly tasty
with:
    diced onions
    apple slices
    herring fillets, cut in strips
    potato salad (mixed)
    strips of celeriac (from a
    jar)
    sweet pickled cucumber
    (from a jar)

Celeriac Salad, cooked, from
a jar.
As a tasty salad, to be recommended, particularly if enriched with:
    thinly-sliced apples
    diced onions
    pickled peppers (from a
    jar)
    grated nuts

Carrot Salad, from a jar.
May be enriched with:
    grated apples
    lemon juice and sugar
    cream as a dressing
    parsley as garnish
    canned sweet-corn (which
    is mixed into it)

Potato Pancakes, deep-frozen,
cooking-time 3—5 minutes.
As main dish to be particularly recommended, if:
    served with rendered-down
    rashers of bacon
    filled with sauerkraut
    served with fried onion
    rings
    served with beetroot salad
    served with green salad
    served with a mixture of
    cinnamon and sugar
    served with apple purée
    served with cranberries

**Ready-to-Serve Ravioli, Pasta
and Rice Dishes**, canned or in
packets.
As main dishes, these are
particularly tasty if:
    enriched with diced ham
    or green peas
    gratinated with an egg,
    cheese and cream mixture
    served with chicory or
    celeriac salad
    garnished with chopped
    fresh herbs

Goulash from a can.
As main dish particularly
good, if:
    served with rice or mashed
    potatoes

enriched with peppers or
tomato eighths
improved by the addition
of soured cream
seasoned with paprika
sprinkled over with onion
rings or parsley

Ragoût Fin, canned.
As main dish particularly
recommended, if:
    enriched with deep-frozen
    peas
    enriched with asparagus
    tips
    enriched with diced ham
    rounded off with cream
    seasoned with curry pow-
    der
    enriched with prawns or
    shrimps
    gratinated with a mixture
    of egg, cheese and cream
As filling for:
    puff-pastry patties
    omelettes
    tomatoes

Ready-to-Serve Dishes

Corned Beef, from the can.
As main dish serve:
    cut in slices and fried with
    fried eggs on toast
    mixed with mashed pota-
    toes and pickled cucum-
    bers as accompaniment to
    fried eggs
    with beetroot salad into
    which you have mixed
    diced pickled cucumber
    in a light sauce (ready-
    made)
    with risi pisi (rice and
    green peas mixed)

Herring Fillets in a sharp
sauce, from a can.
As main dish, serve:
    with fried potatoes and
    salad
    with mashed potatoes,
    baked in the oven
    as accompaniment to
    scrambled eggs on toast
    with hardboiled eggs and
    black bread

Prawns or Shrimps, already
cooked, deep-frozen or from
a can.
As salad with:
    cornichons
    ready-bought spicy sauces
    chopped hardboiled egg
    asparagus tips
    mushrooms
    pineapples or peaches
    buttered toast
As filling for:
    omelettes
    tomatoes
    hardboiled eggs
As ingredient in:
    poultry salad
    chicken fricassée
    egg salad
    steamed sole
    delicate sauces

Ready-to-Serve Dishes

Brown Sauces
Basic ingredient: a small packet of gravy dissolved, according to instructions, in ¼ litre (½ pint) of liquid.

Variations:	*Goes well with:*
Burgundy Sauce Dissolve gravy in $1/8$ litre (¼ pint) of Burgundy wine and in it heat 1 tablespoon sliced mushrooms and 1 tablespoon chopped shallots. Season with a pinch of cayenne.	Boiled beef, minced steaks, game stew, grilled steak, rice and pasta.
Orange Sauce Dissolve gravy in $3/16$ litre ($3/8$ pint) of water; fill up with $1/16$ litre ($1/8$ pint) of port wine. In the sauce heat the finely-grated peel of ½ orange and 1 teaspoon of redcurrant jelly. Season with a pinch each of mustard powder and cayenne.	Stewed wild fowl, roast duck, braised fish, venison steaks and roast venison.
Devil's Sauce Dissolve gravy in $3/16$ litre ($3/8$ pint) water, filling up with 1 tablespoon each of white wine and wine vinegar. Stir in 1 tablespoon finely-chopped shallots, ¼ teaspoon bruised peppercorns and 1 tablespoon tomato purée.	Quickly-fried pork, beef or mutton; all grilled meats, fried sausages and rissoles and potato purée.
Bacon Sauce Lightly brown in ½ tablespoon butter the dice of half a small onion. Render down 50g (2 oz) diced bacon and mix everything into the gravy which you have prepared according to instructions.	Stewed or braised beef, boiled beef, all kinds of pasta and mashed potatoes.
Onion Sauce In 1 tablespoon butter lightly fry a diced onion, pour in ½ cup white wine which you allow to all but boil away. Fill up with the dissolved gravy, adding a pinch each of sugar and mustard powder and a dash of vinegar.	Boiled beef, rissoles, corned beef, canned goulash, potato noodles or pasta with minced meat.

Ready-to-Serve Dishes

White Sauces
Basic ingredient: a small packet of white sauce powder dissolved, according to instructions, in ¼ litre (½ pint) water.

Variations:	*Goes well with:*
Mushroom Sauce Slice 100 g (3½ oz) mushrooms and lightly fry in 1 tablespoon of butter. Prepare basic sauce and enrich it with 1 tablespoon of cream. Add mushrooms.	Steamed veal, steamed fish, omelettes, rice with veal meat balls.
Herb Sauce Prepare sauce in $3/16$ litre ($3/8$ pint) water, fill up with $1/16$ litre ($1/8$ pint) cream. Mix in plenty of finely-chopped herbs.	Hardboiled eggs, omelettes, fresh plain boiled potatoes, steamed fish, cauliflower and asparagus.
Mustard Sauce Dissolve sauce powder in $3/16$ litre ($3/8$ pint) water; fill up with $1/16$ litre ($1/8$ pint) milk. Season to taste with 1−2 teaspoons mustard, a few drops of lemon juice and a pinch of sugar.	Poached eggs, boiled or steamed fish, veal, cauliflower, meat balls.
Cheese Sauce Dissolve sauce powder in $3/16$ litre ($3/8$ pint) water, add $1/16$ litre ($1/8$ pint) cream and round off with one wedge of processed cream cheese.	Omelettes, broccoli, cauliflower, salsify, pasta and fried sausage slices.
White Wine Sauce Prepare the sauce with $3/16$ litre ($3/8$ pint) water and $1/16$ litre ($1/8$ pint) white wine. Add 2 tablespoons melted butter and 1 tablespoon chopped dill.	Steamed fish fillets, shrimps or prawns, cold roast veal, asparagus.

Ready-to-Serve Dishes

In Praise of the Deep-Freeze

It may be worthwhile repeating the advice given earlier on, to lay in as large a stock as possible of industrially-produced deep-frozen food — complete dishes, vegetables, meats, fish and poultry. The advantages of such assorted stocks to any housewife intent on saving time can hardly be exaggerated. Quite possibly, her first reaction to the suggestion that she should invest in a deep-freeze chest of her own may be negative, because she is likely to think in the first instance of the time it will take her to stock the freezer with the appropriate stores. Yet, once persuaded, it won't be long before she realises what a boon it is to have such a treasure chest to draw upon. In fact, she'll soon be asking herself how she ever did without it.

Once the initial reluctance is overcome, everything becomes plain sailing. You merely go to the supermarket stocking the widest range of deep-frozen food or, better still, to one of the new freezer-food centres, and let yourself be inspired by the great variety of frozen goodies on offer. In addition to the peas, beans, prawns, shrimps and all the other basic foodstuffs which have long been the stock-in-trade of any housewife, you'll find yourself tempted by a bewildering variety of ready-to-serve dishes — many of them you may have heard of and been waiting to try, if only time had permitted — which all of a sudden are there for the taking, already prepared, needing no more than heating up (if you have to transport your deep-frozen purchases over a long distance, it may be advisable to buy one of the insulated shopping bags now available).

A deep-freeze of your own helps you to save precious time and money in many different ways. It relieves you to a large extent of the need of constant shopping. Bread, butter, curd cheese, cheese and eggs (the latter, however, only separated or whisked), sausages, meat and the various kinds of bakery products a family needs can all be stored for 3—9 months.

As far as bread is concerned, the best thing to do is to buy a large quantity of the various kinds you like all at once. The loaves, if they are not already sliced, are soon sliced and the slices separated into portions, wrapped suitably marked with a felt-pen and deep-frozen. When needed, the slices are quickly defrosted in the toaster. Bread rolls and small fancy cakes or pastries are soon defrosted in the oven.

Butter is divided into portions, wrapped and deep-frozen; it is taken out either 12 hours before use, and kept in the refrigerator, or 6 hours before use and defrosted at room temperature.

Curd cheese can be stored in the original package, unless you prefer to turn it into a tasty dessert or a savoury spread before deep-freezing. As for other cheeses, it is immaterial whether you store them in a piece, in slices or grated; once defrosted they can be used in exactly the same way as if you had just bought them, i.e. they can be eaten on bread, turned into soufflés, gratinated, or grated to garnish soups.

Eggs can be whisked, packed in suitable quantities and stored. Depending on their use, you add a little salt or sugar before whisking them (we suggest about ¼ teaspoon of salt or 3 level tablespoons of sugar per 2 eggs). Egg yolks can also be deep-frozen, salted or sugared separately, as can egg whites which can be deep-frozen without the addition of either salt or sugar. They are as easily whisked stiff as fresh eggs. Take care to mark your deep-frozen egg packets clearly to indicate whether they are sugared or salted.

Cream keeps runny or

Ready-to-Serve Dishes

whisked, provided it is sweetened. You can use it, once defrosted, like fresh cream, but not as coffee cream or heated up.

Sausage can be stored whole or in slices. In wrapping up slices, place a piece of film between each slice so you can separate them when they're still frozen – separated they defrost more quickly. Frying sausages, too, can be wrapped up raw as they are and then stored. When needed, they can be fried as though they were fresh.

Meat, whether in its raw state or cooked, is eminently suitable for deep-freezing. Lean meat can safely be stored for up to 12 months, whereas fat meat keeps fresh 2–4 months, depending on quality. Minced meat, on the other hand, should not be kept for more than 2–4 weeks, although made-up dishes with minced meat may be kept for up to 2 months. Considering that for meals-in-minutes you mostly need meat slices for quick frying, you should mainly store slices, packed in family portions. As in the case of sausages, you'd better place some film between the individual slices. Meat slices, provided they are no thicker than 1½–2 cm (½–¾") can be fried in hot fat without being defrosted first.

Any kind of bread, cake, pastry, gateau, fruit-flan or pizza can safely be stored in the deep-freeze. Fruit-flans, cheese cakes and anything made of a gateau dough should be put in the oven (175–200°C = 350–400°F; gas mark 4–6) for half-an-hour to be re-baked, while being defrosted.

Even if normally you belong to those who make an art of quick cooking, you'll feel from time to time like preparing a large roast or a big bird, or any other meal which requires more time to get ready. In such cases you'll probably be left with enough food to keep for another occasion. Here again your freezer is the answer. In fact, it's advisable, whatever meal you prepare, whether stew, roast, goulash, ragoût, dumplings etc., to make 2–3 portions more than you require in the first instance; these are sure to prove handy on some later occasion, perhaps when you are unable to prepare a meal yourself and have to leave it to your husband to 'knock something up' quickly for the family. With leftovers it's quite immaterial whether you deep-freeze the complete meal or each part separately. The portions destined to be deep-frozen are best not cooked completely, but taken from the heat before they're done (of course, they have to cool before storing in the freezer). Be careful with the seasoning! Some spices tend to change their flavour during deep-freezing, others don't. Among those which remain un-affected are: ginger, capers, caraway seeds, horseradish, cloves, salt, vanilla, lemon and sugar.

On the other hand, aniseed, savory, vinegar, cocoa, marjoram, nutmeg, paprika, pepper and mustard all tend to lose some of their effectiveness, so you may have to add some seasoning when it comes to re-heating the deep-frozen portions. A third group of spices gain in strength through deep-freezing. These are: basil, tarragon, dill, sage and thyme. In their case, the best thing to do is to add them only after defrosting. Un-suitable for deep-freezing are: garlic and wine, which should always be added only during re-heating. The same goes for herbs, whether fresh or frozen.

The best thickening agent for sauces is flour. Other thickening agents like cream, egg yolks or cornflour are, as far as possible, left until re-heating takes place.

Small quantities of ready-to-serve dishes should be re-heated in a saucepan with the lid on. In most cases it will be advisable to add a little liquid. Larger quantities, on the other hand, should be left in

Ready-to-Serve Dishes

their aluminium foil wrapper and re-heated in the oven at low temperature.

Important: As a rule, nothing defrosted should go back into the deep-freeze. The only exceptions are meat and poultry which have been deep-frozen raw, and can be taken out, used for a meal, and then put back in the deep-freeze, cooked.

The Freezers

Two kinds of freezers have been perfected in recent years – the deep-freeze chest and the deep-freeze upright. Both types function on the same principle: they generate the same temperature of minus 18°C (0°F) at which food already deep-frozen can be stored for up to one year. Moreover, it's possible to reduce the temperatures in the freezers further – low enough to be able to deep-freeze fresh or cooked food yourself. Before beginning the deep-freezing process, it's necessary to reduce the temperature level in the fast-freezing compartment from minus 18°C (0°F) to minus 35°C (-30°F). This is done by turning a special switch to 'super' a few hours before the deep-freezing is due to begin. In the fast-freezing compartment the food to be deep-

frozen is in sufficient contact with the ultra-cold bottom of the compartment and its walls. In addition, air circulates freely, which is another important factor for the entire freezing operation. In the end, the freshly-frozen food is stacked together tightly with the remaining contents of the freezer.

The Packing

It's extremely important that all food to be deep-frozen be wrapped up as near airtight as possible. There are various kinds of wrapping material available, aluminium foil for instance, which for the purposes of deep-freezing is offered in an extra-strong variety. In it you can wrap up practically everything, including solid food which, by pressing, squeezing and folding over, you should be able to turn into a compact airtight parcel. No package, however, should weigh more than 1.5 kg (3½ lb). As far as possible, always wrap up in one package what you are likely to need at any one time. Pack the meat portions, for instance, in such a way that, when deep-frozen, they will fit into a saucepan. Saw off bones from the meat and deep-freeze them separately as they are liable to damage the wrapper. Another use for

aluminium foil is to seal off all cans without lids, in which case you should use a double layer; and make the edges fast with a rubber band. **Aluminium containers** can be had in all shapes and sizes, with and without lids. They are especially useful for keeping ready-cooked dishes in their sauce and all other ready-to-serve dishes which you intend to defrost and re-heat in their container. Then there are the aluminium baking tins, round or box-shaped, in which to bake cakes and which you cover up with aluminium foil to store in your deep-freeze. Alternatively, you can put the dough in such a form, freeze it, and finally bake it, all in the same tin.

Plastic containers must be resistant to cold and heat, must be water-repellent, airtight, odourless and tasteless, acidproof and greaseproof. Their lids should close tight; if they don't they must be fastened with freezer tape. Plastic containers are suitable for storing soups, stewed fruit and fruit preserved in sugar. Please note: plastic containers should never be filled right up to the rim; always leave about the breadth of a finger between content and lid.

Bags and sheets of polythene should be 0.05 mm thick. They are used for the packing of bread slices, meat, fish, dumplings and other larger-sized pieces. Narrower sheets come in handy for wrapping up such things as bouillon cubes, herbs and soup vegetables. Each portion is tied fast at either end and can be cut off when needed. Herbs are deep-frozen as they are, the frozen leaves are rubbed fine before use.

The Deep-Freezing Process

Don't forget to label all packets before deep-freezing. Hot dishes must be allowed to cool at room temperature prior to freezing. Cakes are an exception to this rule and may be deep-frozen straight from the oven — this will preserve the flavour of the freshly-baked cake. The size of the deep-freeze determines how much food it's capable of freezing in 24 hours; its capacity is measured in litres of freezing space. For example: a freezing capacity of 100 litres is enough to freeze 7 kg (15 lb) of food in 24 hours. After placing the food you wish to deep-freeze in the freezing chamber, you leave it on 'super' for anything between 12 and 24 hours, depending on the quantity of food. Thereafter you can assume that the food is completely frozen and ready to be stored at the normal temperature of minus 18°C. The length of storing time varies according to the type of food stored. As a general rule, you can take it that fatty foods should be kept no longer than 3 months, whereas non-fatty food may be kept for up to one year in the deep-freeze. Ready-cooked dishes should be consumed within 4–7 months.

Ready-to-Serve Dishes

In Conclusion

There's practically no end to the suggestions one could make to help the housewife intent on saving time and labour. However, in view of the fact that the ingredients, in spite of their great — and still increasing — variety, are limited, the possible permutations are also restricted, and, as a result, repetitions would soon become unavoidable. But once you're completely au fait with all of the meals herein described, you should have no difficulty in inventing new variations yourself.

Just how varied and mouth-watering quickly-produced meals can be you've no doubt discovered by now. Perhaps you've noticed that expression of relaxed satisfaction on the faces of your family and guests and the festive mood that comes from a carefully-composed meal — whether a richly-garnished toast or a delicate soup, a hitherto-unknown salad or an imaginative sweet.

The Party Cookbook

Annette Wolter

The Party Cookbook

Nelson

Thomas Nelson and Sons Ltd
36 Park Street London WIY 4DE
PO Box 18123 Nairobi Kenya

Thomas Nelson (Australia) Ltd
597 Little Collins Street
Melbourne 3000

Thomas Nelson and Sons
(Canada) Ltd
81 Curlew Drive Don Mills
Ontario

Thomas Nelson (Nigeria) Ltd
PO Box 336 Apapa Lagos

First published in Great Britain in
1974

Copyright © 1973 Gräfe und
Unzer, Munich
English edition: Copyright ©
1974 Thomas Nelson, London
Translated and adapted from
the German by G. and
H. Jacobi

ISBN 0 17 147153 9

Printed in Holland by
Smeets Offset, Weert.

Contents

Recipes Grouped in Categories

Recipes Grouped in Categories

Foreword

There is a difference between 'having to invite people' to some formal function, say a wedding, a jubilee celebration or some banquet you cannot get out of, and giving a party. The highly official dinners with their magnificently appointed tables, their sumptuous platters and dishes, containing exactly what they are expected to contain, are more often than not as costly as they are dull. There is hardly a housewife capable of coping in her own kitchen with the classical sequence of dishes the guests expect at an official dinner; it will consequently be left to a respectable hotel or catering firm to supply the lavish quantities of festive food required for such an occasion. In most cases, these outside caterers also provide the cutlery, china and table decorations as well as the serving personnel. The seating order, strictly arranged as it is according to rank and importance, restricts communication to polite conversation which drags on from hors d'oeuvre to dessert. In short, these parties are not the kind with which this book is concerned. *The Party Cookbook* is designed to help all those who love informal conviviality, who enjoy giving hospitality just as much as receiving it and who are as fond of the pleasures of the palate as of sparkling conversation. Party, in the

sense we understand the word, means an informal gathering in a suitable setting for a purpose understood by everybody. There is no reason, for instance, why you should not give, in your two-room flat with standing room only, a party, the purpose of which may be to say goodbye to all your friends before embarking on a trip round the world. Or perhaps you may simply wish to tell everybody you are looking for a new apartment. A house-warming, the desire to have your friends inspect your garden when the flowers are at their best, a won bet or contest in some sport or other, a jubilee or just a birthday — all these may be occasions for a party. Where it is to be held is pretty well immaterial. It may take place on a spacious verandah, a normal-sized flat, an appropriately decorated cellar; what is important, however, is to inform your guests of the precise circumstances in which you intend to hold the party and to plan the festivity to tone in with these circumstances.
The brief introductory remarks to the various recipe chapters and the chapter on Party Tips will remind you of some of the things you will have to do to make your party a success. The quantities of food you prepare depend not only on the number of your guests but

also on what they like to eat. The recipes are, therefore, not all for the same number of persons but vary according to their degree of general popularity from 6 to 8 persons, while some are even enough for 12 people. A point to bear in mind is that 4 to 6 different party-salads are likely to stimulate your guests' appetites more than a single giant bowl of just one salad. If you have no time to prepare a variety of dishes, it may be advisable to serve, in addition to one substantial main dish, several small snacks most of which can readily be bought at your local delicatessen shop. Another point to keep in mind is this: it is never certain at what time a successful party will end, so it's a good idea to hold in reserve a midnight snack for the indefatigable among your guests or, perhaps, even some light refreshment to be served as dawn breaks. Choose for such collations ingredients which keep or can be deep-frozen. If you possess a deep freeze, you have, of course, also the possibility of preparing a great deal in advance and keeping it fresh in the freezer. Alternatively, you could also just store individual ingredients required for the dishes you wish to prepare subsequently.
You may offer only tit-bits to nibble, snacks or canapés to accompany the drinks, serve

Party Tips

filling salads, or run to a slap-up buffet, or throw your kitchen open to your guests, letting them help you to prepare things on toast or even a fondue — whatever you decide to do, you are sure to find under the appropriate chapter headings a great many suitable recipes. Ring the changes by choosing a recipe from one chapter and combine it with one from another composing your own menu to suit your individual tastes, requirements and kitchen potential.

The aim of this cookbook is to ensure that you're well prepared for any party, large or small. Have fun and enjoy yourselves!

Annette Wolter

The kind of party to give and how to plan for it

Parties in the sense of free-and-easy gatherings of people for the purpose of chatting or dancing with one another or eating and drinking together, have become so popular all over Europe that this English term has been adopted into most continental languages. The success of a party depends, of course, to some extent on the physical surroundings in which the party is taking place, but more important still is the inventiveness and originality displayed by all participants, and that includes guests as well as hosts. The most uncomfortable but perhaps least troublesome of all parties is the **Cocktail Party**. Anybody who hears that certain people are meeting somewhere at a certain time for a cosy chat while standing about, drink in hand, is liable to turn up even without having been invited, though usually he'll be made welcome if he can prove that he knows someone close to the hosts or their more intimate circle of friends.

Ideally all parties should proceed in a totally informal atmosphere. Yet this lack of constraint is not synonymous with a complete absence of rules of behaviour. By all means turn up at a cocktail party whenever you like and disappear without bothering to take formal leave, but nobody would dream of arriving in his working clothes, and even in casual dress you should look smart and well-groomed. Even at cocktail parties one behaves with a certain amount of decorum and shows that one is used to party-going. On the other hand, slightly malicious witticisms will not be found out of place, provided they are amusing. The host or hostess welcomes every new arrival by offering him a drink. Nobody expects to be served by professional waiters as he would in the bar of a grand hotel, but the guests are usually offered the choice between a long drink and a cocktail (for more details see page 113). Once the newcomer has been provided with a drink the host takes him to a group of fellow guests who are already in conversation, introduces him as far as possible and then leaves him to his own devices to return to his or her duties as a provider of liquid refreshment. Guests at a cocktail party cannot count on finding comfortable seats or culinary delights. The few available armchairs are soon taken up by the older generation or particularly distinguished guests. The only way to avoid getting tired by

9

Party Tips

too much standing is to 'migrate' from one group to another, from one topic of conversation to the middle of another, from the source of drinks to the small tables on which are displayed attractively arranged tit-bits to nibble — salted almonds, pretzels, olives, biscuits with some simple spread on them or canapés — all as far as possible of a size to convey them to the mouth with the one free hand, the other being required to balance the glass.

How different the **Bottle Party**! It's said to have originated among the practically-minded Americans. The sometimes heavy financial burden of this type of Bacchanalian revelry is frequently spread among all invited guests, each one of whom turns up with a bottle of stimulating cheer. The best way to proceed is by prior agreement between host and guests as to the kind of drinks the latter are to bring with them, for too great a mix-up may have serious consequences for all involved. The idea of a bottle party is frequently extended by the men being asked to contribute the drinks while the women supply the food. The latter may be in the form of an easily transportable salad, a platter of cold meats or a mixture of different party snacks. Suggestions for what to bring

are to be found in the chapters 'Party Salads' and 'Palate-Ticklers to go with Beer and Wine'. There are, of course, many other ways of organising a party which we can safely leave to your imagination to devise. According to the available premises, the party may be dubbed a Cellar Party, a Garden Party, an Alpine Meadow Party, a Terrace Party, a Cavern Party or a Swimming Pool Party. The resourceful owner of a large, old-established garden with magnificent trees once invited his guests to a Tree-Top Party. In the branches he had wooden platforms fixed and even some huts covered with foliage which could be reached only by means of rope-ladders, and all the guests, suitably dressed in jeans, amused themselves hugely by practising the ancient skill of tree-climbing. Not only the locality but also the main activity can determine the name of the gathering. A Dance Party is as popular as a Games Party. Then there are Discussion Parties, Musical Parties, Slide or Film Parties, Skittle Parties or the Crazy Parties during the Carnival period.

Whenever you plan a party, give some thought in good time to the following question: how many people can you comfortably accommodate in your chosen locality without producing a crush or

leaving chilling vacant spaces? At a pleasant party the guests must be provided not only with drinks but also with something to eat. There is no need for all of them to sit down for their food at the same time; nor is there any reason why they shouldn't be divided into several separate groups as long as each group is provided with knife and fork and given the opportunity of eating at a table. If this can't be done you must at least give them a seat and a chance to put down their glasses. In fact, there should be enough seats available for all your guests, for even at the most high-spirited of parties there will be moments when the guests feel like a rest after all that dancing and playing of games and wish to sit down for a talk.

So don't invite too many persons, but also not too few! Consider carefully who is likely to get on well with the others and if possible invite a few unattached people of either sex so that they don't feel too restricted in their choice of a partner for the evening. Send out your invitations in good time, so that you know at least 8-10 days beforehand who is coming for certain. You may have to ask somebody else to make up the numbers, and nobody likes to be asked at the last minute to act as a stop-gap. The invitations may be in writing, by telephone or word

Party Tips

of mouth. But ask all your friends to tell you definitely whether or not they accept. Tell them plainly the reason for the party; if you don't, some of your guests may feel embarrassed when they discover in the course of the evening that the party is held to celebrate a birthday, a jubilee or some other event which would have called for a present. Excessive generosity on the part of your friends is easily avoided by writing on your invitation something like 'I should like you to help me celebrate my birthday. Just in case you feel like making me a present, I collect postcards, beer-mugs, dried flowers.' Up to you to substitute any other inexpensive little present for those suggested, and, who knows, your amusing little idea may turn out to be the start of a real collection.

Don't leave your guests in any doubt about what kind of party you intend to give so that they arrive in clothing suitable for the occasion. Don't run the risk of seeing them turn up in a cocktail dress for a tree-top party or in evening dress at a cellar party, for unsuitable clothing will make them feel ill at ease. Don't forget to tell everybody when the festivities are to begin.

There's little you can do about notorious latecomers, so it's all the more important to make sure that some of your habitually punctual friends arrive at the appointed time to avoid the proceedings being jeopardized by a slow start. See to it that clothes stands are available; these may be improvised but must be sturdy enough not to collapse under the weight of the clothes they will have to support! There should, of course, be adequate space for eating, dancing or playing games, as well as some music, a few original decorations and sufficient, but not too glaring, light.

What to buy, Where and When — the equipment you need

Begin by fixing the amount you wish to spend. Divide this sum by the number of people you want to ask and think about what you can offer them within these limits. Roughly two thirds of the available funds will have to go on drinks. Serve something with a kick to it — a cocktail, an aquavit, vodka — to all your guests as soon as they arrive to put them quickly into a party mood. But after the starter firmly continue either with beer or wine, offering your guests the choice between a light claret or white wine, or you may prefer to serve a cup. In addition, have some mineral water and non-alcoholic beverages on hand as well as some coffee— just in case!

Apart from single considerations, what you offer in the way of food depends on the time you have to prepare and the likes and dislikes of your guests. You may decide in favour of a few salads, or prefer one of the suggested buffets or some cold platters. To accompany the salads, it's a good idea to serve a cold roast or a meat loaf or sweet and savoury pastry. Platters of cold meats are garnished with gherkins, olives, pearl onions, tomatoes, mixed pickles or radishes.

Divide your shopping list into two parts. One part should contain everything that can be delivered or purchased well in advance, such as drinks (which are much cheaper at super-markets or cash-and-carry places than at ordinary off-licences); all fruit preserves; various kinds of mustard; mayonnaise; ready-made spicy sauces; salt sticks and pretzels; canned or powdered soups; canned fish, sausages or meats and, provided you can store them, deep-frozen items.

The second part of your list is reserved for what must be bought at the last moment — fresh sausages, meat, poultry or fish; eggs; butter; cheese;

Party Tips

bread; vegetables or fruit. Don't forget to order in good time at your bakers what you need in the way of fresh bread, rolls, pretzels etc., unless you prefer to do your baking yourself. Your butcher ought to be told the day before the party what roast or roasts you require so that you can get them ready for the oven in the morning of the day.

As for the indispensable little accessories which often help to make a party go without a hitch, you would be well advised to get them in good time also. Choose those things that will be thrown away afterwards to match the colours of the decorations you intend putting up. Don't be afraid to buy more of them than you may need; it is better to have some over than to run short; besides, anything not used will be handy for subsequent use by your family. Here is a list of what you require:

● Paper napkins in two sizes — the larger ones for the main collation and the smaller for in-between nibbles. Possibly also some tablecloths in different sizes but of the same colour and material.

● Plastic skewers for tit-bits, olives, pickles or to pick out the fruit from a fruit cup.

● Disposable plates (in two sizes) and bowls in which to serve the salads, a sweet or possibly a late-night soup.

Important Party Requisities

Throw-away plates and bowls may be made of fine-quality cardboard, with a waxed inside, or of plastic.

● Disposable cutlery of the same colour is extremely practical in that it saves washing up the following day.

● Drinking cups of the same material as the disposable plates are also obtainable, but to drink wine or beer from them is not to everybody's taste. If your valuable crystal glasses are too precious to risk, buy some pressed-glass beakers which are nowadays available in attractive shapes and at little cost. Moreover, there are now water-resistant paints on the market which you may like to use to paint the names of your guests or other distinguishing marks on the glasses.

● Ash-trays of adequate size

are indispensable. Should they not be available in sufficient numbers you could perhaps take some flower-pot saucers of clay or cheap glass trays and decorate them with the same paint you used for the glasses. Scallop shells obtainable from your fishmonger are also excellent substitutes for ash-trays. Don't use plastic receptacles because they melt when coming into contact with hot ash and produce an unpleasant smell.

● A hot-plate (preferably an electric one) on which to keep warm a soup, hot dogs or, later, the coffee and possibly even another soup to be served as the party draws to its close.

● An electric toaster that enables each guest to make his own fresh toast as and when he requires it.

12

Party Tips

Hot Plate

The 'Musts' and the Optionals

Absolutely indispensable are adequate cloakroom facilities with, if at all possible, enough coat-hangers for everybody. If it rains, there should be a sufficiently large umbrella-stand or, failing that, a sizeable bucket to accommodate all wet umbrellas. If need be, use your bedroom as a cloakroom. It is also important to acquaint your guests right from the

start with the geography of your home. Tell them where your children are sleeping, where your own bedroom is and where the washroom and toilet facilities are to be found. Put out sufficient guest-towels, soap, cottonwool, eau-de-Cologne, 'refresher pads', and possibly also some safety-pins as well as needle and thread. If yours is a beer party and there isn't enough room in your refrigerator for all the beer-bottles, put some ice cubes into your bath tub and

use it as an extra cold-storage place.

If, in addition to electric lighting, you wish to use candles, buy the non-drip variety and place them into solidly based candlesticks or use empty liqueur bottles. The bottles should be half filled with either sand or water to make them stand firmly.

If the express purpose of the party is not to watch a thriller or a sporting event on T.V. you had better remove the set either altogether from sight or hide it behind your decorations. It never fails to create a disturbance if one of the guests suddenly takes it into his head to listen to the news or any other programme.

Even if dancing is not the main purpose of the party, background music is always welcome. However, not everybody likes to conduct a conversation to the strains of Bach or Beethoven, so choose only light music on long-playing records or tape so that host or hostess need not constantly see to the record-player.

Give your domestic animals a chance to get through the evening, undisturbed by the guests and the party noise, by putting them into the children's room, your own bedroom or some remote place.

If you don't live in a house of your own and do not feel like

See that your bath and toilet is well equipped

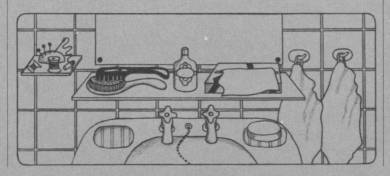

13

Party Tips

After a noisy party —
a present to the neighbour...

inviting all your nearest
neighbours to the party, the
best thing to do is to give them
prior warning and ask their
forbearance, for you may not
be able to reduce the party
noise to an acceptable level. In
which case you would be well
advised to placate them on the
day after with some flowers or
a box of chocolates!
Every party must come to an
end, and you yourself may
want to speed the parting
guests. A good moment to do
this is when the first of your
guests make a move to leave.
This gives you an opportunity
to discuss with the rest of the
party the problem of getting
home. Dissuade the drivers
from using their own cars if
you are in doubt about their
fitness to do so. Order taxis and
and arrange the fares in such a
manner as to avoid all
unnecessary detours. Be

prepared for the possibility of
having to take some of the
guests home in your own car.
On the following day, it's a
good idea to ring up those of
your guests who were the
worst for wear or who had a
particularly long journey to
make and enquire whether
they reached home safely.

The Recipes

Key to the signs following each heading:

△   The recipe is very simple to follow.

△ △   The recipe is not quite so simple and it's therefore advisable to keep strictly to instructions.

△ △ △ The recipe assumes you are prepared to tackle a somewhat more difficult or complicated process with patience.

○   The recipe is in-expensive.

○○   The recipe is in the medium price range.

○○○ The recipe is relatively expensive.

*   The prepared dish can be deep-frozen at a temperature of minus 35° C (-31°F) and will keep for four weeks if stored at minus 18°C (0°F).

**   The prepared dish, after deep-freezing, keeps for up to three months in a temperature of minus 18° C (0°F)

*** The prepared dish, if deep-frozen, and stored at minus 18°C (0°F) keeps for 9-12 months.

You will have noticed in recent years that your local super-markets and grocers have greatly increased the range of foodstuffs for sale. Their shelves now carry many items from foreign countries — sausages, canned and frozen food, spices and cheeses — which not so long ago were completely unknown, if not to you at least to the vast majority of housewives and would have made a cookbook like this pointless. Now it no longer is, for the venturesome among you should find most of the ingredients recommended here readily available. In some cases, however, where availability is still in doubt, some generally known alternative is suggested.
To save time, emphasis has been laid on convenience foods, leaving it to your good judgment to replace these with the fresh variety wherever possible: this applies particularly to herbs which many of you grow in your own garden. Incidentally, it's strongly recommended that you grow some dill; a small packet of seeds should be sufficient to keep you supplied throughout the summer. A sprig or two, finely chopped, will give your salads a pleasant-ly distinctive flavour.

Mustard means either the continental variety or ready-mixed English mustard.
The imperial measures in brackets are approximations only of metric measures.

16

Smoked Eel Appetizer (bottom left); Russian Appetizer (bottom ▷ right); Cossack Appetizer (centre); Florida Appetizer (top). For recipes see pages 18—20

Savoury accompaniments to Beer and Wine

Whenever friends meet at your home over a drink, be it beer, wine, champagne or fruit cup, it's customary to offer them something to nibble such as nuts, potato crisps, biscuits or salt-sticks. Should you prefer, however, to serve in addition some small tit-bits of your own making, you will find some useful hints among the following recipes. Bear in mind that all the recipes in this section are for snacks only, constituting no complete meal in themselves but rather designed to supplement the above-mentioned traditional tit-bits. They are savoury appetizers to form a pleasant basis for the drinks you serve. There is no reason, though, why you shouldn't double the quantities given in your chosen recipe or make two or even three different snacks for your guests, who will most probably bless you for it.

A Russian Appetizer

△ ○ ○

Ingredients for eight people:

Half a stick of French bread
50g (2 ozs) butter
1 teaspoon anchovy paste
200g (7 ozs) cold roast pork
2 sardines
2 tablespoons mayonnaise
A pinch each of celery salt and dried oregano (wild marjoram)
A dash of Worcester sauce
1 tablespoon cream
2 tomatoes
A few olives
Some parsley

Preparation time: 25 minutes

Cut bread into 8 equal slices. Mix butter with anchovy paste and spread on bread. Cut cold pork into fine strips. Divide sardines into small pieces. Stir celery salt, oregano, Worcester sauce and cream into mayonnaise. Add pork strips and sardine pieces and mix well. Distribute mixture over the buttered bread slices. ● Wash and dry tomatoes and cut into thin wedges. Garnish each round with a tomato wedge and slices of olives as well as a sprig of parsley.

Illustration on page 17

A Smoked Eel Appetizer

△ ○ ○ ○

Ingredients for 8 people:

A packet of pumpernickel containing 16 round slices (if unobtainable, buy packet of oblong slices and cut into rounds with a cutter)
1 teaspoon hot mustard (not powder)
3 eggs
A pinch each of salt, pepper and paprika
1 tablespoon oil
200g (7 ozs) smoked eel
Parsley

Preparation time: 20 minutes

Spread pumpernickel with thinnest layer of mustard. Whisk eggs together with salt, pepper and paprika and scramble them in a frying-pan in hot oil. ● Distribute scrambled egg over the rounds of pumpernickel. Peel and fillet smoked eel and put pieces of fillet on the scrambled eggs. Decorate with parsley. If you can't get smoked eel, use buckling or kipper, which will be a lot cheaper.

Illustration on page 17

Savoury accompaniments to Beer and Wine

Assorted Tit-Bits

△○○

Ingredients for 12 people:

400g (14 ozs) Emmental
*   cheese (or Gruyère or*
*   Jarlsberg)*
2 tablespoons sharp mustard
4 tablespoons caraway seeds
2 packets salt sticks
2 packets salt pretzels
1 grapefruit
100g (3½ ozs) salted almonds
1 jar of stuffed green olives
32 crackers
2 portions Gervais cheese
3 tablespoons cream
2 level teaspoons paprika
Small bunch of chives
1 jar of small gherkins

Preparation time: 15 minutes

Dice the cheese into small cubes and place on large wooden board. Put mustard and caraway seeds into small bowls and place them next to cheese on the board (each guest is given a small fork, used to spike a cheese cube, which is dipped lightly into first mustard and then caraway seeds). • Place salt sticks into either one or two glasses. Stick a skewer into grapefruit, hang pretzels onto it and display on board. Heap salted almonds on board. The olives are rinsed briefly in cold water then drained and dried before also being put on board. • For the crackers filled with creamed cheese, mix Gervais together with cream paprika and finely chopped chives. The gherkins are drained and put with the cream cheese between the crackers.

Illustration below

Assorted Tit-Bits, recipe above

Cossack Appetizer

△○○○

Ingredients for 8 people:

2 eggs
Half a stick of French bread
1 clove garlic
50g (2 ozs) butter
½ onion
2 teaspoons capers
200g (7 ozs) raw minced steak
1 dash Tabasco sauce
1 pinch each of dried oregano,
*   sage and salt*
2 teaspoons oil
1 jar caviar (or caviar
*   substitute)*

Preparation time: 30 minutes

Savoury accompaniments to Beer and Wine

Boil eggs for 10 minutes, place into cold water, then peel and slice them. Cut bread into 8 slices of equal thickness. Peel garlic and crush with knife blade or use garlic crusher. • Mix garlic with butter and spread on bread. Peel onion and dice finely. Chop capers. • Mix the minced steak together with chopped onions and capers, Tabasco sauce, oregano, sage, salt and oil and spread resulting mixture on the bread, topping each portion with a slice of egg and the caviar.

Illustration on page 17

Florida Appetizer
△○○

Ingredients for 8 people:

Half a stick of French bread
50g (2 ozs) butter
1 small tin pineapple pieces
100g (3½ ozs) peeled
    shrimps (tinned, fresh or
    frozen)
1 tablespoon mayonnaise
1 tablespoon cream
A dash Tabasco sauce
A pinch each of salt and
    paprika
2 tablespoons finely-chopped
    dill

50g (2 ozs) sliced smoked
    salmon

Preparation time: 15 minutes

Cut the loaf into 8 equally sized slices and butter them. Drain the pineapple. • Mix the mayonnaise with cream, Tabasco sauce, salt, paprika and finely-chopped dill. Fold shrimps into mayonnaise.
• Arrange pineapple pieces on outside of each slice and fill the centre with one tablespoon of shrimp mayonnaise.
• Cut the smoked salmon into 8 slivers, fold one or two stalks of dill into each and use to decorate each snack.

Illustration on page 17

Curried Eggs
△△○

Ingredients for 6 people:

6 eggs
50g (2 ozs) butter
75g (3 ozs) cream cheese
1 level teaspoon curry powder
1 quarter teaspoon salt
A pinch of sugar
Chopped parsley for decora-
    tion

Preparation time: 30 minutes

Boil eggs for 10 minutes, place in cold water, then peel and cut lengthways into halves.
• Take out yolks and press these through a sieve. • Cream the butter and stir the cream cheese, sieved egg yolks, curry powder, salt, sugar and chopped parsley together with the butter to a smooth mixture. Fill into a piping bag and pipe into the egg halves. Decorate each half with a sprig of parsley.
Goes well with toast or crisp bread and butter.

Illustration on facing page

Curried Eggs (centre); Cucumber and Cheese Skewers (bottom left); ▷
Sausage Rolls with a Difference (top); recipes on pages 20 and 22

Savoury accompaniments to Beer and Wine

A Sausage Roll with a Difference

Ingredients for 8 people:

200g (7 ozs) flour
200g (7 ozs) butter
200g (7 ozs) curd cheese
1 level teaspoon salt
1 level teaspoon paprika
500g (18 ozs) pork sausages
1 egg
1 tablespoon caraway seeds

Preparation time: 45 minutes

Baking time: 30 minutes

To make the pastry, first sift flour onto board. Distribute butter in small pieces over it; then add curd cheese, salt and paprika and knead quickly to a smooth dough. If the curd cheese is too moist add a little more flour. Wrap dough in aluminium foil or waxed paper and leave to rest in refrigerator for at least two hours. Preheat oven to 250° C (475° F or gas mark 8). Roll out dough to ½ cm (less than ¼″) thickness and cut into 10 cm X 10 cm (4″ X 4″) squares. Place one sausage on each square. ● Separate egg. Moisten edges of square with egg white and press together firmly. Eggwash the rolls and sprinkle caraway seeds over them. Bake in preheated oven for 30 minutes (this pastry is a very good substitute for puff pastry and less troublesome to make).
The rolls are best eaten warm with cold beer.

Illustration on page 21

Cucumber and Cheese Skewers

△○

Ingredients for 8 people:

Half a stick of French bread
3 tablespoons sandwich spread
2 pickled cucumbers
300g (11 ozs) semi-soft cheese in a piece
½ cup preserved peppers
½ jar pearl onions

Preparation time: 20 minutes

Cut loaf into 8 slices and cover with sandwich spread. Slice cucumbers and cut cheese into cubes. Put cucumber, paprika pieces, cheese cubes and onions in turn onto a wooden skewer and stick it into the bread slices.

Illustration on page 21

Assorted Snacks

△△○○

Ingredients for 12 people:

24 crackers
100g (3½ ozs) butter
1 jar mayonnaise
1 jar sandwich spread
200g (7 ozs) sliced bread
3 eggs
1 bunch radishes
1 green and 1 yellow pepper
1 tub cottage cheese
Grated horseradish
4 tomatoes
1 jar pickled herrings
Ready-mixed mustard
1 onion
1 egg yolk
200g (7 ozs) freshly minced beefsteak
1 small tin truffles
200g (7 ozs) cream cheese
3 tablespoons cream
1 jar red caviar
200g (7 ozs) semi-soft cheese
2 slices canned pineapple
6 walnut halves
6 cocktail cherries
100g (3½ ozs) salami sausage
3 gherkins
6 stuffed olives
Salt, pepper, paprika, parsley

Preparation time: 1 hour

Spread eight crackers with butter, eight crackers with mayonnaise and eight with sandwich paste. Cut sandwich loaf into oblongs or squares and spread each eight of them

Savoury accompaniments to Beer and Wine

in a similar manner. • Boil eggs for 10 minutes, rinse in cold water, peel and slice with egg slicer. Wash radishes and cut into slices. Cut peppers into rings. Remove seeds, wash and dry. • Mix cottage cheese with a little horseradish, finely chopped parsley, salt and pepper and spread on the crackers with sandwich spread. Garnish with radish slices and pepper rings. • Wash and slice tomatoes. The bread slices with the sandwich spread are now covered with the pieces of pickled herring and the onion rings, capers and cucumber strips from the herring jar.

Garnish with tomato slices. • Turning to the slices of bread with the mayonnaise spread on them, first put the thinnest of layers of mustard on top of the mayonnaise. Then peel the onion and dice it finely; mix this with egg yolk, salt, pepper, paprika and minced beef and distribute the resulting mixture over the eight slices. Garnish each with an egg slice on which you have placed a tiny piece of truffle. • Mix together the cream cheese, cream, salt and pepper and fill into a piping bag. Pipe mixture in a circle on the buttered crackers. Fill centre with caviar. • Slice the semi-soft cheese and cover the buttered bread slices with it. Decorate each with a piece of pineapple, a walnut half and a cocktail cherry. • Finally, put slices of salami onto the crackers with mayonnaise. Decorate with a gherkin half, a little horseradish and an olive slice. Arrange on a large platter as illustrated on page 23.

Assorted Snacks, recipe on facing page

Savoury accompaniments to Beer and Wine

Cevapcici in Pastry

△△○○

Ingredients for 6 people:

1 packet deep-frozen puff
    pastry
2 onions
1 clove garlic
500g (18 ozs) minced
    beefsteak
¼ teaspoon pepper
1 teaspoon salt
2 egg yolks

Preparation time: 40 minutes

Baking time: 25 minutes

Pre-heat oven to 250°C
(475° F or gas mark 8). Roll
out thawed puff pastry to a
thickness of 2-3 mm (⅛″)
and cut into squares of
approximately 10 cm
(4″). • Peel onions and dice
very finely. Peel the garlic
clove, cut into small pieces and
squash with the back of a knife
or in a garlic press. Mix onion
dices with garlic and beef, add
salt and pepper and divide
meat into as many portions as
you have squares. • Each
portion of meat is now rolled
into the shape of a sausage and
placed on a square. Eggwash
the edges of the squares and
press together firmly. What
remains of the dough should
be rolled out again and cut into
narrow strips. Decorate the
top of each roll with these
strips by attaching them with
egg yolk. Eggwash the roll all
over.
Rinse a baking sheet with cold
water, put meat rolls on it and
bake in the pre-heated oven for
20-25 minutes.
Serve warm with beer.

Illustration on facing page

Meat Balls on Skewers

△○

Ingredients for 8 people:

2 bread rolls
500g (18 ozs) mixed minced
    meat (pork and beef)
1 large onion
2 eggs
1 level teaspoon salt
¼ teaspoon pepper
1 cup breadcrumbs
½ cup grated cheese
6 tablespoons oil or dripping
1 small jar gherkins
1 small jar pearl onions
½ cup pickled red peppers
½ cup canned mandarin
    segments
½ cup canned pineapple slices

Preparation time: 30 minutes

Soak rolls in lukewarm water
and squeeze well, before
mixing them with the minced
meat. Peel onion and cut into
small dice. Mix the onion, salt
and pepper together with the
minced meat and with wet
hands form into walnut-sized
balls. Mix breadcrumbs with
the cheese and roll meat balls
in this mixture, pressing it
gently round the meat balls.
• Heat oil or dripping in a
frying-pan and fry meat balls at
medium temperature until
crisp and brown. Drain on
kitchen paper and allow to
cool. • The meat balls are

◁ Cevapcici in Pastry, recipe on this page

Savoury accompaniments to Beer and Wine

served cold on skewers on which are stuck either gherkin halves and a pearl onion each, a piece of pickled red pepper and a pearl onion, or tangerine wedges and pine-apple pieces.

Cold Meat Roll
△△○*

Ingredients for 8 people:

1 packet deep-frozen puff
*   pastry*
1 green pepper
1 onion
500g (18 ozs) mixed minced
*   meat (pork and beef)*
½ teaspoon paprika
½ teaspoon freshly-ground
pepper
1 teaspoon salt
2 eggs
2 tablespoons breadcrumbs
3 pairs Vienna or Frankfurt
*   sausages*
1 egg yolk

Preparation time: 50 minutes

Baking time: 1 hour

Allow several hours for puff pastry to thaw. Pre-heat oven to temperature of 200° C (400° F, gas mark 6). • Halve green pepper, remove seeds, then wash and cut into very small dice. Peel and dice onion.

Knead the minced meat together with the paprika, pepper, salt, diced green pep-per and onion, raw eggs and the breadcrumbs until smooth. • Roll out puff pastry thinly, placing half the meat mixture, shaped into a loaf, on it. Lay sausages on top of meat and cover with remaining meat. Fold the dough over the loaf, moisten edges with a little water and press firmly together. • Cut the remaining dough into nice strips, eggwash the meat roll and decorate the top with the strips. Bake it in the pre-heated oven for an hour and allow to cool. • Serve in slices.

Illustration on facing page

Twisted Cheese Straws
△△○○

Ingredients for 10-12 people:

2 packets deep-frozen puff
*   pastry*
100g (3½ ozs) butter
300g (11 ozs) grated cheese
3-4 egg yolks
2 tablespoons coarse salt
2 tablespoons caraway seeds

Preparation time: 35 minutes

Baking time: 25 minutes

Thaw puff pastry and roll out thinly on a surface dusted with flour. • Melt butter without heating it and mix with the grated cheese. Spread this mixture on the rolled out dough, fold over and roll out again with a rolling pin. Re-peat this process 2-3 times, until the cheese mixture has been well absorbed. Now roll out dough to a thickness of ½ cm (¼") and cut it into strips 1-2 cm (½"-¾") wide. Pre-heat oven to 200°C (400°F or gas mark 7). • Sprinkle a little flour on a baking sheet. Eggwash dough strips and turn them carefully into spirals. Sprinkle coarse salt over one half of them and caraway seeds over the other half. Bake for 25 minutes.

Savoury accompaniments to Beer and Wine

Meat Balls with Almonds

△△○○*

Ingredients for 6 people:

70g (2½ ozs) butter
¼ teaspoon salt
¼ litre (½ pint) water
200g (7 ozs) flour
4 eggs
100g (3½ ozs) grated
Emmental cheese, (or any
other cheese of comparable
properties)

2 cups almond splinters
Sufficient oil or fat for deep-
frying

Preparation time: 40 minutes

Melt butter in saucepan, add salt and water and bring to the boil while stirring. Sieve flour quickly into saucepan and continue stirring until mixture comes off the bottom of the pan easily, in one lump. Take pan off the stove and mix the eggs one by one into the dough. The grated cheese is stirred in last. • Spread out almond splinters on a board. With wet hands form cheese mixture into little balls; roll them in the almonds. Heat sufficient oil or dripping in a deep-fryer and fry the balls until golden brown. • When cooked lift them out of the fat with a skimming ladle, drain them on kitchen paper and serve hot or cold.

Cold Meat Roll, recipe on facing page

Savoury accompaniments to Beer and Wine

Pizza Variations

△△○*

Ingredients for the Pizza dough (sufficient to make 4 pizzas, each the size of a dinner plate):

400g (14 ozs) flour
20g (¾ oz) yeast
¼ litre (½ pint) lukewarm
*   water*
4 tablespoons oil
1 level teaspoon salt

Preparation time: 50 minutes

Baking time: 30 minutes

Sieve flour into bowl and make well in centre into which you crumble the yeast. Mix with 2 spoons lukewarm water and a little flour, cover and allow to rise for 10 minutes.
• After 20 minutes work the remaining lukewarm water, the oil, salt and flour into a smooth dough, kneading it until it comes off easily from the bottom of the bowl. Cover dough, put it in a warm spot and allow it to rise for 20 minutes. •
Grease 2 baking sheets. Pre-heat oven to 200° C (400° F or gas mark 6). • Roll out yeast dough, cut into four circular shapes the size of dinner plates, raise the edges a little and place them on two greased baking sheets. Brush a little oil on each pizza, before decorating

them with the various specialities.

Anchovy Pizza

Ingredients for 1 pizza:

2 cups canned peeled
*   tomatoes, well-drained*
50g (2 ozs) grated cheese
½ level teaspoon salt
¼ teaspoon pepper
¼ teaspoon paprika
4 stuffed olives
6 anchovy fillets

For the anchovy pizza cut the canned tomatoes into small pieces, mix with the grated cheese, salt, pepper and paprika and spread this mixture on one of the four flat shapes. Halve the olives and place them and the anchovy fillets on top. Bake pizza in pre-heated oven for 25-30 minutes.

Spinach Pizza

Ingredients for 1 pizza:

120g (4 ozs) deep-frozen
*   spinach*
1 tablespoon cream
1 onion
50g (2 ozs) grated parmesan
*   cheese*

50g (2 ozs) bacon
½ teaspoon salt
A generous pinch garlic
*   powder*
5 black olives
4 anchovy fillets

Put deep-frozen spinach into saucepan together with the cream, cover and allow to thaw at moderate heat until it can be stirred into a smooth paste. Peel onion and chop very finely. Dice bacon. • Now stir spinach together with the onion and bacon dice, the parmesan cheese, salt and garlic powder and spread on the dough. Halve the black olives, distribute them over the pizza and place the anchovies on top. Then bake in pre-heated oven as in previous recipe.

Cheese Pizza

Ingredients for 1 pizza:

75g (3 ozs) processed cheese
2 egg yolks
2 tablespoons cream
1 tablespoon parsley
½ level tablespoon paprika
200g (7 ozs) canned mush-
*   rooms*

Cut cheese into small pieces and stir together with egg yolks, cream, parsley and paprika. Spread mixture on rolled-out dough. Drain mushrooms, cutting the larger one

◁ Pizza Variations, recipes on this page and on page 30

Savoury accompaniments to Beer and Wine

into halves, and place them on top of mixture. Bake as before.

Orange Pizza

Ingredients for 1 pizza:

100g (3½ ozs) streaky bacon
50g (2 ozs) processed cheese in 2 portions
2 tablespoons cream
2 egg yolks
1 generous pinch each of pepper and paprika
¼ teaspoon salt
8 slices peeled orange

Distribute bacon slices over pizza base. Cut cheese into small pieces and whisk together with cream, egg yolks, pepper, paprika and salt. Spread cheese mixture over the bacon and garnish with orange slices. Bake as before.

Island Pizza

Ingredients for 1 pizza:

100g (3½ ozs) streaky bacon
1 jar preserved mussels (preserved in brine or deep-frozen)
150g (5½ ozs) deep-frozen shrimps
2 tomatoes

4 thin cheese slices
½ teaspoon salt
1 pinch each of paprika and oregano

Distribute bacon slices over pizza base. Drain mussels and separate shrimps. Place mussels and shrimps on bacon. Wash tomatoes, dry them, cut them into slices and place them on top of mussels. Cut cheese slices into little strips and place them on the tomatoes. Sprinkle salt, paprika and oregano over the lot. Bake as before.

Salami Pizza

Ingredients for 1 pizza:

2 tablespoons cream
2 egg yolks
50g (2 ozs) grated cheese
1 small jar or can artichoke bottoms
6 stuffed green olives
50g (2 ozs) thin slices salami
½ tablespoon parsley

Stir cream together with egg yolks and grated cheese. Put mixture on pizza base. Drain artichoke bottoms, halve them and distribute on the pizza. Cut olives into thin slices and also put them on pizza. Roll salami slices into little cornets and stick them into the pizza.

Sprinkle parsley over everything and bake in oven as described in previous recipes.

Illustration on page 28

Rhenish Bacon Cake
△△○*

Ingredients for 8 people:

500g (18 ozs) flour
25g (barely 1 oz) yeast
¼ litre (½ pint) lukewarm milk
60g (2 ozs) margarine
1 level teaspoon salt
1 teaspoon lemon zest
500g (18 ozs) fat bacon
2 eggs
2 tablespoons caraway seeds

Preparation time: 50 minutes

Baking time: 30 minutes

Put flour into a bowl, making a well in the middle. Crumble yeast into the well, add 6 tablespoons of lukewarm milk and a little flour and stir. Sprinkle a little flour over the yeast mixture, put into warm place and allow to rise until surface shows signs of crevices. ● Melt margarine but don't heat it. Mix yeast mixture with the melted margarine, the salt,

Rhenish Bacon Cake, recipe on this page ▷

Savoury accompaniments to Beer and Wine

lemon zest, the remainder of the milk and the flour, and stir quickly into a smooth, supple dough, then knead and beat it until bubbles begin to appear. Cover dough and allow it to rise for a further 20 minutes in a warm place. • Grease a baking sheet. Pre-heat oven to a temperature of 220° C (400° F or gas mark 6). Cut uncured bacon into small dice. Whisk eggs. • Roll out dough to 1 cm (½″) thickness and put on baking sheet. Spread the whisked eggs on dough and distribute bacon dice over it. Sprinkle caraway seeds over it and bake in pre-heated oven for 25-30 minutes. *Rhenish Bacon Cake* is best eaten warm, with cool beer.

Illustration on page 31

Herring Tit-bits

△△○

Ingredients for 8 people:

8 rounds pumpernickel
2 tablespoons sandwich spread
1 big apple
Juice of half a lemon
1 portion cream cheese (Gervais)
4 tablespoons milk
A pinch each of salt, pepper and sugar
8 'Matjes fillets' (Matjes is the Dutch term for young herrings, literally: 'Maiden Herring')
2 glacé cherries

Cover pumpernickel rounds with sandwich spread. Peel apple, remove the core and cut it into 8 thin slices. Place them on the pumpernickel rounds and sprinkle with lemon juice. • Stir cream cheese together with salt, pepper and sugar. Around each apple slice arrange a Matjes herring fillet, decorating the centre by squirting the cheese mixture into it. Cut cherries into quarters and place each quarter in the centre of each little heap of cheese.

Cheese Truffles

△○

Ingredients for 8 people:

225g (8 ozs) square of Gervais cheese
1 level teaspoon paprika
A pinch of salt and pepper
1 tablespoon parsley
4 slices pumpernickel

Preparation time: 10 minutes

Time to cool: 30 minutes

Mix together the cheese, paprika, salt, pepper and parsley. Place resulting mixture in a bowl and put into refrigerator to harden for 30 minutes. Crumble pumpernickel finely onto a board. Using two teaspoons which have been dipped into hot water, cut off small quantities from the cheese mixture which, using wet fingers, can be formed into small balls. Roll these in the pumpernickel crumbs, pressing the crumbs lightly into surface of the balls. Heap the cheese truffles into a glass dish and return them once more to the refrigerator for 30 minutes.

Party Salads

Attractively displayed, salads add great variety to a buffet. Unfortunately, to prepare them takes time, for most contain ingredients which must be peeled or cut or diced. However, if you're the fortunate possessor of a deep-freeze there's nothing to prevent you starting these somewhat laborious preparations a week or two in advance of the party date. Do something whenever you have a little spare time and put the prepared bits like pepper pods, cooked rice or noodles, or salad dressings into the deep-freeze. Even completely prepared salads, with the exception of lettuce, potato and horseradish, can be treated in the same manner. Some of your salads should be filling, while others could contain lettuce or other fresh leaves; the latter must be prepared at the last minute, but as relatively small quantities of these are required you may decide to make up just a little in the first instance and, if necessary, replenish your stock in the course of the evening (washed leaves, stored in the refrigerator in plastic bags, keep their freshness, as do salad dressings). • If you display several kinds of bread and cheese, some butter, crackers, fruit and a dessert on your salad buffet, you will have no difficulty in keeping your guests in the best of spirits.

Aniza Salad
△○

Ingredients for 8 people:

2 cans of tunny fish
6 boiled potatoes
3 pickled cucumbers
3 onions
4 carrots
5 peppercorns
3 tablespoons wine vinegar
1 cup cream
½ beaker yoghurt
Juice of half a lemon
½ teaspoon salt
A gererous pinch of sugar

Preparation time: 40 minutes

Marinating time: 6-12 hours

Shred the tunny fish into small pieces. Peel and slice potatoes. Dice cucumbers. Peel onions and cut them into rings. Wash carrots and cut them into small strips. Mix all ingredients and put mixture into an earthenware or glass dish. Sprinkle the peppercorns over it. • Mix vinegar with the cream, lemon juice, salt and sugar; flavour to taste, which should be savoury, and pour over salad ingredients. Cover dish and allow to marinate for half a day or, better still, a whole day. To serve, put salad in a bowl and stand it on ice cubes.

Illustration below

Vegetable-and-Ham Salad
△○○

Ingredients for 8 people:

4 eggs
450g (16 ozs) deep-frozen peas
2 onions
3 pickled cucumbers
400g (14 ozs) boiled ham in one piece
8 tomatoes
4 tablespoons tomato ketchup

Aniza Salad, recipe above

Party Salads

3 tablespoons mayonnaise
2 tablespoons yoghurt
1 teaspoon salt
1 level teaspoon paprika

Preparation time: 45 minutes

Boil eggs for ten minutes, dip into cold water, peel and cut into dice. Put peas into very little salt water, cover saucepan and cook for 6 minutes; when ready drain. • Peel onions and cut into rings. The cucumbers and the ham are then cut into small dice, and the tomatoes washed, dried and cut into eighths. Mix all these ingredients together. • Mix tomato ketchup with the mayonnaise, yoghurt, salt and paprika, and pour the resulting mixture over the salad. Don't mix the salad together thoroughly until you are about to serve it.

Illustration on facing page

Fruit Salad with Curry Mayonnaise

△○

Ingredients for 8 people:

2 red apples
2 bananas
2 teaspoons lemon juice
1 orange
4 canned peach halves
300g (11 ozs) black grapes
6 tablespoons mayonnaise
3 tablespoons yoghurt
1 level teaspoon curry powder
½ teaspoon each of mustard,
   sugar and salt

Preparation time: 40 minutes

The apples should be washed, dried, quartered and cored; the quarters are then sliced finely. Peel bananas, halve them lengthways and cut into thin slices. Sprinkle the lemon juice over apples and bananas. Peel orange, separate wedges and cut these into tiny pieces, removing the pips. Drain peach halves and cut into small pieces. Wash, drain and halve grapes, removing pips. Mix all the fruit together. • Stir mayonnaise together with yoghurt, curry powder, mustard, sugar and salt and pour over salad.

Illustration on facing page

Summer Salad in Melon Halves

△○○

Ingredients for 8 people:

4 small honeydew melons
1 salad cucumber
6 tomatoes
1 carton of cress
4 tablespoons oil
2 tablespoons wine vinegar
½ teaspoon salt
¼ teaspoon pepper
¼ teaspoon sugar

Preparation time: 35 minutes

The melons must be washed, halved, have their seeds removed and flesh cut out; this is then cut into small dice. Wash and drain the cucumber and cut on a slicer. Wash tomatoes, drain, and cut them into thin slices. • Clean the cress with a pair of kitchen scissors, wash it briefly in a sieve under cold running water and drain well. Carefully mix together the melon cubes, cucumber, tomato slices and cress and fill the 8 melon halves with this mixture. • Stir together oil, vinegar, salt, pepper and sugar and distribute over the melon halves.

Illustration on page 34

◁ Summer Salad in Melon Halves (top); Chicory-and-Crab Salad (left); Vegetable-and-Ham Salad (right); Fruit Salad with Curry Mayonnaise (bottom), recipes on pages 33–36

35

Party Salads

Chicory-and-Crab Salad

△○○

Ingredients for 8 people:

4 heads chicory
2 pickled cucumbers
2 sour apples
280g (10 ozs) canned crab
    (white meat only)
1/8 litre (¼ pint) cream
1 beaker yoghurt
1 teaspoon lemon juice
½ teaspoon sugar
¼ teaspoon white pepper
1 pinch of powdered ginger
1 teaspoon salt

Preparation time: 40 minutes

Remove any bad outside leaves from the chicory, cut out a wedge from the root ends and slice into strips. Dice cucumbers. Peel and quarter the apples, remove cores, and cut quarters into small dice. Shred the crab meat, wash briefly under cold running water and drain it. Mix chicory strips with the cucumber and apple dice and the crab meat. ● Beat cream till stiff. Stir together yoghurt, lemon juice, sugar, pepper, ginger powder and salt. Fold mixture under the cream and pour over salad, leaving the mixing until shortly before serving.

Illustration on page 34

Zurich Cheese Salad

△○○

Ingredients for 6 people:

1 jar mixed pickles
250g (9 ozs) Emmental cheese
    in one piece
100g (3½ ozs) blue-veined
    cheese
1 red pepper
½ fresh cucumber
1 onion
2 tablespoons mayonnaise
3 tablespoons cream
2 generous tablespoons
    chopped herbs
1 pinch of garlic powder
½ teaspoon salt
10 drops Tabasco sauce

Preparation time: 40 minutes

Drain mixed pickles and cut finely. Cut both Emmental and blue cheese into cubes. Halve pepper pod, removing pips, wash and cut into fine strips. Wash and drain cucumber and cut it, unpeeled, into fine slices with a slicer. Peel onion and cut into rings. Mix these ingredients together. ● Stir together mayonnaise, cream, herbs, garlic powder, salt and Tabasco sauce and add gently to salad ingredients. Allow to stand in refrigerator for some time before serving.

Illustration on facing page

New York Salad

△○○*

Ingredients for 6 people:

1 green pepper
1 yellow pepper
4 tomatoes
200g (7 ozs) canned crabs or
    shrimps
200g (7 ozs) semi-soft cheese
2 tablespoons wine vinegar
4 tablespoons oil
½ teaspoon salt
1 tablespoon chopped herbs
A little pepper and garlic
½ teaspoon celery salt

Preparation time: 25 minutes

Halve peppers crossways, removing pips, then wash and slice them. Wash, drain and dice tomatoes. Wash crabs (or shrimps) under cold running water and drain them. Cut cheese into small cubes. ● Mix together vinegar, oil, salt, herbs, pepper, garlic powder and celery salt. Stir gently into salad.

Illustration on facing page

Party Salads

Amsterdam Cheese Salad

△○○*

Ingredients for 6 people:

300g (11 ozs) Edam cheese in one piece
150g (5½ ozs) celeriac
3 slices canned pineapple
1 sour apple
3 tablespoons mayonnaise
3 tablespoons yoghurt
1 tablespoon pineapple juice

1 pinch cayenne pepper
1 pinch powdered ginger

Preparation time: 30 minutes

Cut Edam cheese into fine strips. Peel celeriac thickly, remove brown marks and grate it finely. Cut pineapple slices into pieces. Peel and quarter apple and, after removing core, cut quarters into very thin slices. Mix together cheese strips, pineapple pieces, the grated celeriac and apple slices. • Stir together mayonnaise, yoghurt, pineapple juice, the cayenne pepper and powdered ginger and pour this mixture over the salad ingredients.

Illustration on page 37

Beyruth Salad (left); Amsterdam Cheese Salad (bottom); Zurich Cheese Salad (right); New York Salad (top); recipes on pages 36—38

Party Salads

Beyruth Salad

△○○

Ingredients for 6 people:

3 slices canned pineapple
½ can mandarin segments
250g (9 ozs) semi-soft cheese
*   in one piece*
2 lettuce hearts
2 tablespoons each of canned
*   pineapple and mandarin*
*   juice*
350g (12½ ozs) roast or
*   boiled spring chicken*
1/8 litre (¼ pint) cream
¼ teaspoon salt

Preparation time: 25 minutes

Drain pineapple slices and cut them into small pieces. Halve mandarin segments. Cut cheese into even-sized pieces. Separate lettuce hearts into leaves, wash, drain and dry them thoroughly. Remove bones and skin from spring chicken and cut meat into small, even-sized cubes. Mix together pineapple and mandarin pieces, the cheese, lettuce leaves, chicken meat, mandarin and pineapple juice. • Whisk cream until semi-stiff, stir in salt and pour over salad.

Illustration on page 37

Mushroom-and-Rice Salad

△○○*

Ingredients for 8 people:

4 cups rice
1 teaspoon salt
6 eggs
2 cans mushrooms
1 onion
1 bunch dill
1 bunch chives
1 cup cream
½ cup yoghurt
½ teaspoon salt
A generous pinch white pepper

Preparation time: 40 minutes

Wash rice thoroughly. Bring about 2 litres (4 pints) salted water to the boil, pour rice into it and cook at high temperature for 15-16 minutes. Put in sieve under cold running water and drain. • Boil eggs for 10 minutes, put under cold running water, peel and cut into eighths. • Drain mushrooms and cut larger ones into small pieces, or, if button mushrooms, into quarters. Peel and dice onions. Wash, drain and chop dill and chives. • Mix rice with the mushrooms and onions, garnishing with egg eighths. Stir together cream, yoghurt, salt, wine vinegar, sugar, pepper and finely chopped herbs and pour resulting mixture over salad.

Illustration on facing page

Mushroom-and-Rice Salad, recipe on this page ▷

Party Salads

Fruit Salad Garda

△○○

Ingredients for 6 people:

500g (18 ozs) black grapes
2 sour apples
Handful of peeled almonds
1 packet vanilla sugar
3 level teaspoons sugar
2 tablespoons lemon juice
2 liqueur glasses brandy

Preparation time: 30 minutes

Cooling time: 2 hours

Wash grapes, removing stalks. Peel apples, remove cores and quarter them; then cut the quarters into slices. Cut almonds into small splinters. Mix the fruit together. • Stir vanilla and ordinary sugar with lemon juice and brandy and pour over fruit. Place in refrigerator to marinate for two hours.

Illustration below

Allgau Potato Salad

△○○

Ingredients for 8 people:

1kg (2¼ lbs) salad potatoes
350g (12½ ozs) spam or
*   breakfast sausage*
350g (12½ ozs) Emmental
*   cheese*
2 cups canned tomatoes
1 jar very small corn-cobs
2 onions
2 gherkins

Fruit Salad Garda, recipe above

Party Salads

½ cup instant stock
1 beaker yoghurt
½ cup cream
Juice of 1 lemon
½ teaspoon sugar
1 teaspoon salt
½ teaspoon white pepper
½ teaspoon dried marjoram

Preparation time: 40 minutes
Marinating time: 20 minutes

Brush salad potatoes and cook for 25 minutes. • Remove skin, if any, from sausages and cut into strips. Cut cheese and tomatoes into strips. Drain corn-cobs, cutting them into halves or quarters. Peel and dice onions. • Put potatoes under cold running water, peel and slice them. Mix all these ingredients, pour instant stock over mixture, cover and leave to marinate for 20 minutes at room temperature. • Mix yoghurt with the cream, lemon juice, sugar, salt, pepper and marjoram and pour over salad before serving.

Illustration below

Rich Party Salad
△○○

Ingredients for 8 people:

1½kg (3½ lbs) small salad
  potatoes
6 eggs
400g (14 ozs) boiled ham
400g (14ozs) breakfast
  sausage or spam
400g (14 ozs) semi-soft cheese
  in one piece
3 red peppers

Allgau Potato Salad, recipe above

Party Salads

200g (7 ozs) canned button
    mushrooms
4 pickled cucumbers
2 onions
2 bunches parsley
10 tablespoons mayonnaise
10 tablespoons yoghurt
20 drops Tabasco sauce
1 level teaspoon salt
2 tablespoons wine vinegar
¼ teaspoon powdered onion
¼ teaspoon garlic salt

Preparation time: 50 minutes

Marinating time: 2 hours

Brush potatoes and cook in
boiling water for 25 minutes.
• Boil eggs for 10 minutes,
cool under running cold
water, peel and cut into
eighths. Cut ham, sausage and
cheese into strips
of equal size. Halve pepper
pods, removing seeds, and cut
into strips. Drain mushrooms
and cut the larger ones into
halves or quarters. Dice
cucumbers. Peel and dice
onions. Wash, drain and chop
parsley. • Let cold water run
over cooked potatoes, then
peel and cut them into slices.
Mix the lot together. • Now
stir together mayonnaise,
yoghurt, Tabasco sauce, salt,
vinegar, onion powder and
garlic salt and add to salad.
Allow to marinate in
refrigerator for at least
2 hours.

Illustration on facing page

◁ Rich Party Salad, recipe page 41

Avoto Salad

△ ○ ○

Ingredients for 8 people:

4 eggs
3 heads chicory
2 avocados
4 tomatoes
2 apples
2 bananas
2 tablespoons lemon juice
1 beaker yoghurt
4 tablespoons mayonnaise
2 level teaspoons sugar
½ teaspoon salt
¼ teaspoon pepper
¼ teaspoon paprika
4 tablespoons chopped parsley

Preparation time: 40 minutes

Boil eggs for 10 minutes, cool
in cold water, peel and cut into
eighths. Clean chicory, cut
into strips and wash in cold
water several times. Halve
avocados, cut out stones and
remove flesh; cut this into thin
slices. Wash and dice tomatoes.
Peel, core and quarter apples,
cutting quarters into thin
slices. Sprinkle lemon juice
over apple and banana slices.
• Now mix yoghurt,
mayonnaise, sugar, salt, pepper and paprika together and
pour over salad ingredients.
Garnish with parsley.

Toasted white bread goes well
with *Avoto Salad*.

Illustration below

Avoto Salad,
recipe above

Egg Salad

△○*

Ingredients for 8 people:

12 eggs
150g (5½ ozs) mayonnaise
1 beaker yoghurt
2 tablespoons sharp mustard
    (ready-mixed)
5 tablespoons tomato ketchup
½ teaspoon paprika
1 level teaspoon sugar
3 apples
2 pickled cucumbers
4 tomatoes
1 bunch chives
1 cup milk

Preparation time: 40 minutes

Boil eggs for 10 minutes, pour cold water over them, then peel and cut them into not too thin slices. • Stir together mayonnaise, yoghurt, mustard, tomato ketchup and sugar. • Peel and halve apples, removing core, then dice them finely.
To peel tomatoes make a slight incision at the bottom end, pour boiling water over them, and allow them to lie in the water for several minutes. Then remove their skin and cut them into pieces. Wash, drain and chop finely the chives and add, together with the mayonnaise, to the other salad ingredients. Leave this to marinate for two hours in the refrigerator. • As egg salad tends to dry out during marinating add a cup of milk to it shortly before serving. We advise you to prepare the egg salad the day before and to keep it in the refrigerator well covered.

Illustration below

Egg Salad, recipe above

Midnight Soups

Soups are soothing to the stomach, whether served as a prelude to a party or in its later stages when sorely-tried stomachs cry out for something to calm them down. There is one small, but nevertheless significant difference between the kind of soup to start a meal with and the soup you offer your guests in the later or concluding stages of a party. It is this: the soup served as a starter should as a rule be something in the way of light refreshment and therefore not highly seasoned, whereas the soup you give towards midnight should have a stronger taste — something that overrides the variety of tastes — in liquid and in solid form — with which you have tempted your guests in the course of the evening. This soup is meant to help your friends to quieten down or, as the case may be, get their second wind for a few more hours of merry-making. Serving a midnight soup to revive flagging spirits is well worth trying. Use pepper, paprika or other seasoning a little more liberally than usual, or serve, together with the soup, some highly-seasoned snacks — some tit-bits like anchovies on toast or some raw minced beef, seasoned with chilli powder or merely some cottage cheese mixed with paprika or pepper.

In preparing your midnight soup allow for generous portions, for you will be surprised how many takers there are. Keep what remains warm for the indefatigable ones who are liable to ask you for a second helping long after others have gone.

Ukrainian Bortsch
△○○**

Ingredients for 6 people:

150g (5½ ozs) haricot beans
6 medium-sized beetroots
    (preferably uncooked)
750g (1¾ lbs) beef (chuck
    steak)
1 bay leaf
4 peppercorns
1 clove garlic
Soup vegetables (1 carrot,
    1 leek, 1 stick of celery or a
    piece of celeriac)
1 onion
6 tomatoes
¼ firm cabbage
150g (5½ ozs) streaky bacon
2 tablespoons vinegar
2 teaspoons salt
1 level teaspoon sugar
2 level tablespoons flour
4 tablespoons butter
2 cups soured cream

Preparation time: 40 minutes

Cooking time: 1½ hours

Wash the haricot beans and soak for 12 hours in plenty of water. Brush the raw beetroots under cold running water. Cook four of them in water and when soft peel and dice. The remaining two are peeled and grated raw and kept with their juice. • Cut the beef into even-sized dice, cover with water and cook for 20 minutes. Skim and add drained beans, bay leaf, peppercorns and garlic clove. Clean, wash and dice soup vegetables, peel and cut up the onion and add to the meat. Cover saucepan and simmer for 45 minutes. You may have to add water at some stage of the cooking process. • Make a slight incision into the bottom-end of the tomatoes, pour boiling water over them and leave to soak for a few minutes. It will now be easy to remove the skin. Dice the tomatoes. Remove outer leaves and stalk from cabbage and slice it finely. Add tomatoes and cabbage to the soup and simmer for another thirty minutes. • Dice bacon and add it, together with the salt, vinegar, sugar and the grated and diced beetroot, to the soup. Dissolve flour in a little water, stir and bring to the boil several times. Remove soup from stove, add butter and thin down with more water if required. Serve in a soup tureen into which you should put a dollop of

Midnight Soups

soured cream just before serving.

An alternative: deep-freeze the soup, but without the soured cream.

Illustration on front cover of book

Goulash Soup with Grapes

△○○**

Ingredients for 8 people:

500g (18 ozs) chuck steak
3 tablespoons oil
4 onions
4 tablespoons tomato purée
1½ litres (3 pints) instant meat broth
1 tablespoon ready-made chilli sauce
¼ teaspoon freshly-ground pepper
¼ teaspoon cayenne pepper
1 tablespoon pickled pearl onions
1 small can sliced mushrooms
1 small jar button mushrooms
300g (11 ozs) green grapes
2 level teaspoons flour
6 tablespoons cream
1 liqueur glass brandy
½ tumbler port
2 teaspoons salt
1 level teaspoon paprika

Preparation time: 40 minutes
Cooking time: 40-50 minutes

Cut meat into cubes, removing skins and sinews. Heat oil and lightly fry meat in it on all sides. Peel and dice onions and fry them lightly with the meat at low temperature. Stir in tomato purée, fill up with instant meat broth, cover, and cook at low temperature for about 40 minutes or until meat is ready. • Then add chilli sauce, pepper, cayenne, and the pearl onions, stirring thoroughly. Drain mushrooms, cut the larger ones in halves and add to soup. Wash and halve the grapes, remove their pips and put into soup. Mix flour with the cream and stir into the soup, which should once more be brought briefly to the boil. Round off with the brandy, port, salt and paprika, before serving piping hot in soup bowls.

An alternative: by all means deep-freeze the soup, but preferably without the grapes, the flour-cream thickening and the alcoholic ingredients.

Illustration on facing page

Irish Game Soup

△○○*

Ingredients for 8 people:

1kg (2¼ lb) venison (odd bits with bones will do)
100g (3½ ozs) bacon
2 onions
1 bunch soup vegetables
4 juniper berries
2 bay leaves
2 teaspoons salt
1½ litres (3 pints) water
2 level tablespoons flour
2 tablespoons butter or margarine
½ teaspoon sugar
2 egg yolks
2 cups red wine

Preparation time: 20 minutes
Cooking time: 1½ hours

Divide venison into pieces. Dice bacon. Peel onions and cut into eighths. Put all this into saucepan, together with water, the soup vegetables, juniper berries, bay leaves and salt and cook at low heat for 1½ hours. Strain broth. Remove all sinews, bones and gristle and cut remaining meat into small pieces. • Knead the flour with butter or margarine and add little by little, to the hot broth, whisking all the while and bringing to the boil several times. Return meat to the soup. Add sugar, red wine and last of all the egg yolks, and stir thoroughly.

46

Goulash Soup with Grapes, recipe on this page ▷

Midnight Soups

Puszta Soup

△○○*

Ingredients for 8 people:

2 onions
500g (18 ozs) green pepper
4 tablespoons oil
1kg (2¼ lbs) lean minced
    beef
1 teaspoon salt
½ teaspoon pepper
2 level tablespoons paprika
1 jar sweetcorn
2 small cans tomato purée
2 litres (4 pints) water
2 egg yolks
1 cup soured cream
1 level teaspoon instant meat
    concentrate
1 generous pinch marjoram
½ cup finely-chopped parsley

Preparation time: 20 minutes

Cooking time: 30 minutes

Peel and dice onions. Halve
pepper pods, removing seeds,
and wash and cut them into
strips. Heat oil in large saucepan, and lightly fry onions
while stirring. Add minced
meat and also lightly fry while
stirring. Season with salt,
pepper, paprika and pepper
pod strips. Drain sweetcorn
and add it to meat together
with tomato purée. Mix everything well together, fill up
with water, cover and cook
at low heat for 30 minutes.
• Whisk egg yolks with
soured cream. Stir instant
meat concentrate and
marjoram into soup. Take
off stove and bind with egg
yolk and cream mixture.
Garnish with parsley before
serving piping hot. The *Puszta
Soup* is a favourite among
peasants of the Hungarian
plains.

Balkan Soup

△○*

Ingredients for 8 people:

400g (14 ozs) lean pork
4 onions
4 carrots
2 tablespoons lard
2 small jars tomato purée
3 bay leaves
2 level teaspoons ground
    caraway seeds
2 teaspoons salt
½ teaspoon dried oregano
1 level teaspoon thyme
2 small packets ready-made
    goulash soup
1½ litres (3 pints) water
3 level tablespoons paprika
1 cup red wine
1 generous pinch garlic
    powder
1 cup soured cream
1 pinch sugar

Preparation time: 50 minutes

Cut pork into even-sized
cubes. Peel and dice onions.
Scrape, wash and dice
carrots. Heat lard in large
saucepan and in it lightly
fry first the meat, on all
sides, and then the onions and
carrots. Add tomato purée,
bay leaves, salt, caraway seeds,
thyme and oregano, stirring
well. Cover and let stew for
20 minutes over low heat.
• Stir the goulash soup
powder into a little water and
add it with the remainder of

Midnight Soups

the water to the soup, letting it cook for another 10 minutes. Season to taste with the paprika, garlic powder, red wine, soured cream and sugar, before serving piping hot.

Hessian Bean Soup

△○＊＊

Ingredients for 8 people:

4 tablespoons oil
4 level tablespoons flour
1 litre (barely 2 pints) instant meat broth
600g (22 ozs) deep-frozen green beans (runner or French)
¾ litre (1½ pints) water
1 teaspoon salt
1 good pinch each of pepper and dried thyme
A dash of wine vinegar
¼ litre (½ pint) cream
2 level teaspoons paprika

Preparation time: 30 minutes

Heat oil in large saucepan and, while continually stirring, sprinkle flour into it until it is deep brown. Slowly add instant meat broth, continue stirring and let it come to the boil several times. Cover and keep this brown stock warm.
• Put the beans into another saucepan, add water and salt, cover and boil for 6 minutes.

Add contents of second saucepan to the brown soup. Season generously to taste with salt, pepper, the dried thyme and the vinegar. • Whisk cream till stiff. Serve in soup bowls, putting on each 1-2 tablespoons of cream which in turn should be dusted with a little paprika powder.

Illustration below

Chicken Curry Soup

△○○

Ingredients for 8 people:

1 boiling chicken of about 1.5 kg (3½ lbs)
2½ litres (5 pints) water
1 bunch of soup vegetables
1 onion
2 teaspoons salt
150g (5½ ozs) rice
2 cups deep-frozen peas
2 level teaspoons curry powder
6 tablespoons cream
4 tablespoons deep-frozen parsley

Preparation time: 40 minutes
Cooking time: 2-3 hours

Hessian Bean Soup, recipe above

Midnight Soups

Wash the inside and outside of the chicken thoroughly under cold running water and drain. Put it into a saucepan, cover it with cold water and bring to boil. Clean and wash soup vegetables. Peel onion and cut it into eighths. Skim before adding salt and onion eighths. Now let chicken boil at medium heat for 2-3 hours. When cooked, take chicken out, remove skin and bones and cut meat into even-sized pieces. Strain broth. • Cook rice in fast-boiling salted water. Drain and rinse in cold water. Put meat, rice and peas into broth and cook for another 6 minutes at low heat. • Mix curry powder with parsley and cream and stir mixture into soup before serving.

Goes well with toasted white bread and a glass of beer.

Illustration below

Chicken Curry Soup, recipe page 49

Do-It-Yourself Snacks

The following hints are not meant for larger parties; they are intended for the more intimate ones at which your guests may find it fun to help you lay the table and prepare the refreshments you've planned for them. Of course, you must know your guests pretty well to risk asking them to such a 'do-it-yourself' party, but provided they are chosen with reasonably good care such informal gatherings can be highly amusing and stimulating.

There are, naturally enough, no hard and fast rules to observe for such get-to-gethers. It's odds-on, however, that some of your guests, if not all, will soon gravitate towards your kitchen where, inspired by what they discover in the refrigerator, they will soon proceed to compose some tasty dishes. The ideal equipment for such common efforts should in-clude a grill, toaster, frying-pan and a deep-fat fryer. Soon these would-be helpers will automatically divide themselves into chefs and menial workers, each eager to contribute to the success of the party according to his or her ability; so see that there are adequate supplies of aprons and kitchen paper. Depend on the good humour of your voluntary helpers should something go wrong, and be prepared for the least

popular chores to fall on you. Problems are least likely to arise if the meal is consumed in the kitchen. If it's dished up in another room it will be the responsibility of the hosts to see that their 'kitchen staff' are relieved in time to partake in peace of the meal they have been helping to prepare.

Roast Beef with a sharp Sauce Remoulade
△△○○○ ❋ ❋

Ingredients for 8 people:

1kg (2¼ lbs) joint of beef for
*   roasting*
2 tablespoons oil
A pinch each of salt, pepper,
*   dried sage and thyme*
2 jars mixed pickles
1 jar pickled red peppers
1 small jar gherkins
1 can asparagus tips
3 eggs
1 jar mayonnaise
1 beaker yoghurt
1 apple
1 onion
3 tomatoes
2 small pickled cucumbers
A dash of garlic essence
1 generous pinch each of sugar,
*   salt, pepper and paprika*

Preparation time: 40 minutes

Pre-heat oven to 250° C (450° F, gas mark 8). Rinse joint of beef briefly under cold running water; dry it well and make a few incisions on the top before brushing it with oil. Rub salt, pepper, sage and thyme into the roast and put it on the middle sliding tray of the oven to roast for 30 minutes (the roasting time varies, of course, according to whether you like your beef well, medium or underdone, but for the size of roast recommended in this recipe 25 minutes should be the minimum). • At the end of the roasting period, switch off the oven and leave the roast in it for another 10 minutes. Then take it out, allow it to cool down and cut into slices. Place the slices on a platter. The mixed pickles, red peppers, gherkins and asparagus tips are best arranged in separate little dishes. • Boil eggs for ten minutes, rinse under cold running water, peel and dice them. Stir yoghurt into mayonnaise. Peel and halve apple, removing core; then grate it. Peel and dice onion. Dice also tomatoes and pickled cucumbers. Now stir the chopped eggs, onions, tomatoes and pickled cu-cumbers as well as the grated apple, garlic essence, sugar, salt, pepper and paprika in with the mayonnaise. The resulting *Sauce Remoulade* should be served separately

Do-It-Yourself Snacks

from the roast beef. • Roast beef prepared in this manner is highly suitable for a help-yourself service, because every guest adds to his meat what he likes best of the sour side-dishes, the only 'must' being the mouthwatering *remoulade*.

Serve with a choice of different breads

Illustration below

Improvising with the Toaster

△ ○ ○

Ingredients for 6-8 people:

1 large sliced toasting loaf
1 small rye bread
1 small wholewheat loaf
750g (1½ lbs) of various sliced sausages
1 can sliced pineapples
½ can peach halves
½ can mandarin segments

1 jar olives
1 jar pickled cucumbers
2 onions
8 tomatoes
1 fresh cucumber
8 hardboiled eggs
1 packet deep-frozen mussels
1 packet crab meat
500g (18 ozs) assorted cheese slices
Butter, mayonnaise, sandwich spreads, ready-made spicy sauces and spices.

Preparation time: as long as

Roast Beef with a sharp Sauce Remoulade, recipe page 51

Do-It-Yourself Snacks

you and your guests like to spend.

Arrange all ingredients attractively on wooden boards or dishes. Pre-heat grill. Invite every guest to put whatever he likes on the toast or bread and toast it over. Distribute samples of any particularly successful creations to encourage the others.

Illustration below

Shrimps on Spiced Toast

△ ○ ○

Ingredients for 6 people:

12-18 slices of toasting bread
1 jar sandwich spread
1 jar Russian dressing (a ready-made spicy sauce)
1 jar mustard (also ready-made)
1 cup mayonnaise

2 tablespoons grated horse-radish
600g (22 ozs) shrimps, canned or deep-frozen
A few lettuce leaves
1 can asparagus tips
6 tomatoes
1 jar caviar substitute

Preparation time: 40 minutes

Have the toaster ready and use it to keep up with demand. Put out sandwich spread and spicy

Improvising with the Toaster, recipe above

Do-It-Yourself Snacks

sauces as well. Mix mayonnaise with the horseradish. ● Remove shrimps from can, rinse them under cold running water and drain them (deep-frozen shrimps will, of course, have to be thawed). Wash and drain lettuce leaves and drain asparagus tips. Wash, dry and slice tomatoes. Open the tin of caviar and put it into a jar ready for use. ● Each guest seasons his own toast to taste with the aid of the spicy sauces provided and covers it with shrimps, garnishing them with whatever he or she likes — lettuce leaves, asparagus tips, slices of tomato or caviar.

Illustration below

Shrimps on Spiced Toast, recipe page 53

Swiss Asparagus Toast

△○○○

Ingredients for 6 people:

4 tablespoons butter
6 slices white bread
*6 slices raw smoked ham of the
    same size as the toast slices*
*About 36 canned white
    asparagus stems*
*6 thin slices Tilsit cheese
    (Cheddar or Cheshire or
    any other more readily
    available sliceable cheese
    will do)*
A pinch of salt per slice
3 tomatoes
6 sprigs dill

Preparation time: 25 minutes

Pre-heat oven or grill to highest temperature. Heat butter in frying-pan and lightly fry bread slices on both sides. Cover each slice with a slice of ham and distribute asparagus over the ham, salting them lightly. Having put the cheese slices on top, bake the lot in the oven or under the grill until cheese begins to melt but don't brown. ● Wash and slice tomatoes, putting some on each toast. Garnish with a sprig of dill.

Illustration on facing page

Skewer Compositions

△△○○○

Ingredients for 8-10 people:

*500g (18 ozs) 'beer sausage' (a
    parboiled sausage consist-
    ing of a mixture of minced
    beef, pork and bacon — also
    available in cans)*
2 green peppers
*250g (9 ozs) Gouda cheese in
    one piece*
1 jar canned red peppers
*500g (18 ozs) deep-frozen
    scampi*
1 fresh cucumber

Swiss Asparagus Toast, ▷
recipe on this page

Do-It-Yourself Snacks

200g (7 ozs) smoked eel
200g (7 ozs) streaky bacon
1 jar stuffed green olives
200g (7 ozs) canned button
    mushrooms
250g (9 ozs) bacon in one
    piece
250g (9 ozs) boiled ham in
    one piece
250g (9 ozs) pork fillet
4 onions
2 red peppers
Salt
Pepper
Paprika
Mustard
Oil
An assortment of spicy sauces

Preparation time: 1½ hours

Cut into cubes or pieces the ingredients intended to be spiked on the skewers. Drain scampi and mushrooms. Display all ingredients attractively to inspire your guests: each guest spikes on his skewer the ingredients he likes best. We suggest one of the following combinations:
(1) Sausage, green pepper, Gouda cheese and red pepper. (2) Scampi, fresh cucumber, smoked eel, streaky bacon, green olives and button mushrooms. (3) Bacon, boiled ham, pork and red pepper.
Each person seasons his skewer to taste, brushes it with oil and grills it himself. This snack is best eaten with bread, tomato or lettuce salad.

56

Pancake Variations
△○

Ingredients for 6-8 people:

10 eggs
¼ litre (½ pint) milk
⅛ litre (¼ pint) water
1 teaspoon salt
250g (9 ozs) flour
6 tablespoons oil
An assortment of:
1 cup finely-chopped mixed
    fresh herbs
100g (3½ ozs) sliced bacon
1 can wild mushrooms called
    'chanterelles'
1 can button mushrooms
Canned breast of chicken in
    jelly
Apple purée
Cranberries
Apricot jam
2 peeled apples in slices
Cinnamon and sugar
1 jar gherkins
1 jar mayonnaise
1 can tunny fish
1 can sardines in oil
1 jar olives
1 jar capers
2 finely-chopped onions
200g (7 ozs) ready-prepared
    herring salad

Preparation time: 1 hour

Whisk eggs together with milk, water and salt. Slowly stir flour into mixture until it reaches a thick running consistency. Pour a small quantity of the

batter into a small frying-pan in which you have previously heated a little oil and make a thin pancake of roughly similar size. Repeat process till all batter is used up. Each guest can fill his pancake with a savoury or a sweet filling and eat it warm or cold as he wishes. Eaten warm, it tastes particularly good with the chanterelles, the button mushrooms or the breast of chicken, if baked together with some apple slices, cinnamon and sugar, or with apple purée, cranberries or apricots. Those preferring to eat their pancakes cold have the choice between:
1) The finely cut-up gherkins and mayonnaise.
2) A mixture of tunny fish and olives, sardines, capers and diced onions.
3) The ready-prepared herring salad.

Sausage Variations
△○○

Ingredients for 8-10 people:

6-8 of both Vienna and Frank-
    furt sausages
An assortment of thin smoky
    sausages from your delica-
    tessen shop
2 cans cocktail sausages
2 packets chipolatas

Do-It-Yourself Snacks

*200g (7 ozs) sliced streaky
  bacon*
*400g (14 ozs) cheese in one
  piece*
Several kinds of mustard
Diverse spicy sauces
1 jar mixed pickles
*1 large can or jar pickled
  cucumbers*
10 tomatoes (minimum)

Preparation time: 1 hour

The boiling sausages are put in
a large pot with boiling water;
keep them warm for as long as
necessary but don't keep the
water boiling. As for the
frying or grilling sausages,
leave these uncooked for
each guest to prepare as his
fancy strikes him. Your
guests may decide to
wrap them in slices of bacon
or may prefer to cut them up
and spike them on skewers,
together with tomato and
cucumber pieces, and grill
them. Season with some of the
various mustards or spicy
sauces and serve with different
kinds of bread, bread rolls and
pretzels.

Chicken Drumsticks with Mango Sauce

△○○

Ingredients for 6 people:

*12 chicken drumsticks from
  the deep-freeze*
10 tablespoons oil
2 liqueur glasses whisky
¼ teaspoon pepper
1 teaspoon salt
2 tablespoons butter
1 packet almond splinters
*1 bottle mango sauce (ready-
  made spicy sauce)*
2 bananas
Juice of ½ lemon

Preparation time: 35 minutes

Wash deep-frozen chicken
drumsticks briefly under cold

Chicken Drumsticks
with Mango Sauce,
recipe above

running water, dab dry and let
thaw in a mixture of oil,
whisky, pepper and salt,
turning them several times in
the marinade. Grill them one
after the other under the pre-
heated grill, brushing them
with oil and whisky while they
are cooking. ● Heat butter in
saucepan and fry almond
splinters till golden brown.
Add Mango sauce. Peel and
slice bananas and, together
with the lemon juice, add them
to the sauce which should then
be cooked for a while. The
Mango sauce is served with the
chicken drumsticks.

Goes well with toasted white
bread and mushroom-and-rice
salad (for recipe see page 38).

Illustration below

Do-It-Yourself Snacks

Scrambled Eggs with Salami

△○○

Ingredients for 6 people:

6 slices white bread
12 slices salami
6 eggs
1 tablespoon cream
1 pinch of salt and pepper
1 can button mushrooms
2 tablespoons dripping

2 tablespoons parsley
3-4 tomatoes

Preparation time: 20 minutes

Lightly toast white bread slices and while they are still warm place salami slices on them. • Beat together eggs, cream, salt and pepper. Drain button mushrooms, cutting larger heads into smaller pieces. Heat dripping and pour egg mixture into it, adding also mushrooms and parsley. Scramble till eggs

are set. • Wash, dry and slice tomatoes. Spread scrambled eggs on the salami slices and garnish each slice of toast with tomatoes.

Illustration below

Scrambled Eggs with Salami, recipe above

Do-It-Yourself Snacks

Mussels and Cheese on Toast △○○

Ingredients for 6 people:

1 onion
100g (3½ ozs) streaky bacon
2 cans mussels (or deep-frozen mussels)
6 slices toast
6 teaspoons butter
1 bunch chives
1 pinch garlic powder per slice
6 thin slices cheese (Cheddar, Cheshire, Gouda or Gruyére)

Preparation time: 25 minutes

Pre-heat oven to 250° C (450° F; gas mark 8) or turn on grill to maximum temperature. Peel and finely dice onion; dice bacon. Drain or de-freeze mussels. Lightly toast bread slices and butter them. Wash and dry chives and chop them finely. Place half the quantity of chopped chives on the buttered toast. • Fry diced onions lightly in a sauce-pan together with diced bacon. Add mussels (the canned mussels need only be heated up thoroughly, whereas the frozen ones must be allowed to cook for 4-5 minutes). Distribute mixture over slices of buttered toast, season each with garlic powder and cover with a slice of cheese. Place into oven or under grill till cheese melts. • Sprinkle each slice of toast with remaining chives.

Illustration below

Mussels and Cheese on Toast, recipe above

Fun with Fondues

Fondues are among the few dishes the very preparation of which helps to get a party going with a swing: all of your guests can — and probably will — take a hand in the cooking, serving and handling, if only in the capacity of adviser. The connoisseurs among them will know that the work which goes into the making of a fondue will prove to be well worthwhile, while the un-initiated will be pleasantly surprised at the agreeable taste of the dish they have helped to prepare.

Fondue is French for 'melted', which is short for melted cheese for originally, in Switzerland where fondues were first thought of, it was melted Swiss cheese that was used as the main ingredient of the new creation.

Since then, the fondue habit has spread to many other countries, undergoing various changes in the process, as you will see from the selection of recipes in the following section. So while you are sitting round the table, getting the fondue of your choice ready for eating, you may like to think for a moment of the many Japanese who at the same time are concocting their delicious 'Sukiyaki', which like the fondue, originally stemmed from the little Swiss canton of Neuchâtel.

The equipment you need for making any kind of fondue consists of: 1) A 'Caquelon', or fire-proof earthenware pot with a handle in which to melt the cheese; 2) A copper or enamel dish for meat or fish fondues; 3) A spirit-burner (sometimes called 'rechaud') with an easily-adjustable flame, needed on the table to keep the dish hot throughout the meal; 4) Long-handled fondue forks, one for each guest, who will need it either to dip small pieces of bread into the melted cheese or to hold various raw ingredients (meat or fish) to cook in the rechaud. Each guest places his cooked piece on either an ordinary dinner plate or, better still, a special fondue plate with several compartments to hold the various sauces and side-dishes which are essential to make your fondue party the complete success it deserves to be.

Neuchâtel Cheese Fondue

△△○○

Ingredients for 6 people:

1 clove garlic, cut in half
600g (22 ozs) Emmental or Gruyère cheese, or a mixture of both
1/8 litre (¼ pint) Neuchâtel wine or any other fairly dry white wine
1½ liqueur glasses kirsch
2 level teaspoons cornflour
Pepper
Grated nutmeg

Preparation time: 35 minutes

Rub a fairly large fireproof earthenware pot (caquelon) with the cut garlic clove. Grate the cheese and place it on the bottom of the caquelon. Pour wine over it and put pot on stove. Stir with a wooden spoon, always describing the figure 8; slowly the cheese will melt, then thicken and become creamy. Dissolve cornflour in kirsch and stir it into the fondue. Add seasoning and bring to boil before transferring caquelon to spirit burner. ● Cut white and farm bread into even-sized, not-too-small cubes, distributing them among your guests.
● Each of them sticks one of the cubes on his (fondue) fork and dips it into the fondue, turning it around thoroughly so that the bread soaks up the cheese.

Serve with the same white wine or kirsch — but on no account with beer.

Illustration on facing page

◁ Neuchâtel Cheese Fondue, recipe on this page

Fun with Fondues

A tip: should the fondue become too thick while it is being eaten, add a little warmed white wine and kirsch, stirring it well with a whisk.

Fondue Bourguignonne

△△△○○**

Ingredients for 6 people:

2-2½ lbs tender fillets of beef, pork or veal
1 litre (2 pints) oil

Preparation time: 40 minutes

Remove skin, sinews and fat from meat and cut it into even-sized cubes of 1.5 cm (¾'') each. Dab dry before serving.
• Heat oil thoroughly in caquelon and test heat by dipping one meat cube into it to see whether it becomes crisp and brown quickly. If this is the case, transfer caquelon to spirit burner to maintain oil at same heat. Each member of the party sticks a piece of meat on his (fondue) fork and holds it in the fat until it is browned on all sides. The meat cube is then removed from the fork and put on a plate, seasoned to taste and eaten with knife and fork

together with the various side-dishes. In the meantime another piece of meat is being browned in the fat for the next helping.

Illustration on facing page

To serve with *Fondue Bourguignonne*, there are various sauces, the recipes for which you will find further on in this section. Also, there are ready-made sharp sauces, mixed pickles, cornichons, pearl onions, mustard pickles and an assortment of bread. Beer or not too heavy red wine are the recommended drinks.

A tip: keep meat cubes for a fondue in deep-freeze in readiness for unexpected guests; meat cubes left over from a fondue dinner may likewise be deep-frozen.

Sauces for Meat Fondues

Curd Cheese Sauce with Herbs

△○

Ingredients for 6 people:

1½ cups curd cheese
½ cup cream
Salt, pepper and ground caraway seeds
6 tablespoons finely-chopped fresh herbs (parsley, chives, cress, mint, dill and chervil)

Preparation time: 15 minutes

Stir the cream, salt, pepper, caraway seeds and the finely-chopped herbs into the curd cheese and serve in a bowl.

Fondue Bourguignonne, recipe on this page

Fun with Fondues

Apple-Curry Sauce
△○

Ingredients for 6 people:

*3 medium-sized apples
1 tablespoon lemon juice
1 level teaspoon sugar
4 tablespoons curd cheese
1 level teaspoon curry powder*

Preparation time: 15 minutes

Peel apples and cut into quarters, removing cores. Grate them, then stir together with the lemon juice, sugar, curd cheese and curry powder.

Illustration below

Brandy Sauce
△○○

Ingredients for 6 people:

*1 egg yolk
$1/8$ litre (¼ pint) oil
1 liqueur glass brandy
1 dash of Worcester sauce
Salt
Some small capers*

Preparation time: 15 minutes

Whisk egg yolk and stir it drop by drop into the oil. To the resulting mayonnaise add brandy, Worcester sauce and capers (should the latter be too large, cut them into smaller pieces).

Illustration below

Herb Mayonnaise
△○

Ingredients for 6 people:

*1 cup finely-chopped mixed herbs (parsley, chives, chervil, tarragon, dill and cress)
2 cups mayonnaise
1 teaspoon lemon juice
1 pinch sugar*

Preparation time: 15 minutes

Mix together the herbs, mayonnaise, lemon juice and sugar shortly before serving.

A tip: if you don't have enough fresh herbs available add an additional tablespoon of dried herbs, rubbing them fine before adding to the mayonnaise; then, let the mayonnaise marinate for 30 minutes before adding the fresh herbs shortly before serving.

Illustration below

Herb Mayonnaise, Apple-Curry Sauce, Brandy Sauce, recipes on this page

Fun with Fondues

Sauce Chantilly

△○

Ingredients for 6 people:

1 cup mayonnaise
2 tablespoons sherry
1 teaspoon lemon juice
½ teaspoon sharp mustard
A generous pinch of both salt
    and pepper
$1/8$ litre (¼ pint) cream

Preparation time: 10 minutes

Mix together the mayonnaise, sherry, lemon juice, mustard, salt and sugar. Whisk cream till stiff and fold under mayonnaise.

Illustration below

Sauce-Bozen Style

△○*

Ingredients for 6 people:

3 eggs
2 pickled cucumbers
1 onion
2 anchovy fillets
1 tablespoon capers
2 tablespoons finely-chopped
    mixed herbs (fresh for
    preference)
1 teaspoon sharp mustard
1 tablespoon wine vinegar
4 tablespoons oil

*Salt, pepper, cayenne and
  garlic powder*

Preparation time: 15 minutes

Boil eggs for 10 minutes, cool under cold running water and peel and dice them. Dice also the pickled cucumbers, peeled onions, the anchovy fillets and capers. Mix all this with the finely-chopped herbs, the mustard, wine vinegar, oil, salt, pepper, cayenne and garlic powder.

Illustration below

Sauce Chantilly, Sauce Bozen-Style, recipes on this page

Curry and Almond Sauce

△○

Ingredients for 6 people:

1½ cups mayonnaise
4 tablespoons cream
1 level teaspoon curry powder
1 teaspoon lemon juice
½ teaspoon sugar
6 tablespoons ground almonds
½ cup mandarin segments

Preparation time: 15 minutes

Stir together the mayonnaise, cream, curry powder, lemon juice, sugar and ground almonds. Cut the mandarins into very small cubes and mix them, and their juice, with the curry mayonnaise.

Illustration on page 66

65

Fun with Fondues

Horseradish Sauce

△ ○

Ingredients for 6 people:

1 cup mayonnaise
4 tablespoons apple purée
4 tablespoons grated horse-
*   radish*
1 teaspoon lemon juice
½ teaspoon sugar
2 egg yolks
2 tablespoons cream

Preparation time: 10 minutes

Stir well together the mayonnaise, apple purée, horseradish, lemon juice, sugar, egg yolks and cream. Place in a small bowl.

Illustration below

Fruity Tomato Sauce

△ ○

Ingredients for 6 people:

½ can (the equivalent of two
*   soup plates) tomato soup*

3 tablespoons mayonnaise
3 tablespoons cream
2 tablespoons tomato ketchup
1 level teaspoon paprika
1 pinch each of salt, celery salt
*   and garlic powder*

Preparation time: 10 minutes

Stir well together all the above-mentioned ingredients and serve cold with meat fondue.

Illustration below

66   Curry and Almond Sauce (top left); Horseradish Sauce (top right);
Fruity Tomato Sauce (bottom), recipes on pages 65 and 66

Fun with Fondues

Sukiyaki — Japanese Style

△△○○○

Ingredients for 6 people:

750g (1½ lbs) fillet of beef
300g (11 ozs) leeks
1 onion
1 handful spinach or lettuce leaves
250g (9 ozs) button mush-rooms (fresh or canned)
1 carrot
1 small can bamboo shoots
1 tablespoon oil or hard vegetable fat
2 tablespoons soya sauce (ready-made spicy sauce)
2 teaspoons sake (Japanese rice wine)
100g (3½ ozs) transparent noodles
1 litre (2 pints) instant chicken broth
6 eggs
About 300g (11 ozs) rice, boiled, drained and dried

Preparation time: 40 minutes

Remove skin and sinew from fillet of beef and cut into wafer-thin slices. Wash leeks thoroughly and slice thinly. Peel onion and cut likewise into thin slices. Wash spinach or lettuce leaves and cut into strips. Clean mushrooms, drain and cut into fine slices. Scrape and wash carrot and cut it into strips. Drain bamboo shoots.
• Melt fat in a special Sukiyaki pan or in your 'Caquelon' over

Sukiyaki-Japanese Style, recipe on this page

Fun with Fondues

the spirit burner. Mix soya sauce, sugar and sake together and pour it into the fat (which should be very hot). • Add the vegetables to this nearly boiling mixture and allow them to stew for 10 minutes. Now pour in the pre-heated chicken broth. • The meat slices are then added one by one to cook. Throw the transparent noodles into boiling water, bring them to the boil once, drain and cut them into pieces, before putting them into the pan. • Break eggs into 6 small bowls and beat them. Fill a further 6 small bowls with the boiled rice. • Each member of the Sukiyaki party helps himself to a few cooked slices of meat and a little of the vegetables from the pan, dips this mixture into the beaten egg and eats it together with the rice. But don't forget to cook only a small number of meat slices at any one time; the process can be repeated several times during the meal as and when required.

Illustration on page 67

Chocolate Fondue
△△○○

Ingredients for 6-8 people:

400g (14 ozs) chocolate (milk or bitter)
1½ cups cream
2 tablespoons chopped candied ginger
2 liqueur glasses rum
500g (18 ozs) white bread cut in cubes
Some stewed fruit of your own choice (slightly acidy for preference)

Chocolate Fondue, recipe above

Preparation time: 10 minutes

Break chocolate into small pieces. Heat cream in a fireproof earthenware saucepan on the spirit burner, adding chocolate gradually and stirring all the time. Mix in the finely-chopped pieces of candied ginger and the rum. Reduce heat. • Each participant can then stick a piece of bread onto his fondue fork and dip it into the chocolate fondue and eat it with the stewed fruit.

Illustration below

Buffet Parties

'Permitted is what tastes good' is about the only rule to observe in planning a Buffet Party. However regally you feel like treating your guests, true hospitality demands that your arrangements should never be so grand as to over-awe them and thus disturb the informal atmosphere which is perhaps the most essential ingredient of any successful party. Informality — a spirit of gay abandon — must remain the keynote even in the face of the choicest and costliest things like salmon in aspic or lobster Newburg. Make what you have to offer as varied as possible; arrange everything in such a manner as to make it easy — and a pleasure — for your guests to help themselves, leaving it entirely to them whether they want to gorge themselves or just have a little nibble. Supplement the recipes suggested in this section by a large assortment of breads; see that there is enough butter, a variety of cheeses, fresh fruit and gateaux as well as an ample supply of tit-bits with-in easy reach. Provide an adequate stock of (disposable) plates and cutlery. Some flowers will, no doubt, be useful in making your buffet as attractive a sight as possible, but take care the flowers don't fade before they have produced their intended effect. Hot dishes should be placed on hot plates in readiness for the moment you give the signal for their consumption. If you're considering suggesting toast snacks, place the slices with their fillings next to the grill in readiness for toasting by your guests.

Keep the buffet tidy through-out the evening, clearing the debris regularly and unobtrusively providing any fresh supplies of plates, cutlery or anything else that may be needed.

Buffet for the Discerning

For 8 people

Bean Soup Elche

△△○○ *

Ingredients for 8 people:

2 large cans haricot beans
3 large onions
1 leek
4 tomatoes
3 bouillon cubes
5 cups hot water
2 tablespoons oil
1 clove garlic
1 pinch coarsely-ground pepper
1 pinch cayenne
1 pinch salt
1 pinch fresh savory
500g (18 ozs) minced meat
1 teaspoon salt
1 generous pinch coarsely-ground pepper
1 generous pinch dried oregano
1 egg
$1/8$ litre (¼ pint) oil
½ litre (1 pint) soured cream

Preparation time: 25 minutes

Drain haricot beans. Peel and finely slice onions. Halve the leek lengthwise, wash thoroughly and cut into thin slices. Make an incision, cross-wise, at the bottom end of the tomatoes, pour boiling water over them and leave them for a

Buffet for the Discerning (see picture on pages 70–71; recipe on ▷ pages 69–73)

Buffet Parties

few minutes in the water. Peel and dice them. Dissolve the stock cube in the hot water. Heat the oil in a sufficiently large saucepan, add the onions and leek slices and fry them lightly. Add the juice of the garlic clove and the diced tomatoes. • Cover and cook for a short time over low heat then add the beans and the stock. Season with salt, pepper, cayenne and savory. Cook the soup over low heat for 15 minutes. • Season the minced meat with salt, pepper and oregano. Mix everything together with the egg and shape into small balls. Heat the oil and fry the meatballs in the hot fat until they are golden brown all round. Add them to the finished soup and let stand for a few minutes before serving. Serve the soured cream separately.

Illustration on pages 70/71

An alternative: freeze the soup, but without the soured cream.

Plowman's Board
△○

Ingredients for 8 people:

300g (11 ozs) cheese made from ewe's milk (or any white cheese)
2 level teaspoons paprika
450g (1 lb) garlic sausage
1 jar pearl onions

Preparation time: 15 minutes

Cut the cheese into thick slices, arrange them on a board and sprinkle with paprika. Slice the garlic sausage thinly. Drain the pearl onions. Place 4–5 folded sausage slices on a skewer, alternating them with onions. Finish every skewer with a pearl onion.

Illustration on pages 70/71

Celery Dip with Pepper Strips
△○

Ingredients for 8 people:

3 red peppers
3 green peppers
1 onion
200g (7 ozs) curd cheese
100g (3½ ozs) blue cheese (Danish blue or Gorgonzola)

1/8 litre (¼ pint) soured cream
1 clove garlic
½ teaspoon curry powder
1 level teaspoon celery salt

Preparation time: 15 minutes

Cut the peppers in half, removing the pips. Wash the halves, cut them into strips and stand them up in a glass. Peel the onion and chop it very finely. Stir together the curd cheese, blue cheese, onion, soured cream, the juice of the garlic clove, curry powder and celery salt. Serve with the pepper strips.

Goes well with French bread.

Illustration on pages 70/71

Buffet Parties

Peperoni Eggs

△○

Ingredients for 8 people:

8 eggs
2 canned red peperoni (small
   peppers)
1 small onion
1 tablespoon sharp mustard
A good pinch of coarsely-
   ground pepper
A pinch of cayenne
A pinch of salt
1 clove garlic
1 teaspoon wine vinegar
2 teaspoons oil
1 level teaspoon paprika

Preparation time: 20 minutes

Hardboil the eggs for
10 minutes and cool them
under running cold water. Peel
and cut them in half lengthwise. Slice the peeled onion
and then chop peperoni and
onion together very finely. •
Lift the egg yolks from the
whites. Mash the yolks with a
fork. Mix them together with
the onion and peperoni
mixture, the mustard, pepper,
cayenne, salt, the juice of the
garlic clove, the wine vinegar
and oil. Pipe this mixture into
eight egg halves. Place the
other eight egg halves over the
filling and sprinkle them with
paprika.

Illustration on pages 70/71

Shrimp Salad

△○○*

Ingredients for 8 people:

1 egg
450g (1 lb) shrimps, cooked in
   their shells, or 8 ozs frozen
   shrimps
1 onion
1 bunch parsley
Juice of one lemon
A pinch of salt
2 tablespoons oil
1 tomato

Preparation time: 25 minutes

Hardboil egg for 10 minutes,
cool under running cold water,
peel and cut into eight wedges.
Put the peeled shrimps into a
bowl. Chop the peeled onion
very finely. Wash and dry the
parsley; keep one sprig back
and chop the rest. Mix together onion, parsley, lemon
juice, salt and oil and pour
this mixture over the
shrimps, stirring very carefully. Wash and dry the tomato and cut into 8 wedges.
Arrange the egg and tomato
wedges on top of the salad
and garnish with the parsley
sprig.
Goes well with either white
bread or Westphalien black
bread and butter.

Illustration on pages 70/71

Buffet Parties

New Year's Eve Buffet

For 8 people

Lobster Bouchées
△○○○

Ingredients for 8 people:

100g (3½ ozs) frozen
    shrimps
4 eggs
400g (14 ozs) canned lobster
    meat cut up small
1 cup preserved pumpkin
2 pickled cucumbers
½ onion
1/8 litre (¼ pint) cream
A good pinch each of cayenne,
    curry powder and salt
1 liqueur glass brandy
8 bouchées (bought ready-
    made)
1 jar caviar substitute
2 tomatoes
Fresh parsley

Preparation time: 30 minutes

Pre-heat the oven to 180° C
(360° F or gas mark 5).
Defrost the shrimps and reserve the 16 best tails. Cut up
the rest. Hardboil the eggs for
10 minutes, rinse under cold
water, peel and chop them. •
Wash the lobster meat quickly,
break it up with a fork and
drain. Drain also the pumpkin
and cut into small cubes. Dice

the cucumber. Chop the
peeled onion finely. Mix the
cut-up shrimps, chopped
eggs, lobster meat, pumpkin,
cucumber and chopped onion
with the cream, cayenne
pepper, curry powder, salt
and brandy. • Warm the
bouchées for 10-12 minutes
in the oven. Heat the lobster
mixture for 10 minutes over
hot water and fill into the
bouchées. Garnish each
bouchée with two shrimp tails
and a little caviar. • Wash and
dry tomatoes, and cut into
eight wedges. Wash and drain
the parsley and separate into
small sprigs. Arrange tomato
wedges and parsley sprigs
between the bouchées.

Illustration on facing page

Chicken Salad
△○○

Ingredients for 8 people:

½ chicken, already cooked
350g (12 ozs) cooked veal
2 cups frozen peas
2 tablespoons water
1 teaspoon salt
1 cup diced carrots (tinned)
1 cup cooked cauliflower
    sprigs
½ jar sweetcorn
6 tablespoons mayonnaise
3 tablespoons yoghurt
2 tablespoons cream
A good pinch each of salt,
    pepper and garlic powder
A few drops of soya sauce

Preparation time: 25 minutes

Remove the skin and bones
from chicken. Cut both
chicken and veal into large
cubes. Cook the frozen peas in
salt water for six minutes and
drain them. • Mix together
chicken, veal, cooked peas,
carrots, cauliflower sprigs and
sweetcorn. • Stir the
mayonnaise with the yoghurt,
cream, salt, pepper, garlic
powder and soya sauce and
pour over the salad.

Illustration on page 75

New Year's Eve Buffet, recipes pages 74–76 ▷

Buffet Parties

Champagne Jelly

△△○○○

Ingredients for 8 people:

450g (1 lb) frozen straw-
    berries or raspberries
16 white gelatine leaves
1 bottle white wine
100g (3½ ozs) sugar
½ lemon
1 half-bottle champagne or
    other sparkling wine
¼ litre (½ pint) cream

Preparation time: 15 minutes
Cooling time: 2 hours

Defrost the strawberries (or
raspberries) at room
temperature for several hours.
Soak the gelatine in cold
water. • Heat the white wine
and the sugar, stirring until the
sugar is dissolved. Grate the
rind of the half lemon into the
liquid. Squeeze out the
gelatine, add it to the wine
and stir until dissolved. •
Cool the wine, stirring
occasionally. Just
before setting, stir in the
champagne. Divide the fruit
into eight dessert glasses and
pour the cold jelly over it.
Place jelly in the refrigerator
to set. • Whisk the cream
and pipe a large rosette onto
each dessert glass.

Illustration on page 75

The recipes for Apple Punch,
English beerdrink, the
Champagne Cocktail and the
Champagne-Orange Cocktail
are in the beverages section on
pages 117/120/123.

Buffet with Salads

For 8 people

Fruit Salad with Cheeseboard

△○*

Ingredients for 8 people:

Fruit from jars or cans
200g (7 ozs) gooseberries
250g (9 ozs) morello cherries
400g (14 ozs) apricot halves
4 pineapple slices
4 canned pear halves or 2 fresh
    pears
Juice of one lemon

Preparation time: 15 minutes

Drain the fruit. Peel the fresh
pears, core them and cut them
into eight wedges. Stew them
in 4 tablespoons mixed juice
(from the tins). If tinned pears
are used, cut them into wedges
and mix them with the other
fruit and the lemon juice. •
This fruit salad goes well with
all kinds of cheeses, like
Roquefort, Chester, Gouda,
Edam, Emmental, Brie,
Munster, Cream Cheese,
Camembert, Goat Cheese in
vine leaves, Cottage cheese and
other mild cheeses.

Buffet Parties

Serve with different kinds of bread and butter.

Illustration on page 78

Sweetcorn Chowder

△○**

Ingredients for 8 people:

3 large onions
1 bunch fresh parsley
12 fat bacon slices cut thin
1 tablespoon oil
2 level tablespoons flour
2 litres (4 pints) milk
2 tins sweetcorn
1 teaspoon salt
¼ teaspoon pepper

Preparation time: 40 minutes

Chop the peeled onions. Wash, dry and chop the parsley. Cut the bacon into strips and fry them in the oil in a large saucepan until crisp. Remove the bacon from the pan and keep aside. • Add the onions to the fat and fry them to a golden brown. Sprinkle the flour over the onions and let it slightly brown. Then add the milk slowly and bring several times to the boil, stirring continuously. Remove from the heat. • Add the sweetcorn to the soup and season well. Reheat the soup to

warm the sweetcorn. • Serve the soup in soup dishes and garnish with the bacon strips and parsley.

Illustration on page 78

Herring Salad Old Henry

△○*

Ingredients for 8 people:

6 matjes fillets (young, salted herring fillets)
2 pickled cucumbers
2 apples
3 pineapple slices
5 tablespoons mayonnaise
3 tablespoons cream
1 tablespoon wine vinegar
1 good pinch pepper

Preparation time: 30 minutes

Wash the matjes fillets thoroughly under running cold water, dry them carefully and cut them into strips. Dice the cucumbers. Peel and core the apples, cut them into quarters and then into thin slices. Drain the pineapple slices and cut into small pieces. Mix together the matjes strips, diced cucumbers, apple slices and pineapple pieces, fill into a dish and let marinate for a little time. • Stir together the mayonnaise, cream, vine-

gar, pepper and a few drops of the pineapple juice and pour this mixture over the herring salad.

Illustration on page 78

Rice Salad with Ham

△○

Ingredients for 8 people:

250g (9 ozs) rice
2½ teaspoons salt
300g (11 ozs) frozen peas
300g (11 ozs) cooked ham
200g (7 ozs) mushrooms (canned)
6 tablespoons mayonnaise
2 tablespoons yoghurt
2 tablespoons lemon juice
1 good pinch each of salt, sugar and pepper

Preparation time: 35 minutes

Wash the rice thoroughly. Add two teaspoons salt to four pints of water and bring to the boil, put in the rice and boil rapidly for 16 minutes. Pour the rice onto a sieve, refresh with cold water and let drain. • Bring two tablespoons of water with the rest of the salt to the boil, add the frozen peas, cover and cook over a slow heat for 6 minutes. Let them drain on a sieve. • Cut

Buffet Parties

the ham into even cubes. Drain and slice the mushrooms. Mix together carefully the rice, peas, ham cubes and mushroom slices. • Stir together thoroughly the mayonnaise, yoghurt, lemon juice, salt, sugar and pepper. Fold the mayonnaise mixture carefully into the ham mixture, cover and let marinate before serving.

Illustration below

Savoury Tuna Salad

△ ○ *

Ingredients for 8 people:

300g (11 ozs) noodles
1 teaspoon salt
4 onions
3 tablespoons oil
2 pickled cucumbers
6 tomatoes
1 bunch fresh dill (or dried or
*   frozen)*
2 tins tuna fish

2 tablespoons wine vinegar
A good pinch each of salt,
*   paprika and sugar*

Preparation time: 35 minutes

Cook the noodles in four pints of boiling, salted water for 12 minutes. • Pour the noodles onto a sieve, rinse with cold water and allow to drain. Chop the peeled onions. Heat the oil and fry the onions lightly in it for a few minutes. • Dice the

Buffet with Salads, recipes pages 76–79

Buffet Parties

cucumber, wash the tomatoes and dry them, cutting them into eight wedges. Wash the dill, dry and chop. Using a fork, break the tuna fish into even pieces. • Mix the noodles with the onions, oil, cucumber, tomatoes, tuna fish and the dill. • Stir together wine vinegar, salt, paprika and sugar, pour resulting mixture over the salad and let marinate.

Illustration on facing page

Sausage Salad Teen
△○○＊＊

Ingredients for 8 people:

1 large onion
3 tablespoons oil
A pinch each of sugar, salt and
    pepper
1 tablespoon wine vinegar
100g (3½ ozs) sweet pickled
    cucumber
100g (3½ ozs) sour pickled
    cucumber
4 pairs Vienna sausages

Preparation time: 30 minutes

Peel the onion and chop it finely. Heat the oil and fry the onion in it. Add sugar, salt, pepper and vinegar, stir in well and remove pan from heat. Cut the sweet and sour cucumbers into small cubes and add to the onions. • Slice the sausages thinly. Pour the still warm sauce over the sausage slices, cover and marinate in the refrigerator.

An alternative: mix the sausage salad with half a cup of tomato ketchup.

Illustration on facing page

Carnival Buffet

For 8 to 10 people

Piquant Rollmops
△○＊＊

Ingredients for 8 people:

4 Bismarck herrings
1 pepper
2 onions
$^1/_8$ litre (¼ pint) vinegar
¼ litre (½ pint) water
1 level teaspoon salt
3 peppercorns
1 bay leaf
1 apple
1 pickled cucumber
¼ litre (½ pint) soured
    cream
2 tablespoons mayonnaise

Preparation time: 15 minutes
Marinating time: 12 hours

Cut the Bismarck herrings into fillets. Halve the pepper, remove the pips and cut lengthwise into strips. Cut the peeled onion into rings. Place pepper strips and onion rings into the vinegar, pour the water over it, add the salt, pepper corns and bay leaf and bring to the boil. Remove from heat and allow to get cold. • Peel the apple and cut into wedges. Cut the cucumber into strips. Place onto each herring fillet a few

Buffet Parties

pepper strips, apple wedges, onion rings and cucumber strips, roll up and secure with a cocktail stick. Place the rollmops into a high glass. • Whisk the cream together with the mayonnaise, pour over the rollmops and leave them to marinate overnight. Serve the rollmops with the soured cream.

Illustration on pages 82/83

Buckling Salad Harlequin

△○*

Ingredients for 8 people:

5 bucklings (smoked herrings)
4 tomatoes
2 apples
3 pickled cucumbers
¼ litre (½ pint) soured
 cream
1 teaspoon lemon juice
A pinch each of salt, sugar,
 pepper and curry powder
3 cups cooked rice

Preparation time: 35 minutes

Halve the bucklings length-wise, remove bones and skin and cut into small pieces. Wash and dry the tomatoes, then dice them. Quarter the peeled and cored apples and dice them. Dice the

cucumbers. • Season the soured cream well with the lemon juice, salt, sugar, pepper and curry powder. • Mix the rice with the prepared ingredients, fold in the soured cream, cover and leave at room temperature for about 20 minutes.
If you can't get bucklings use kippers instead.

Illustration on pages 82/83

Liver Pâté

△△○○○*

Ingredients for 8 people:

3 bread rolls
750g (1½ lb) calves' liver
1 bunch parsley
5 shallots
125g (4 ozs) fat bacon
75g (3 ozs) butter
3 egg yolks
A good pinch each of salt,
 pepper, dried marjoram
 and dried thyme
250g (9 ozs) fat bacon rashers
 cut very thin

Preparation time: 40 minutes
Baking time: 1½ hours

Cut the crust off the rolls and soak the bread in water. Skin the liver, remove the sinews and cut into dice. Wash and dry the parsley, removing the

hard stalks only. Peel the shallots and quarter them. Cut up the fat bacon. • Squeeze out the bread and mince together with the liver, parsley, shallots and bacon. Put the ingredients twice through a fine mincer. Cream the butter until fluffy, add the egg yolks, salt, pepper, marjoram and thyme. Combine the two mixtures. Line a round, fireproof soufflé dish with the bacon rashers, fill in the liver mixture and cover with bacon rashers. Bake the pâté in the pre-heated oven at 180° C (360° F, gas mark 5) for 90 minutes.
If you can't get calves' liver use chicken liver.

Goes well with toasted white bread and butter.

Illustration on pages 82/83

80

Buffet Parties

Toast Elvira

△○

Ingredients for 8 people:

8 slices toasting bread
8 teaspoons butter
2 tablespoons oil
8 eggs
8 gammon slices
8 slices Gouda cheese

Preparation time: 30 minutes

Heat the oven to 250° C
(480° F, gas mark 8 or 9) or
light the grill to the highest
temperature. Toast the bread
lightly and butter. • Heat oil
in a pan and fry the eggs.
Remove them. Cook the
gammon in the fat and place
onto the toast. Place onto each
piece a fried egg and cover with
a slice of cheese. • Bake the
bread in the oven or under the
grill until the cheese starts to
melt.

Illustration on pages 82/83

Fisherman's Toast

△○○

Ingredients for 8 people:

8 good lettuce leaves
4 eggs
8 slices toasting bread
8 teaspoons butter or
    margarine
150g (5-6 ozs) salmon pieces
10 ozs canned shrimps or
    prawns
8 tablespoons soured cream
A good pinch each of salt,
    pepper, paprika
1 tomato
Parsley

Preparation time: 30 minutes

Wash the lettuce leaves
thoroughly and dry them.
Hardboil the eggs for
10 minutes, then plunge them
into cold water; peel them and
cut them into slices. • Fry
the bread on one side only —
in the butter or margarine —
to a light brown. Place the
salad leaves on the unfried
side of the bread and cover
with egg slices. Top
these with salmon pieces.
• Separate the shrimps.
Season the soured cream with
salt, pepper and paprika, mix
with the shrimps and divide
this onto the bread. Wash the
tomato and cut into 8 wedges.
Wash the parsley and divide
into eight small sprigs. Garnish
each piece of toast with a
tomato wedge and a little
parsley.

Illustration on pages 82/83

Pickled Pork with Horseradish

△○○**

Ingredients for 10 people:

1kg (2¼ lb) pickled spare
    ribs of pork
1 apple
¼ litre (½ pint) cream
A pinch of salt
A pinch of sugar
A few drops lemon juice
1 tablespoon grated horse-
    radish
Sprig parsley

Preparation time: 20 minutes
Cooking time: 50 minutes

Roast the pork in a pre-heated
oven at 220° C (425° F, gas
mark 7), without additional
fat, for 50 minutes. • Remove from heat, let it cool;
then remove the bones and
slice the meat carefully. •
Peel the apple and grate it.
Whip the cream and mix in
lightly the grated apple, salt,
sugar, lemon juice and horseradish. Serve separately from
the pork. Garnish the dish
with the parsley, washed.

Carnival Buffet (see pages 82−83); recipes pages 79−84 ▷

Buffet Parties

Goes well with farmhouse or black bread.

A tip: any leftover meat can be frozen, but not the horseradish.

Illustration on pages 82/83

Almond Fritters

△△○○

Ingredients for 8 people:

500g (18 ozs) flour
2 level teaspoons baking powder
3 eggs
1 tablespoon rum
100g (3½ ozs) ground almonds
About 2 pints oil for frying
1 cup cinnamon sugar

Preparation time: 1¼ hours

Sift the flour and baking powder onto a pastry board. Make a well in the centre; put eggs, rum, almonds and butter in flakes into the well. Mix first the ingredients in the centre and then mix in the flour quickly. Wrap the paste in foil or oiled greaseproof paper and rest in the refrigerator for at least 30 minutes. Roll out the paste 1 cm (³/₈″) thick and cut out small diamonds or

other shapes. Fry the fritters in the hot oil until crisp and golden brown. Remove the fritters, drain them on kitchen paper and roll them in cinnamon sugar.

Illustration on pages 82/83

Garden Party Buffet

For 8 to 10 people

Vegetable Salad with Chicory

△○

Ingredients for 8 people:

400g (14 ozs) canned green beans
400g (14 ozs) canned small garden peas
400g (14 ozs) canned asparagus tips
250g (9 ozs) canned baby carrots
250g (9 ozs) canned mushrooms
3 chicory heads
1 onion
¹/₈ litre (¼ pint) soured cream
2 tablespoons oil
Juice of 1 lemon
1 teaspoon salt
¼ teaspoon pepper
¼ teaspoon sugar

Preparation time: 20 minutes

Drain the beans, peas, asparagus, carrots and mushrooms. Keep 1 tablespoon liquid from each tin. Remove any bad outside leaves from the chicory and remove a wedge from the hard root end.

Buffet Parties

Cut the chicory into strips, wash and drain. Chop the peeled onion. • Stir together the vegetable juice, soured cream, oil, lemon juice, salt and sugar and pour over the salad. Cover the salad and let marinate.

Illustration below

Tomato Roll
△△△○ **

Ingredients for 10 people:

For the pastry:
250g (9 ozs) flour
1 egg
2-3 tablespoons water
*1 level teaspoon baking
  powder*
A good pinch of salt
*100g (3½ ozs) butter, in
  flakes*

For the filling:
2 onions
300g (11 ozs) ham
4 tablespoons butter
8 tomatoes
½ teaspoon salt
¼ teaspoon pepper
Pinch dried thyme
*5-6 tablespoons white bread-
  crumbs*
2 eggs
*1 tablespoon chopped fresh
  herbs*
For the glaze:
1 egg yolk

Buffet Parties

Preparation time: 50 minutes
Cooking time: 45 minutes

Sift the flour and baking powder onto a pastry board and make a well in the centre. Put into it the egg, water, salt and butter flakes, and work all these ingredients quickly into a pastry. Form into a roll, wrap into foil or oiled greaseproof paper and leave to rest for two hours in refrigerator. Pre-heat the oven to 220° C (425° F, gas mark 7). • Peel the onion and chop it finely. Cut the ham into small cubes. Melt the butter in a sufficiently large saucepan and fry the onion and the ham lightly in it. Wash and dry the tomatoes, and cut into eight wedges. Mix with the salt, pepper, thyme, ham and onion. Cook over a low heat until the liquid has evaporated. • Knead together the bread-crumbs, eggs, chopped herbs and the tomato mixture. • Roll out the pastry into an oblong, spread the filling on to it, roll up, press the ends together and brush over with egg yolk. Bake the roll for 45 minutes and cut into slices.

Illustration on page 85

Baked Meat Pasties

△△△○ *

Ingredients for 8 people:

For the pastry:
250g (9 ozs) flour
250g (9 ozs) curd cheese
250g (9 ozs) butter
For the filling:
1 clove garlic
2 onions
2 tablespoons dripping
300g (11 ozs) minced meat
1 level tablespoon paprika
A pinch each of salt, pepper and cayenne pepper
2 tablespoons tomato purée
For the glaze:
1 egg yolk

Preparation time: 50 minutes
Cooking time: 30 minutes

Sift the flour onto a pastry board, add the curd cheese and the butter cut into small pieces and work these ingredients quickly into a pastry. Cover the pastry with foil or oiled greaseproof paper and leave to rest for two hours in the refrigerator.
Peel the garlic clove, chop it up and then crush it. Peel and chop the onion finely. Heat the fat in a frying-pan, add the onion and garlic and fry for a short time. Stir in the minced meat, paprika, salt, pepper, cayenne pepper and tomato purée and keep over the heat, stirring continuously. •

Preheat the oven to 220°C (425° F, gas mark 7). Roll out the pastry thinly and cut out even-sized squares. Place onto each square 1 tablespoon of the meat filling, press the sides well together and brush the pasties over with egg yolk. Bake for 30 minutes until golden brown.

Illustration on page 85

Cheese and Minced Meat Skewers

△△○○

Ingredients for 8 people:

1 bread roll
500g (18 ozs) minced beef
2 tablespoons tomato purée
2 eggs
½ teaspoon salt
2 tablespoons finely-chopped parsley
A good pinch of pepper
A good pinch of paprika
2 tablespoons dripping
300g (11 ozs) Gouda, Edam or Emmental cheese in one piece

Preparation time: 30 minutes

Soak the bread roll in water and then squeeze out well. Mix together the bread, minced beef, tomato purée, eggs, salt, parsley, pepper and paprika.

Buffet Parties

Form small balls from this mixture. Fry these in the fat at medium heat for 6 - 8 minutes. ● Cut the cheese into even cubes. Place the meat balls and cheese cubes alternating on small skewers and serve with a ready-made *Schaschlik* sauce.

Illustration on page 85

Curd Cheese Dessert

△○

Ingredients for 8 people:

500g (18 ozs) fresh or canned bilberries
³⁄₈ litre (¾ pint) cream

2 packets vanilla sugar
10 level tablespoons sugar if you use fresh fruit, 2 tablespoons if you use canned
500g (18 ozs) curd cheese

Preparation time: 25 minutes

Pick over the fresh bilberries, wash and drain them (in the case of canned bilberries, just drain). Whip the cream and stir in the vanilla sugar. Mix two tablespoons sugar with the curd cheese and fold the cream into it. Mix the rest of the sugar with the fresh bilberries. ● Layer the cheese mixture with the bilberries in glasses, finishing with a dome of bilberries.

Illustration on page 85

Italian Buffet

For 4 to 6 people

Dainty Green Soup

△○○**

Ingredients for 6 people:

2 lettuce
400g (14 ozs) spinach
100g (3½ ozs) green celery leaves
2 leeks
200g (7 ozs) sorrel
1 bunch each of parsley, chives, chervil and dill
1 onion
2 tablespoons butter
1 tablespoon oil
1½ litres (3 pints) instant beef stock
1 teaspoon salt
A pinch of pepper
A pinch of grated nutmeg
For the egg garnish:
½ tablespoon oil
2 eggs
2 tablespoons stock
¼ teaspoon salt
1 pinch grated nutmeg
1 pinch pepper

Preparation time: 1 hour

Pick over the lettuce, wash and break into small pieces. Pick over and wash the spinach. Wash the celery leaves and drain. Halve the leeks lengthwise, wash thoroughly

and slice. Wash and drain the sorrel and chop a little. Chop the peeled onion finely. Heat the butter with the oil in a sufficiently large saucepan. Stir in the onion and fry gently. Add the vegetables, cover and cook until tender. Remove the vegetables and pass them through a sieve into the saucepan. Pour the stock over the vegetables, season with the salt, pepper and grated nutmeg, cover and heat over medium heat. • For the egg-garnish heat water in a large shallow saucepan for the *bain marie*. Oil a small flat mould (or a cup). Whisk the eggs with the stock, the salt, nutmeg and pepper and pour into the oiled mould. Place the covered egg mixture into the *bain marie* and simmer for 15-20 minutes until set. The water must not be allowed to boil. • Turn out the set egg mixture and cut into dice or diamonds. Serve the soup in cups, with egg shapes on top.

Illustration on pages 88/89

Pizza Napolitana

△△○○ *

Ingredients for 6 people:

For the dough:
300g (11 ozs) flour
20g (¾ ozs) yeast
½ cup lukewarm milk
50g (2 ozs) butter
A good pinch of salt
1 egg (optional)
1 level teaspoon paprika
For the filling:
500g (18 ozs) firm tomatoes
200g (7 ozs) cooked ham
20 green stuffed olives
A pinch each of salt, pepper,
    dried oregano and dried
    thyme
1 garlic clove
100g (3½ ozs) thinly-sliced
    salami
3 slices Edam cheese

Preparation time: 1½ hours

Sift the flour into a bowl, and make a well in the centre. Break the yeast into the well and mix with the lukewarm milk and a little flour. Sprinkle some more flour over the yeast and allow to stand for 20 minutes in a warm place. • Melt the butter and, together with the salt, paprika and egg (if used), add to the flour. Make it quickly into a dough and beat it until bubbles appear. • Leave the dough again for about 20 minutes, then roll it out into

a round, put it onto a baking sheet and prick it several times with a fork. Pre-heat the oven to 220° C (425° F, gas mark 7). • Wash and dry tomatoes and cut them into rounds. Cut the ham into strips and the olives into thin rounds. Divide the tomato slices, the ham strips and the olive slices over the dough and sprinkle with salt, pepper, oregano and thyme. Peel the garlic clove, chop and crush it. Divide over the pizza. Bake the pizza in the pre-heated oven for 25-30 minutes. • Ten minutes before finishing time place the salami slices, formed into cornets, between the tomatoes and cover with the cheese slices cut into strips. Bake the pizza until the cheese starts to melt and brown. Serve the pizza warm.

Illustration on pages 88/89

Buffet Parties

Stuffed Dessert Oranges

△○

Ingredients for 4 people:

4 oranges
300g (11 ozs) raspberries
100g (3½ ozs) redcurrants
2 level tablespoons sugar
1 liqueur glass orange liqueur
1 liqueur glass kirsch
¹/₈ litre (¼ pint) cream

Preparation time: 30 minutes

Wash the oranges with hot water, dry them and cut off the top third to serve as cover. Remove the flesh from the orange. Free it from pips and pith and cut into dice. Pick over the berries and wash them. Mix together the berries and orange flesh (keep back some redcurrants). • Mix the orange liqueur, kirsch and sugar with the fruit and fill into the orange hollows. Let the filled oranges macerate for about an hour in the refrigerator. • Whip the cream and pipe onto the oranges. Garnish by sprinkling the retained redcurrants over the cream.

Illustration on pages 88/89

Melon with Ham

△○○

Ingredients for 4 people:

½ Honeydew melon or
¼ water melon
200g (7 ozs) cooked (or uncooked) ham, cut into very thin slices

Preparation time: 10 minutes

Cut the melon into 4 (or 8) thin wedges and remove the pips. Place the melon wedges onto a flat dish. Place the ham — rolled up — between the melon wedges.

Illustration on pages 88/89

Jolly Kitchen Buffet

For 8 to 10 people

Ham Quiche

△△○*

Ingredients for 10 people:

For the pastry:
200g (7 ozs) flour
2 level teaspoons baking powder
1 level teaspoon salt
4 tablespoons water
125g (4½ ozs) butter
For the filling:
375g (14 ozs) fat bacon
2 large onions
¼ litre (½ pint) soured cream
2 eggs
2 heaped teaspoons flour
¼ teaspoon pepper
¼ teaspoon paprika
A good pinch of grated nutmeg
4 tablespoons finely-chopped parsley or chives
100g (3½ ozs) grated Emmental cheese

Preparation time: 30 minutes
Cooking time: 45 minutes

Sift the flour onto a board. Sprinkle the baking powder and the salt over the flour. Make a well in the centre and

Buffet Parties

pour the water into it. Cut the butter into flakes and distribute over the flour, mixing the whole quickly to a smooth paste. Cover the dough with foil or oiled greaseproof paper and leave for two hours in the refrigerator. Chop the fat bacon very finely. Chop the peeled onions finely and mix with the bacon. ● Whisk the soured cream with the eggs, flour, pepper, paprika, grated nutmeg and finely-chopped herbs. Pre-heat the

oven to 200° C (400° F, gas mark 6). ● Roll out the pastry on the baking sheet and sprinkle with the grated Emmental cheese. Spread the ham-onion mixture over the pastry and pour the soured cream mixture over it. Bake the cake to a golden brown (35-45 minutes).

Best served hot.

Illustration below

Piquant Pirate Soup

△○○ * *

Ingredients for 8 people:

4 onions
3 tablespoons oil
3 tablespoons tomato purée
1 level tablespoon paprika
400g (14 ozs) diced beef
1 teaspoon salt
A pinch of ground caraway seed
A pinch of dried marjoram

Buffet Parties

2 level tablespoons flour
2 tablespoons wine vinegar
1½ litres (3 pints) hot water
*⅛ litre (¼ pint) soured
  cream*
2 tablespoons frozen parsley
2 tablespoons tomato ketchup

Preparation time: 15 minutes
Cooking time: 1 hour,
20 minutes

Chop the peeled onions finely.
Heat the oil in a rather large
saucepan and fry the onions in
it for a few minutes, stirring
occasionally. • Add the
tomato purée and the paprika
and heat quickly, stirring all
the time. Add the meat cubes,
fry them on all sides. Add salt,
ground caraway seed and dried
marjoram and fry these briefly.
Dust the meat with the flour
and stir until brown. Add the
wine vinegar and slowly pour
in the hot water. Cover the
soup and cook for 60 minutes
over medium heat. • Stir the
tomato ketchup and the
parsley into the soured cream.
Remove soup from heat and
mix in the soured cream.

Our advice: if the soup is to be
frozen, add the soured cream
mixture only when re-heating.

Illustration opposite

Macaroni Salad Pépé

△○

Ingredients for 8 people:

300g (11 ozs) macaroni
1 level teaspoon salt
3 eggs
6 tomatoes
*⅛ litre (¼ pint) soured
  cream*
1 teaspoon lemon juice
*2 tablespoons finely-chopped
  chives*
½ teaspoon salt
*A pinch each of pepper,
  paprika and sugar*
2 pickled cucumbers
*200g (7 ozs) cooked ham in
  one piece*
*150g (5½ ozs) Edam cheese
  in one piece*

Preparation time: 40 minutes

Break macaroni into small
pieces and cook in 2 litres
(4 pints) boiling, salted water
for 16 minutes. Pour the
macaroni into a sieve, rinse in
cold water and drain. • Hardboil the eggs, put into cold
water, peel and mash them.
Make an incision at bottom
end of tomatoes, pour boiling
water over them and leave for
a few minutes in the water,
then peel off the loosened skin.
Cut the tomato into strips.
• Mix the soured cream with
the lemon juice, chives, salt,
pepper, paprika and sugar. Cut

the pickled cucumbers, ham
and Edam cheese into
even-sized cubes. • Combine
the macaroni with the tomato
strips, the cucumbers, ham and
cheese. Mix the soured cream
with the mashed egg and fold
into the salad. Cover the salad
and let it marinate for some
time.

Illustration opposite

Chipolata Rolls

△△○

Ingredients for 8 people:

1 packet frozen puff pastry
2 egg yolks
8 pork chipolatas

Preparation time: 30 minutes
Baking time: 25 minutes

Defrost the puff pastry for
several hours. Pre-heat oven to
250° C (480° F, gas mark 7).
Roll out puff pastry on a
floured pastry board and cut
out 8 pieces (sized about
10 cm × 12 cm (4″ × 5″).
Brush the edges over with egg
yolk. Place a pork sausage into
the centre of each piece and
envelop it completely in the
pastry. Pinch the ends
together. • Roll out the left-
over pastry again, cut into neat
strips, brush them over with

Buffet Parties

egg yolk and stick them on top of the sausage envelopes. Place the rolls on a baking sheet and bake for 20-25 minutes till crisp and golden brown.

Illustration on page 92

A tip: the baking can be done several hours before the party and the rolls can merely be reheated when they are required.

Television Buffet

For 6 to 8 people

Tunny and Rice Salad
△ ○ ✳

Ingredients for 8 people:

250g (9 ozs) rice
⅛ litre (¼ pint) soured cream
½ cup mayonnaise
A good pinch each of salt, pepper and curry powder
1 pickled cucumber
3 tomatoes
1 apple, not too sweet
2 cans tunny fish

Preparation time: 25 minutes

Wash the rice several times, pour it into boiling, salted water and boil for 15 minutes at a high temperature. Pour the rice onto a sieve, rinse under cold water and allow to drain. • Mix the soured cream with the mayonnaise, salt, pepper and curry powder. • Cut the pickled cucumber into dice, and also the tomatoes. Peel the apple, quarter and core it, then cut the quarters into dice. Using a fork, break the tuna fish into even pieces and mix these with the rice, the diced

cucumber, the tomato, apple and mayonnaise. Cover the salad and leave to marinate for at least 30 minutes at room temperature.

Illustration on pages 96/97

Viennese Cheese Soup
△ ○

Ingredients for 8 people:

5 tablespoons butter
4 level tablespoons flour
1½ litres (3 pints) instant stock
100g (3½ ozs) macaroni
200g (7 ozs) grated cheese
⅛ litre (¼ pint) cream
A pinch of salt
A pinch of pepper
4 tablespoons deep-frozen parsley

Preparation time: 25 minutes

Heat the butter in a large saucepan, add the flour and stir until it is light brown. Pour in stock slowly and bring to boil several times. • Put the macaroni into boiling salted water and boil for 16 minutes at high temperature. Pour onto a sieve, rinse under cold water, drain and cut into small ends. • Stir these and the cheese into the soup. Finish soup off

Buffet Parties

with the cream, and season with salt and pepper. Sprinkle parsley over it.

Illustration on pages 96/97

Special Potato Salad

△ ○

Ingredients for 8 people:

750g (1½ lbs) potatoes
½ cup white wine
½ cup instant stock
A good pinch each of salt and
    pepper
1 tablespoon wine vinegar
4 tomatoes
200 g (7 ozs) canned mush-
    rooms
250g (7 ozs) cooked ham
¹/₈ litre (¼ pint) soured
    cream
2 tablespoons deep-frozen
    parsley
A good pinch of sugar

Preparation time: 40 minutes
Marinating time: 1 hour

Scrub the potatoes, boil them in their skins for 25 minutes, peel and slice them. ● Mix the white wine with the stock, salt, pepper and vinegar, boil up once and pour hot over the still warm potatoes. ● Wash and dice tomatoes. Drain mushrooms and slice

them thinly. Dice ham.
● Mix soured cream with parsley and sugar and fold into the potatoes, together with the tomatoes, mushrooms and ham. Cover the salad and allow to marinate for one hour at room temperature.

Illustration on pages 96/97

Tomato baskets

△△○

Ingredients for 8 people:

4 eggs
250g (9 ozs) Emmental
    cheese in one piece
4 tablespoons mayonnaise
4 tablespoons soured cream
A good pinch each of salt and
    pepper
½ teaspoon mustard
5 tablespoons finely-chopped
    fresh herbs
8 tomatoes

Preparation time: 20 minutes

Hardboil eggs for 10 minutes, rinse under cold water, peel and dice them. Cut the cheese into very fine strips or grate it coarsely. ● Stir together mayonnaise, soured cream, salt, pepper, mustard and finely-chopped herbs. Mix mayonnaise with the diced eggs and cheese strips. ●

Wash tomatoes, cut off top third of each to serve as lids. Hollow out the tomatoes and season them with salt and pepper. Cut a strip from each lid and shape into a handle for the baskets. Fill the cheese salad into the tomatoes and put a handle on to each basket.

Illustration on pages 96/97

Toast Appetizer

△○

Ingredients for 8 people:

8 slices toasting bread
100g (3½ ozs) butter
1-2 tablespoons grated horse-
    radish (from a jar)
½ teaspoon salt
½ teaspoon lemon juice
¼ teaspoon sugar
2 apples
8 slices cooked ham

Preparation time: 20 minutes

Pre-heat oven to 220° C (425° F, gas mark 7), or put the grill on full. Fry the bread lightly on one side only. ● Cream the butter with the horseradish, salt, lemon juice and sugar until fluffy. Spread the horseradish butter on the unfried side of the bread. ● Peel and core the apples, then cut them into thin slices.

Television Buffet (see pages 96—97); recipes on pages 94—98 ▷

Buffet Parties

Cover the horseradish butter with the apple slices and place a slice of ham on top. Grill the bread (or bake it in the hot oven) until the ham starts to browns.

Illustration on pages 96/97

Nut Boats
△△○○*

Ingredients for 8 people:

For the pastry:
140g (5 ozs) flour
1 egg yolk
70g (2½ ozs) sugar
Grated rind of ½ lemon
70g (2½ ozs) ground almonds
140g (5 ozs) butter, in flakes
A little butter and about 2 tablespoons breadcrumbs for the small moulds
For the filling:
200g (7 ozs) ground hazelnuts
100g (3½ ozs) sugar
1 level teaspoon cinnamon
A pinch ground cloves
¹/₈ litre (¼ litre) milk
A few whole hazelnuts for garnish
1 cup chocolate couverture

Preparation time: 40 minutes
Baking time: 50 minutes

Sift the flour onto a pastry board, make a well and put into it the egg yolk, sugar, grated lemon rind, ground almonds and flaked butter. Work quickly to a smooth pastry. Grease 8 boat-shaped moulds with butter and dust with the breadcrumbs. Line the moulds with ²/₃ of the pastry. Pre-heat the oven to 180° C (360° F, gas mark 4½). •
For the filling mix the ground hazelnuts with the sugar, cinnamon, cloves and hot milk, allow to cool and fill into the lined moulds. Cover the moulds with lids cut from the left-over pastry, and press these on firmly. • Bake the boats for 40-50 minutes, then cover them with chocolate couverture and garnish with hazelnuts.

Illustration on pages 96/97

Lovers' Knots
△△○**

Ingredients for 8 people:

210g (8 ozs) flour
1 egg yolk
70g (2½ ozs) sugar
2 packets vanilla sugar
140g (5 ozs) butter, in flakes
White of 1 egg
About ½ cup nib sugar

Preparation time: 20 minutes
Baking time: 20 minutes

Sift the flour onto a pastry board, put the egg yolk into the centre, sprinkle over the sugar, vanilla sugar and flaked butter. Knead together to a paste. Cover with foil and allow to rest for two hours. • Pre-heat the oven to 200° C (400° F, gas mark 6). Form a roll out of the paste, cut into slices and from each slice form a pretzel (also called 'lovers' knot'). Brush over with egg white, sprinkle with nib sugar and bake for about 20 minutes until light brown.

Illustration on pages 96/97

Buffet Parties

Special Summer Buffet

For 12 to 16 people

Salmon Cutlets

△△○○○

Ingredients for 16 people:

16 salmon cutlets, each
weighing 200 g (7 ozs)
16 pieces foil
150g (5½ ozs) butter
2 lemons
8 bay leaves
A pinch each of salt and white
pepper per cutlet
8 tablespoons mayonnaise
6 tablespoons cream
2 tablespoons grated horse-
radish (from a jar)
16 slices fresh cucumber
16 lemon wedges

Preparation time: 1 hour,
including 25 minutes cooking
time

Pre-heat the oven to 175° C
(350° F, gas mark 4). Wash
salmon cutlets quickly under
cold water and dry them.
Grease the foil well with
butter. Lay onto each piece of
foil 1 thin lemon slice
(unpeeled) on ½ bay leaf.
Season the salmon cutlets with
salt and pepper and wrap them
in the foil.
Bake the cutlets in the oven for

25 minutes and then let them
cool in the foil. ● Stir the
mayonnaise together with the
cream and the horseradish.
Place the now-cooled cutlets
onto a flat dish. Roll the
cucumber slices into cornets,
filling each cornet with a tablespoon of the horseradish
mayonnaise. Add to each
salmon cutlet a lemon wedge.
Put a lightly-dressed lettuce
into the centre of the dish.

Illustration on page 101

Cold Gammon

△△○○○ ＊＊

Ingredients for 12 people:

2kgs (4½ lbs) smoked
gammon in one piece
2 onions
2 carrots
1 bay leaf
4 peppercorns
20 cloves
About 4 tablespoons brown
sugar
½ litre (1 pint) cider

Preparation (including
cooking): 4½ hours

Soak gammon in cold water
for an hour. Remove and dry
well, then place it into a large
saucepan with the skin side at
the bottom. Cover the
gammon with fresh cold

water and bring to the boil,
skimming frequently. ● Peel
onions and cut into eighths.
Wash and peel the carrots and
cut into pieces.
Add the onions and carrots,
the bay leaf, peppercorns and
three cloves to the gammon,
and let simmer for one hour.
● Then lift gammon out of
liquid, dry well and place in a
roasting tin, together with
1 pint cider. Cover with foil.
Now bake gammon in a pre-
heated oven at 180° C (360°
F, gas mark 4½) on the
middle shelf for 1 hour. ●
Next, after removing foil,
take off rind and score
fat layer crosswise. Stick
the cloves into the fat and
sprinkle brown sugar over it.
Bake the gammon for another
30 minutes at 230° C (450° F,
gas mark 8) – during this time
you may like to sprinkle a little
more sugar over the gammon.
● Leave the gammon for
another 20 minutes in the
oven, but with the door open.
Then take out and leave to get
completely cold.

Illustration opposite

Choose a salad from among
the following to serve with
the gammon and offer your
guests an assortment of bread.

Buffet Parties

Lettuce Hearts with Cucumber

△○

Ingredients for 16 people:

3 fresh cucumbers
8 lettuce hearts
10 tablespoons oil
7 tablespoons wine vinegar
1 level teaspoon salt
½ teaspoon white pepper
½ teaspoon sugar
5 liqueur glasses apricot juice

Preparation time: 20 minutes

Wash the cucumbers and slice very finely on a mandoline. Remove the larger ribs from the lettuce hearts and separate them into single leaves. Wash the lettuce several times and drain well. • Mix the oil with the wine vinegar, salt, pepper, sugar and apricot juice. Gently mix the lettuce leaves with the cucumber slices. Pour dressing over the salad just before serving.

Illustration opposite

Walnut Curd-Cream

△○○

Ingredients for 12 people:

500g (18 ozs) curd cheese
2 cups cream
1 cup finely-chopped onion
2 cups coarsely-ground walnuts
1 level teaspoon salt
½ teaspoon pepper
2 tablespoons tomato ketchup
A few walnut kernels for garnish

Preparation time: 15 minutes

Stir together the curd cheese, cream, onion, ground walnuts, salt, pepper and tomato ketchup. Fill the walnut cream into a dish and garnish with the walnut kernels.

Serve with crackers, salt biscuits and salt pretzels.

Illustration opposite

Pepper Rings

△○

Ingredients for 12 people:

4 green peppers
4 red peppers
2 onions
2 bunches chives
400g (14 ozs) cottage cheese
1/2 cup cream
4 tablespoons mayonnaise
½ teaspoon salt
½ teaspoon white pepper
A pinch of garlic powder

Preparation time: 20 minutes

Cut the peppers into rings, removing the ribs and pips. Wash the rings well and dry them. Chop the peeled onions very finely. Wash the chives, drain and chop finely. • Stir together the cottage cheese, mayonnaise, onions, chives, salt, pepper and garlic powder. Arrange the pepper rings on a flat dish and fill the centres with the cottage cheese mixture.

Illustration opposite

Special Summer Buffets; recipes on pages 99–102 ▷

Buffet Parties

Tongue in Aspic

△△○○○

Ingredients for 16 people:

1½kg (3 lbs) pickled ox
    tongue
8 peppercorns
1 carrot
1 onion
3 cloves
1 bay leaf
2 tomatoes

Preparation: wash the tongue
well and soak in cold water for
12 hours.
Cooking time: 3 hours
Final touches: 40 minutes

Place tongue in a large
saucepan, cover with cold
water, put a lid on and bring to
the boil. Skim. Peel carrot, cut
it into pieces and add, with the
peppercorns, to the tongue.
Stick the cloves into the peeled
onions and, together with the
bay leaf, also add to the
tongue. Bring again to the boil
and simmer for three hours.
• Then remove from the
liquid and place for a minute
or so into cold water. Skin
the tongue while still hot and
remove the small bones at the
end of the tongue. Replace
tongue into the cooking liquor
and let it get cold in it. • Cut
the cold tongue into slices and
arrange them in a large round
soufflé dish lined with foil.
Reduce the cooking liquor and

then let it cool until it starts
setting. If necessary add some
gelatine to help the setting
process. Pour the liquor over
the tongue and allow to set.
• To serve, unmould onto a
flat dish and surround with
narrow tomato wedges.

Illustration on page 101

Tomato and Onion Salad

△○

Ingredients for 16 people:

20 tomatoes
5 onions
2 cups French dressing
6 tablespoons finely-chopped
    parsley
2 tablespoons dried marjoram

Preparation time: 30 minutes

Wash and dry the tomatoes
and cut them into thin slices.
Chop the peeled onions very
finely. Place the tomato
slices into a shallow dish and
sprinkle the onions over
them. Add the parsley and
marjoram to the French
dressing and pour over
the tomatoes and onions.

Illustration on page 101

Buffet Parties

Gay Buffet for People in a Hurry

For 6 to 8 people

Seafood Platter

△○○

Ingredients for 6 people:

2 eggs
6 rollmops
1 can smoked herring fillets
1 tub creamed cod roe
2 cans (or jars) mussels
280g (10 ozs) canned shrimps
3 tablespoons remoulade sauce
  (from jar)
2 slices pineapple (canned)
1 cocktail cherry
2 tablespoons grated horse-
  radish (jar)
4 tablespoons mayonnaise
1 tablespoon canned pineapple
  juice

Preparation time: 20 minutes

Hardboil eggs for 10 minutes, rinse under cold water, peel and chop finely. Arrange the rollmops and herring fillets neatly on a large flat dish. Garnish with the creamed cod roe. Drain mussels, mix with eggs and also arrange on the dish. • Separate the shrimps, wash them quickly and drain.

Mix the remoulade sauce with chopped pineapple and combine with shrimps. Fill this mixture into a small dish, garnish with the cherry and place it in the centre of the platter. • Mix together the grated horseradish, mayonnaise and pineapple juice and pour over the rollmops.

Illustration on pages 104/105

Two Soups in One

△○**

Ingredients for 6 people:

1 can 'Jägersuppe' (Hunter's
  Soup) for 4 people
1 can goulash soup for
  2 people
4 tablespoons tomato ketchup
½ teaspoon paprika
1 dash Tabasco sauce
2 liqueur glasses sherry
3 'Landjäger' sausages (or any
  heavily-smoked sausage of
  pork and beef)
1 cup frozen or canned peas

Preparation time: 15 minutes

Heat the Hunter's soup and the goulash soup together according to instructions on the cans. Stir the tomato ketchup, paprika, Tabasco sauce and sherry into the soup. Cut the smoked sausage into

slices and add with the peas to the soup. Cover the soup and cook for 6 minutes over medium heat.

Our advice: if the soup is to be frozen use canned peas instead of frozen ones.

Illustration on pages 104/105

Garnished Sausage Platter

△○○

Ingredients for 6 people:

200g (7 ozs) mortadella
200g (7 ozs) uncooked ham
200g (7 ozs) salami
300g (11 ozs) canned 'Ochsen-
  maulsalat' (muzzle of beef-
  salad) also a favourite salad
  in France, called 'salade de
  museau de boeuf'
3 tablespoons chilli sauce,
  ready-made
3 tablespoons mustard sauce,
  ready-made
1 jar mixed pickles

Preparation time: 10 minutes

When buying the mortadella, the uncooked ham and the salami, have them cut into very thin slices. Arrange the slices neatly on a platter. Place in the centre a small

Buffet Parties

dish with the 'Ochsenmaul-salat'. Pour the chilli sauce over it. Drip the mustard sauce over the ham and garnish the mortadella and the salami with the mixed pickles.

Illustration on pages 104/105

Cheese Salad Hawaii
△○○

Ingredients for 6 people:

250g (9 ozs) Edam cheese in one piece
250g (9 ozs) uncooked ham
4 slices canned pineapple
2 tablespoons chopped wal-nuts
2 tablespoons wine vinegar
3 tablespoons oil
1 pinch each of salt, pepper and cayenne

Preparation time: 20 minutes

Cut the Edam cheese into fine strips, also the raw ham. Cut up the pineapple slices. Combine the cheese and ham strips, the pineapple and the chopped walnuts. • Mix together vinegar, oil, salt, pepper and cayenne and stir lightly into the salad.

Illustration on pages 104/105

Jester's Buffet

For 10 to 12 people

Marinated Herrings
△○**

Ingredients for 10 people:

10 fresh herrings
About 2 tablespoons salt
3 onions
4 bay leaves
8 peppercorns
5 coriander seeds
2 level teaspoons sugar
½ teaspoon salt
½ litre (1 pint) wine vinegar

Start preparations one week in advance

Actual preparation time: 30 minutes

Open the herrings on the underside, take out the intestines and clean out thoroughly. Cut off heads and tails. Rub the herrings thickly with salt. Layer the herrings closely in a bowl, cover and allow to stand for 24 hours. Then wash the herrings thoroughly and dry them. Cut them once lengthwise and then cut in half across. Roll up the pieces and secure with a cock-tail stick. Cut the peeled onions into rings. Layer the

herring rolls with the onion rings, bay leaves, peppercorns and coriander seeds in a high jar. • Dissolve the sugar and the salt in the wine vinegar and pour over the herrings (they should be covered by the liquid). Close the jar and let marinate in a cool place for one week. • For service remove the herring rolls from the liquid and serve with the onion rings.

Illustration on page 108

Pickled Sausage slices

△ ○ * *

Ingredients for 12 people:

½ litre (1 pint) wine vinegar
¼ litre (½ pint) water
1 dash Worcester sauce
1 dash Tabasco sauce
½ teaspoon sugar
½ teaspoon salt
1kg (2 lbs) 'Extrawurst' (or any other mild pork sausage)
2 large onions
2 pickled cucumbers
3 bay leaves
10 peppercorns

Preparation time: 40 minutes
Marinating time: 2 days

Bring the vinegar and the water to the boil, stir in the Worcester sauce, Tabasco sauce, salt and sugar. Cool the marinade. • Cut the sausage in half lengthwise and then into not too thin slices. Cut the peeled onions into thin rings. Cut the pickled cucumbers into long strips. Layer the sausage slices, onion rings, cucumber strips, bay leaves and peppercorns into a high jar and pour the nearly cold marinate over it. Cover the jar and let it stand for two days in a cool place.

Illustration on page 108

Bread Rolls with Herbs

△ △ ○ * * *

Ingredients for 10 people:

500g (18 ozs) flour
30g (1 oz) yeast
1 teaspoon salt
¼ litre (½ pint) lukewarm milk
1 large onion
1 bunch parsley
1 bunch chives
1 level teaspoon salt
2 level teaspoons ground caraway seed
8 tablespoons oil
1-2 egg yolks

Preparation time: 1 hour
Baking time: 15 minutes

Sift the flour into a bowl, break the yeast into a well in the centre and stir it in with the salt, a little milk and flour. Dust the yeast mixture with some flour, cover and let prove in a warm place for 20 minutes. When the thin flour cover on the yeast shows cracks it has proved enough. • Chop the peeled onion finely. Wash and dry the herbs and chop them very finely. Mix the yeast with the onions, herbs, the rest of the milk, the salt, caraway seed, rest of the flour and the oil. Knead and beat until the dough is smooth and shows bubbles. Form 20 small balls from the dough (about the size of an egg), place them on a greased baking sheet, dust lightly with flour, cover with a tea towel and put in a warm place. Pre-heat the oven to 220° C (425° F, gas mark 7). • After 20 minutes brush over the rolls with egg yolk and cut a cross on top with a sharp knife; according to taste, sprinkle either caraway seed or coarse salt over the rolls and bake for 15 minutes.

Illustration on page 108

Buffet Parties

Tomato and Anchovy Squares

△ △ ○ * *

Ingredients for 10 people:

For the dough:
500g (18 ozs) flour
30g (1 ozs) yeast
¼ litre (barely a ½ pint)
*   lukewarm milk*
8 tablespoons oil
1 level teaspoon salt
4 tablespoons breadcrumbs

For the topping:
750g (1¾ lbs) firm tomatoes
200g (7 ozs) smoked bacon
*   rashers*
1 can mushrooms
½ teaspoon salt
¼ teaspoon pepper
2 jars anchovy fillets

Preparation time: 1 hour
Baking time: 20 minutes

Sift the flour into a bowl and make a well in the centre. Break the yeast into it and mix it with a little milk and flour. Dust some more flour over the yeast mixture, put the bowl in a warm place and let prove for about 20 minutes. ● Then knead the yeast together with the remaining milk, the oil, salt and the rest of the flour. Knead and beat until the dough is smooth and shows bubbles. Roll the dough out on a floured board and put it on a greased baking sheet. Sprinkle the breadcrumbs over the dough, cover with a cloth and

Jester's Buffet, recipes on pages 106−109

let prove for 20 minutes in a warm place. Pre-heat the oven to 220° C (427° F, gas mark 7). • Wash, dry and slice the tomatoes, and cover the dough with them. Cut the bacon rashers lengthwise and place them on top of the tomatoes. Drain the mushrooms, slice them thinly and spread over the tomatoes. Season with salt and pepper. Drain the anchovy fillets, cut them in half lengthwise and also spread over the top. Bake for 20 minutes, cut into rectangles while still hot and serve as warm as possible.

Illustration opposite

Three Cheese Dips

△ ○ ○

Ingredients for 12 people:

1. *150g (5½ ozs) blue cheese (Danish Blue, Gorgonzola etc)*
   1/8 litre (¼ pint) cream
   1 teaspoon Worcester sauce
   1 tablespoon finely-chopped parsley
   A pinch of celery salt
   A pinch of sugar
2. *1 onion*
   150g (5½ ozs) cream cheese
   2 level teaspoons paprika
   1 teaspoon tomato purée

½ teaspoon salt
1 dash Tabasco sauce
1 pinch sugar
1 tablespoon mayonnaise
1 pinch cayenne
3. *2 portions cream cheese*
   4 tablespoons canned milk
   1 tablespoon grated horse-radish
   ¼ teaspoon salt
   1 pinch sugar
   2 level tablespoons ground almonds

Preparation time: 15 minutes

1. Mash the blue cheese with a fork and mix with the cream, Worcester sauce, finely-chopped parsley, celery salt and sugar. •
2. Chop the peeled onion very finely. Mix the cream cheese with the onion, paprika, tomato purée, tabasco sauce, sugar, mayonnaise and cayenne. •
3. Mash the cream cheese with a fork and mix with the canned milk, horseradish, salt, sugar and ground almonds. • With the dips serve small savoury biscuits like crackers, salt pretzels, cheese biscuits or crisp bread.

Illustration opposite

Buffet for a Stag Party

For 4 to 6 people

Swedish Crispbread

△ ○ ○

Ingredients for 2 people:

2 good lettuce leaves
4 slices crisp bread
1 small can goose liver paté
1 tablespoon mayonnaise
2 tablespoons finely-chopped dill
2 round oranges slices

Preparation time: 10 minutes

Wash and dry the lettuce leaves. Spread the goose liver pâté on the crisp bread, put two together and place them onto the lettuce leaves; stir the finely-chopped dill into the mayonnaise and put a dab of it on each sandwich. Cut the round orange slices, with the skin on, into half moons and garnish the sandwiches with them.

Illustration on page 112

Buffet Parties

Open Herring Sandwiches de la Maison

△ ○

Ingredients for 2 people:

2 slices wholemeal bread
2 teaspoons butter
2 Bismarck herrings
A few small capers
1 small onion
1 teaspoon oil
1 good pinch mixed herbs

Preparation time: 10 minutes

Butter the bread slices. Cut the Bismarck herrings into small strips and cover the bread with them. Cut the peeled onion into rings and place on top of the herrings. Sprinkle the capers over the onion rings. Stir the mixed herbs into the oil and drip it over the bread.

Illustration on page 112

Edam Slices

△ ○

Ingredients for 2 people:

2 slices rye bread
2 teaspoons butter
2 teaspoons finely-chopped walnuts
2 slices Edam cheese

2 tomatoes
A pinch each of salt, pepper and paprika

Preparation time: 10 minutes

Spread the butter on the rye bread slices and sprinkle the chopped walnuts over them. Lay the cheese slices on top. Wash, dry and slice the tomatoes and arrange in fan-fashion on the cheese. Season the tomato slices with salt, pepper and paprika.

Illustration on page 112

Gipsy Goulash

△ ○ * *

Ingredients for 4 people:

600g (1¼ lbs) canned beef goulash
1 cup red pepper (from jar or can)
½ cup pickled pearl onions
1 pickled cucumber
10 olives
1 dash wine vinegar
A generous pinch of cayenne

Preparation time: 15 minutes

Heat the beef goulash. Cut the peppers into thin strips, quarter the pearl onions, dice the pickled cucumber and slice

the olives. Add everything, together with the wine vinegar and cayenne, to the goulash and warm over low heat.

Serve with: farm loaf or white bread

A tip: you can keep the gipsy goulash on a warming plate — in readiness for a late snack.

Illustration on page 112

Toast Tartare

△ ○ ○

Ingredients for 2 people:

1 egg
2 slices toasting bread
2 teaspoons butter
1 small onion
300g (11 ozs) minced raw beefsteak
A good pinch each of salt, pepper, paprika and caraway seed
1 teaspoon oil
1 tablespoon mayonnaise
1 teaspoon cream
½ teaspoon curry powder (depending on taste)

Preparation time: 15 minutes

Hardboil egg for 10 minutes, rinse under cold water, peel and cut into slices. Fry the

110

Buffet Parties

bread slices on one side in the heated butter. • Chop the peeled onion finely. Mix the minced beefsteak with the onion, salt, pepper, paprika, caraway seed and oil and spread onto the bread. Divide egg slices over the steak. • Mix the mayonnaise with the cream and curry powder and distribute over the eggs.

Illustration on page 112

Flamed Fruit Salad

△ △ ○ ○

Ingredients for 4 people:

2 bananas
4 slices canned pineapple
4 canned green figs
1 tablespoon butter
2 tablespoons sugar
4 liqueur glasses rum
4 tablespoons juice from the figs and the pineapple

Preparation time: 20 minutes

Peel the bananas and cut in halves lengthwise. Drain the pineapple slices and figs. • Melt butter in a Flambé pan, add the sugar and stir until light brown. Add the drained fruit to the butter, heat thoroughly and fry until light brown, turning them over carefully. • Pour the rum

over the fruit and set alight. Let it burn for about 1 minute, then douse flame out with the fruit juice.

Illustration on page 112

Party Steak

△ ○ ○

Ingredients for 4 people:

4 fillet steaks of about 200 g (7 ozs) each
2 tablespoons oil
1 good pinch each of garlic powder, pepper, dried oregano and finely-chopped parsley
2 eggs
3 tablespoons mango chutney
250g (9 ozs) canned mush-rooms
1 tablespoon butter

Marinating time: 2 hours
Preparation time: 20 minutes

Wash the steaks quickly and dry carefully. Turn the steaks in the oil and season with the garlic powder, pepper, oregano and chopped parsley. Leave them in the oil for 1-2 hours. Hardboil the eggs for ten minutes, rinse under cold water, peel and cut into slices. • Pour the oil from the

steaks into a pan and heat. Fry the steaks in the hot oil on both sides for 4-5 minutes, salt slightly and keep warm. • Heat the mango chutney in the left-over fat, stirring all the time. Add the mushrooms to the pan, also the egg slices and butter and heat everything, stirring gently. • Finally, add the steaks again and reheat well over low heat.

Illustration on page 112

111

Drinks - The Long and Short of it

What to serve?

A good drop to drink belongs to any celebration as much as music does to dancing. But drinking habits vary considerably according to local custom, personal taste and the occasion, with the result that it's hardly possible to lay down any generally valid rules.

Cocktail Parties

Yet when it comes to a party, some guidelines can be given. The first one is never to offer too wide a choice. As mentioned earlier, the guest at a cocktail party is normally asked on arrival to choose between a long and a short drink. Having expressed his preference, he can usually decide between two different concoctions of the long or the short variety. At grander cocktail parties which may go on for hours, you will find either that all guests are served the same drink or that everyone may have his favourite tipple. This he may mix himself or get the bartender to mix for him. The latter type of cocktail party often comes to a premature end, however, for the well-known reason that mixtures paralyse brain and tongue more quickly than pure drinks. This is why it's advisable to serve cocktails only as a starter before food is served or the party gets going. Thereafter it's better to offer something that can be imbibed over longer periods without devastating effects.

Pouring out Beer

A Beer Party is much less complicated. Whether you serve the beer in bottles, which gives your guests a chance to sample a range of products from different breweries, or whether you order a barrel (these are obtainable in various sizes) depends entirely on your cold-storage space.
Drawing the beer from the tap requires a little practice and is best done in the cellar, the garden or on the balcony. Bear in mind that even the smallest traces of fat in the glass prevent the beer from forming any froth, so wash the glasses first in a detergent solution and rinse them thoroughly in clear, hot water. No matter whether bottled or from a barrel, beer should, when poured out, always have a nice froth on top. This is achieved by pouring it slowly into a cooled glass, held at an angle. Some guests may like to drink a 'chaser' with their beer — usually some kind of 'schnapps' — a dram of something stronger. Up to you to decide the extent you wish to indulge such special tastes. There are many suitable kinds to choose from, such as corn brandy, aquavit or vodka. But in any case, one kind of chaser is ample. Never forget that nothing is more capable of spoiling your party than too great a variety of drinks.

Wine and Cheese Parties

It's fair to say that no nation appreciates wine and cheese more than the French. No wonder, you may say, for they've a greater selection of both in their own country than most others. Yet it's not the French who have invented the Wine and Cheese Party but the English. Whereas in France cheese and wine are expertly matched to finish off most meals, the English nowadays give many parties where a variety of cheeses, eye-catchingly displayed on wooden platters, are the main attraction. As for the wines to

Drinks - The Long and Short of it

serve, you may take the view that, generally speaking, a fairly full-bodied red wine goes best with cheese, particularly the more strongly-flavoured ones. You may prefer to serve one light white wine, medium-dry or dry, in addition to a red wine. The quality you offer depends largely on your purse. But unless you have a gathering of connoisseurs to entertain you needn't be afraid to offer your guests what the French call 'an honest wine'. There are, of course, also parties at which it's left to the guests to choose from a great variety of drinks — beer, various kinds of wine, spirits and possibly even champagne. The latter is often mixed with orange, pineapple or grapefruit juice and these mixtures are very popular among people who do not require a high concentration of alcohol in their blood to enjoy themselves. Champagne being rather expensive, it's quite reasonable to replace it by cheaper varieties of sparkling wine such as German sekt, French mousseux or Italian asti. A light fruit cup according to season or a punch in winter are also very acceptable beverages to imbibe for hours on end and in convivial company. See to it, however, that you never run out of an adequate stock of mineral water, Coca Cola and fruit juices such as grape or tomato juice which are appreciated by guests who prefer non-alcoholic drinks.

The Improvised Cocktail Bar

For a cocktail party you will be well advised to improvise a special bar, for even a highly-practiced mixer using the greatest care can hardly avoid spilling something or making a mess. So even if you have a cocktail bar or cabinet in your living-room, sufficient though it may be for more intimate gatherings, it is not really suitable for a grander occasion demanding a greater variety of drinks. You may find it convenient, therefore, to set up a bar in the kitchen.

Now for the utensils you require as amateur barkeeper:
• 1 mixing beaker for the preparation of long drinks (or, alternatively, a deep bowl normally used to whisk cream in)
• 1 long spoon for stirring long drinks and measuring smaller quantities of ingredients
• 1 measure to determine the correct quantities of the various ingredients (a liqueur glass containing 2 fl. ozs. will do)
• 1 special bar-strainer which keeps ice-cubes or the remnants of fruit back (a shallow tea-strainer will do)
• 1 shaker with a built-in strainer and a screw-cap
• 1 wooden board on which to cut fruit
• 1 sharp knife with which to cut it and to peel off the orange and lemon rind you are sure to need
• 1 fruit-squeezer to press out lime and orange juice
• 1 nutmeg grater
• 1 pepper mill

Utensils for the amateur barkeeper

Cocktail shaker

114

Drinks - The Long and Short of it

- 1 thermos container for ice-cubes
- 1 pair of ice-tongs
- Drinking straws and cocktail sticks
- Some tea towels and dish cloths

As for the basic ingredients required to run an improvised house-bar successfully, they are relatively few in number. A stock of vermouth, gin, brandy, vodka, rum and whisky is, of course, essential. In addition you need mineral and tonic water, lemon, lime and tomato juice, a small bottle of grenadine (a French cordial syrup of pomegranate), and an even smaller bottle of angostura bitter as well as some oranges, lemons and a few sprigs of peppermint. In the following chapter you will find some recipes for a few popular cocktails. Choose from among them some for your party and get the ingredients you need to concoct them. This will enable you to gain some initial experience. Later you will be in a position to choose your own speciality or invent one yourself and, having reached that degree of expertise, you may finally decide to concentrate the activities of your improvised bar entirely on this 'cocktail de la maison'. Have the courage of your own concoction.

What Does one Mix and How?

A mixed drink is produced either by stirring or shaking. The product is called a cocktail – a short drink, meant to be sipped, in contrast to a long drink which is intended for drinking in mouthfuls, such as the 'fizzes'. Besides, there are also the Cobblers, Sodas, Sours and Coolers, to mention but a few from the repertoire of a classical bar. Also included are some recipes for making Punch, Grog, and various kinds of cups. For the classical mixed drinks, the recipes give the ingredients per glass, but this should not stop you making four or five times the quantity at a time to keep pace with demand. Let us start with the most popular among the cocktails.

Cocktails from the Shaker

First of all, measure and prepare all the ingredients you require for a particular cocktail; put three ice cubes into the shaker to cool it thoroughly; pour the iced water away. Then put all the ingredients into the shaker and close it; wrap a napkin around and shake it vigorously, holding it with both hands in a horizontal position. The finished cocktail is finally poured through the strainer into the glasses, the ice cubes remaining behind. Fresh ice-cubes are put into the glasses, should the recipe require it.

Alexander Cocktail

Ingredients per drink:

Put 1 measure cream, 1 measure crème de cacao (a sweet chocolate-coloured liqueur with the flavour of cocoa), 1 measure of brandy into shaker over the ice-cubes; shake vigorously, and pour into glass.

Baby's Special

1 measure each of cream, apricot brandy and peach brandy are poured into shaker over the ice-cubes; shake well and strain into glass.

Bombay Cocktail

Take 1 measure each of lemon juice and curacao (a French liqueur made of the zest of bitter orange) and two measures of arrak (a spirit distilled from fermented dates, rice and palm juice). Shake well over ice-cubes and pour.

115

Drinks - The Long and Short of it

Caruso Cocktail

Take 1 measure each of gin and French vermouth (drier and lighter than the Italian variety) and 1 measure of crème de menthe. Mix well in iced shaker before pouring.

Charlie Chaplin Cocktail

1 measure each of lemon juice and apricot brandy and two measures of gin are shaken well over ice-cubes before being strained into glass.

Cherry Brandy Cocktail

Take 1 measure each of orange juice, brandy and cherry brandy (liqueur distilled from fermented cherries and their crushed stones), 3 dashes each of curacao and grenadine, and shake well over ice cubes. Put a cocktail cherry into glass before pouring.

Columbus Cocktail

Take 1 measure each of lemon juice, apricot brandy and rum. Shake well before straining into glass.

Dixi Cocktail

Take 1 measure each of anisette (French aniseed-flavour liqueur) and French vermouth and 2 measures of brandy. Shake well over ice before straining into glass.

Cocktail Havana

Take 1 measure of white rum, the juice of half a lemon and half an orange and 1 measure of vermouth. Shake briefly before straining into glass in which you have placed a small piece of orange.

Cockatoo Cocktail

Take 2 measures whisky, 1 measure orange juice, a dash of angostura bitter and a spoonful lemon juice. Shake in iced shaker, place a large slice of unpeeled orange in glass and strain cocktail into it.

Merry Widow Cocktail

Take 1 measure each of grapefruit juice, cointreau (orange-flavoured liqueur from France) and vodka. Mix in shaker over ice-cubes before straining into glass.

Paradise Cocktail

Take 1 measure each of orange juice, gin and apricot brandy and shake well over ice-cubes before straining.

Piccadilly Cocktail

Take 1 dash each of absinthe (a spirit distilled from wormwood, aniseed and other herbs) and of grenadine syrup, 1 measure French vermouth and 2 measures gin; shake briefly in iced shaker, then strain into glass.

Queen Mary Cocktail

Take 1 dash strawberry syrup, 1 dash anisette, 1 measure each of cointreau and brandy; mix in iced shaker, put a fresh strawberry into glass and strain cocktail into it.

Royal Cocktail

1 dash maraschino and 1 measure each of gin, cherry brandy and French vermouth are mixed together in iced shaker and strained into glass containing a cocktail cherry.

Drinks - The Long and Short of it

Sidecar Cocktail

1 measure each of lemon juice, cointreau and brandy are briefly shaken and poured into glass.

White Lady Cocktail

1 measure each of lemon juice, gin and cointreau are mixed in iced shaker and poured into glass.

Cocktails which need Stirring

Another group of cocktail is stirred, not shaken. In the case of these concoctions, the ingredients are poured into the mixing beaker or bowl you have in readiness for the purpose (see under 'utensils'), stirred for 10 seconds with the long-handled bar spoon, and the contents then strained into the glass.

Gitta Cocktail

Take 1 measure each of gin and white vermouth and mix together with dash of Pernod (popular French appetizer with aniseed flavour) in mixing beaker over ice cubes. Strain into glass and serve with an ice cube and a small piece of lemon rind.

Panama Cocktail

1 measure each of rum, pineapple juice and maraschino are mixed over some ice cubes in the mixing beaker and strained into a glass. Add 2 fresh ice cubes before serving.

Cocktail Mister

Mix ½ measure each of sherry and dry white vermouth with 2 spoons of orange liqueur in the mixing beaker and strain into glass, adding 2 olives, a small piece of lemon rind and 1 ice cube.

Champagne Cocktail

Fill a champagne glass with finely-crushed ice. Add 1 spoon grenadine syrup, 1 spoon lemon juice, 1 spoon brandy, a dash angostura bitter and 1 slice unpeeled orange. Fill up with champagne or sekt (the German champagne substitute which is cheaper).

Champagne-Orange Cocktail

Stir 1 measure each of orange juice, vermouth, curacao and gin in the mixing beaker over ice cubes, strain into champagne glass and fill up with dry champagne, or sekt.

Adonis Cocktail

A dash of orange bitter, 1 measure sherry and 2 measures Italian vermouth are thoroughly stirred in mixing beaker and then strained into glass.

Kangaroo Cocktail

Stir 3 measures vodka together with 1 measure dry vermouth over ice cubes in mixing beaker before straining. Add a tiny piece of lemon peel to heighten aroma.

Manhattan Cocktail

A dash of angostura bitter, 1 measure red vermouth, 2 measures Canadian club whisky. Mix thoroughly over ice cubes, strain into glass, adding cocktail cherry. If instead of the cherry you put an olive into the glass, the finished product is a 'Manhattan Dry'.

Dry Martini

A dash of angostura bitter, 2 measures gin and 1 measure of Martini vermouth extra dry are stirred together over ice cubes. The resulting

Drinks - The Long and Short of it

concoction is then strained into the glass and 1 olive added.

Perfection Cocktail

1 measure each of French vermouth, Italian vermouth and gin are stirred together over ice cubes and the mixture strained into a glass.

Whisky Cocktail

Take 2 dashes grenadine, 2 dashes angostura bitter and 1 measure whisky; stir well and strain into glass, adding one cocktail cherry.

Famous Fizzes

All fizzes are mixed in the shaker over finely-crushed ice with a dash of soda added to give them their effervescence.

Apricot Fizz

Put the juice of half a lemon and half an orange and one measure apricot brandy into shaker. Shake well over finely-crushed ice, strain into glass and fill up with soda water.

Brandy Fizz

The juice of 1 lemon, 3 spoonfuls of sugar and 1 measure brandy are shaken thoroughly over crushed ice in the shaker and strained into glass.

Cream Fizz

The juice of 1 lemon, 1 measure cream, 3 spoons sugar and 1 measure gin are shaken thoroughly over ice in the shaker and strained into glass.

Egg Fizz

Shake very thoroughly over crushed ice the juice of one lemon, 1 whole egg, 2 spoons sugar and 1 measure brandy in shaker, strain into glass and fill up with soda water.

Gin Fizz

Mix juice of lemon, 3 spoons sugar and 1 measure gin in shaker, fill into tall glass and fill up with soda water. Serve with drinking straw.

Golden Fizz

1 egg yolk, the juice of 1 lemon, 2 spoons sugar, 3 spoons grenadine syrup and 1 measure gin are shaken thoroughly over crushed ice, poured into glass and a dash of soda water added.

Royal Fizz

1 whole egg, the juice of half a lemon and half an orange, 3 spoons grenadine syrup, 2 spoons sugar and 1 measure gin are put into shaker and shaken thoroughly over crushed ice. Strain into tall glass, adding a little soda.

Drinks - The Long and Short of it

Whisky Fizz

Mix in shaker 2 measures whisky, the juice of half a lemon, 1 spoon sugar. Shake well. Strain into tall glass. Fill up with soda water. Add two maraschino cherries and 2 small pieces of ice.

Cobblers to Spoil the Ladies

To produce a 'cobbler' you fill a champagne goblet or any other glass with a wide opening two thirds full of finely-crushed ice. The desired mixture is then poured over it and garnished with fruit. Cobblers. are served with spoon and drinking straw.

Brandy Cobbler

Fill the glass two thirds full of crushed ice. Add 1 spoon grenadine syrup, 3 dashes each of maraschino, curacao and kirsch and 1 measure brandy. Place a few pieces of pineapple and some maraschino cherries on top.

Champagne Cobbler

Put some grapes and a few banana slices onto the crushed ice. Add 3 dashes each of maraschino liqueur, cointreau and curacao and fill up with champagne or German sekt. Serve with spoon and drinking straw.

Sherry Cobbler

Garnish the crushed ice in the cobbler glass with some small pieces of canned peach and a few cocktail cherries. Add 3 dashes each of brandy, kirsch and grenadine syrup. Fill up with sherry.

Sodas for the Thirsty

The best-known among this type of beverage is the Whisky Soda. However, it's just as good to serve a Brandy Soda, a Gin Soda or a Rum Soda. To prepare, pour 50 g (3 tablespoons) of the desired spirits into a tall glass (for Whisky Soda use slightly less) and top up with soda water. Should the drink not be cold enough you merely add 1 or 2 ice cubes.

The 'Sours'

'Sours' are easily digestible and very thirst-quenching beverages which, like the 'Fizzes', are mixed thoroughly in the shaker over crushed ice. The method of preparation is the same in every case: pour the juice of half a lemon over the crushed ice in the shaker and add 2 spoons of sugar. Then pour 1 glass of whisky, gin, brandy or rum into the shaker; shake the mixture vigorously and for a long time, for the drink must be really cool before it's strained into the glass, in which you place 2 cocktail cherries and 1 tiny piece each of lemon and orange. Serve with a spoon and a drinking straw. On particularly hot days, an extra drop of soda water will be appreciated.

The 'Coolers'

'Coolers' are similar to the 'sours'. They, too, are prepared in a shaker over lots of crushed ice. In each case, you need 2 spoons of sugar and the juice of half a lemon, in addition to a glass of gin, whisky, rum or arrack. Shake vigorously until really cool and pour into a medium-sized glass which you top up with ginger ale. Serve with drinking straws.

Drinks - The Long and Short of it

Fruit Cups

The main ingredient of this type of cup is white wine – a light Moselle for preference. Only fresh fruit and herbs should be used. A fruit cup is started by putting a little sugar onto the fruit, which you should have placed into a large bowl; if you wish, you can also pour a little liqueur over the sugared fruit. Then pour the wine onto it – the wine should be really cold. Cover the dish with a lid and keep it for some time in a cool place. Before serving add some champagne, sekt or soda water. No ice cubes should be put into the fruit cup, but the bowl is kept cold by standing it in ice cubes.

Apple Cup

For 6 people:

Peel 6 sour apples and cut them into thin slices. Put the apples into a dish and sprinkle with 1 cup of sugar. After a few hours the apples will have extruded some juice. Then pour 2 measures of rum over the fruit, adding at the same time the zest of 1 lemon and 1 bottle of burgundy. Replace the lid and put the fruit cup back into the refrigerator, leaving it for some time. Before serving, top up with 1 bottle of red champagne or sekt.

Special Raspberry Cup

For 8-10 people:

Wash thoroughly half a lemon and 2 oranges in hot water and cut them unpeeled into thin slices; pour 4 measures of brandy and 2 measures of maraschino liqueur over them. Add 2 tablespoons sugar and 2 bottles of cooled white wine. Allow to stand for 30 minutes before adding some 800-900 g (approx. 2 lbs) of fresh or deep-frozen raspberries and 3 bottles of champagne or sekt.

Strawberry Cup

For 6–8 people:

Put 250g (9 ozs) sugar into a bowl, pour 1 bottle of light white wine over it and stir until sugar is completely dissolved and the wine quite clear. Add 2 lbs fresh, and preferably wild, strawberries – although ordinary garden strawberries will do, provided they are small. Cover and allow to stand for about 1 hour. Shortly before serving add 2 more bottles of white wine and half a bottle of champagne or sekt.

Sangria

For 6 people:

Many people who have in recent years travelled on the Continent and particularly in Spain and the Balearic Islands have returned home full of enthusiasm for the refreshing qualities of Sangria. Indeed this drink is highly acceptable, particularly at a garden party in the height of summer. To prepare, empty two bottles of Spanish red wine into a large jug. Add sugar to taste, four generous slices each of orange and lemon and the juice strained from the rest of each fruit. Stir, add a liqueur glass of brandy. Chill well. Just before serving add ice cubes and about two thirds of a syphon of soda.

Cucumber Cup

For 6–8 people:

Wash thoroughly 1 fresh salad cucumber and cut into thin slices. Pour 1 bottle of white wine over them, cover and allow to stand at room temperature for half an hour.

Drinks - The Long and Short of it

Strain the wine into the serving bowl, stirring 2 tablespoons of sugar into it. When the sugar has completely dissolved and the white wine has become quite clear, add a second bottle of white wine and a bottle of champagne or sekt.

Orange Cup

For 4–6 people:

Wash 2 oranges in hot water, dry and cut them unpeeled into thin, even slices. Place the oranges in a bowl, sprinkle 200g (7 ozs) sugar over them and add 1 glass Malaga, 1½ measures kirsch and 1½ measures curacao. Let stand at room temperature for half an hour. Finally, before serving, add 1 bottle of cooled white wine, half a bottle of champagne and 1 bottle of soda water.

Peach Cup

For 6–8 people:

Stone 6–8 fresh peaches of good quality and cut into quarters. Put these into a bowl, sprinkling about 100g (3½ ozs) sugar over them. Pour 1 measure each of peach liqueur, Malaga and red port onto them. Keep covered in refrigerator for 1 hour to infuse. In a second dish, stir 100g (3½ ozs) into 1 bottle of white wine and then add this to the peaches. Allow to infuse for a short time, before pouring 2 more bottles of white wine and half a bottle of champagne or sekt into it.

Cider Cup

For 6–8 people:

Take two oranges, a lemon, 2 apples, 2 bananas, about 1 inch of good-sized cucumber, some grapes and any berries that may be in season. Take the rind off the oranges and the lemon with a potato peeler; put the rind at the bottom of the bowl and squeeze the juice into it. Slice the other fruit and place it into the bowl, adding a sprig of borage. Now pour over 2 full wine glasses of brandy and 1 wine glass each of sherry, cointreau, lime-juice and lemon-squash. Stir well, squashing the fruit. Place in a

refrigerator to infuse for at least one hour. Before serving, add 2 quarts of medium-sweet cider and stir again.

Peeling a lemon to obtain a spiral for 'Cold Duck'

'Cold Duck'

For 4–6 people:

This German speciality is easy to prepare and, being very refreshing, stands a good chance of becoming popular in English-speaking countries. All you do is pour 2 bottles of chilled white wine into a tureen, wash and dry a lemon and peel it with a sharp knife as thinly as possible and in such a manner as to have the whole peel in one piece, forming a spiral. Leave the peel to infuse in the wine for some 15 minutes, then remove it, before pouring 1 bottle of champagne or sekt and 1 bottle of soda water into the white wine; some may like to add a little sugar.

121

Drinks - The Long and Short of it

Punches and Grogs

Egg Punch

Pour 1 bottle of white wine into a saucepan and heat at a moderate temperature. Whisk together 5 egg yolks, 100g (3½ ozs) sugar and 1 glass of Malaga. Slowly add the hot wine to the egg mixture, stirring constantly, and bring once more to boiling point. Pour the punch into the punch glasses, sprinkling a little nutmeg on each.

Wedding Punch

For 8 people:

Put the juice of 12 lemons, ¼ litre (½ pint) pineapple juice, 1 bottle of white port, half a bottle of brandy, 1 vanilla pod and 250g (9 ozs) sugar into a saucepan and, stirring continuously, bring up to boiling point. Add slowly 1 litre (2 pts) hot water. Allow to infuse at very slow heat for 30 minutes. Let cool and, before serving, stir in 1 jar of cherries.

White Wine Punch

For 8 people:

Dissolve 9 ozs of sugar in 3 bottles of white wine in a saucepan and, continuing to stir, bring to boiling point. Slowly add 1 bottle of rum and allow to infuse for 20 minutes at mild heat. Serve in punch glasses, garnishing each with 3 cherries.

Tea Punch

Half a litre (2 pts) of arrack, 250g (9 ozs) of sugar and the juice of 2 lemons are put in a saucepan and brought to boiling point, while being stirred continuously. Gradually, 2 litres (4 pts) of freshly-brewed hot tea are added, while stirring continuously. Pour the mixture into punch glasses and add a slice of lemon to each.

The classical grog consisted of nothing but sugar candy, rum and hot water. Since then innumerable variations have developed, such as:

Grog with Rum

You will require 1 measure of rum per portion. Pour the rum into a saucepan and add the juice of 1 lemon, 2 spoons of sugar, 2 cloves, a little cinnamon and some fresh, cold water. Bring to the boil once and at low temperature, pour into punch glasses, removing the small piece of cinnamon and the cloves. All other grogs are prepared in exactly the same way; you merely take, instead of the rum, 1 measure of brandy, whisky, gin or arrack.

Mulled Port

Bring 1 litre (barely a quart) of cheap ruby port (or its South African or Australian equivalent) to near boiling point in a saucepan. Add half a litre (1 pt) of boiling water into which you have sprinkled a good pinch of mixed spice and a lemon that has been stuck with cloves and roasted in the oven. Rub 20g (barely 2 ozs) off the rind of another lemon, put it into a jug or bowl, adding the juice of half a lemon. Now pour over the wine. Serve piping hot, but remember: no mull must ever boil.

Drinks - The Long and Short of it

Refreshing Concoctions

Gin and Orange Special

For each glass, put 2 ice cubes into a mixing bowl, pour over 1 measure of gin, the juice of half a lemon, one teaspoon of sugar and ¼ pint of buttermilk. Mix thoroughly before pouring. Stick a thin slice of an unpeeled orange onto the rim of each glass.

South Sea Drink

For each glass, put 2 ice cubes into a mixing bowl and fill up with 1 tablespoon of honey, the juice of ½ lemon, 1 measure of beer and ¼ pint of milk. Mix well. Fill into the glasses, garnishing each with a small spiral of lemon peel.

Good Luck Shake

For each glass put 2 ice cubes into a mixing bowl and fill up with the juice of 1 grapefruit, 1 egg yolk, 3 level tablespoons sugar and ¼ pint of buttermilk. Mix well and pour out. Garnish with a touch of whipped cream.

Mocha Flip

For each glass, put 1 egg yolk, 2 spoons of sugar, 1 measure of mocha liqueur and 2 spoons of double cream into a mixing bowl and mix well with 2 ice cubes before straining into the glasses.

Whisky Flip

Mix thoroughly 1 egg yolk, 2 spoons of sugar and 1 measure of whisky with 1 large ice cube; strain into the glasses, sprinkling a little grated nutmeg over it.

Mocha Blitz

For each glass, mix a ½ measure of brandy with a ¼ of a cup of cream and 1 level teaspoon of powdered coffee. Place 1 ice cube into each glass and add drink, sprinkling 1 teaspoon of sugar over it.

After this detour into the classical repertoire of the professional mixers you should be in a position to try your hand at some inventions of your own. You will find it great fun, but do try out your own creations first of all on a few willing guinea pigs to make sure your concoctions are easy on the stomach.

Drinks - The Long and Short of it

The correct glass for every drink, from left to right:
Sekt, Claret, White Wine, Cocktail, Whisky and Long Drinks,
Brandy, Plum Brandy

Finally, a postscript to the subject of drinks, of interest to all would-be hosts or hostesses:

1 standard-sized bottle of champagne, red or white wine yields on average 6 glasses.

1 bottle of sherry, port or other fortified sweet wine yields 12—16 glasses (according to the size of glasses you use). 1 bottle of whisky, brandy or other concentrated spirits fills 20 glasses of average size.

In Conclusion

If you have inwardly digested all you've been told so far you should now be well-equipped to tackle any kind of party, but should you ever feel confidence flagging just remember that a party is not a stiff, ceremonial affair but something uncomplicated and unconventional where improvisation counts for a great deal. And if in the course of the evening you run into some trouble or difficulty, or if you should be in doubt about something, don't try to hide it from your guests but ask their advice openly — they'll be only too delighted to help.

LIFE
SKILLS

Be SMART, STAY SAFE

Louise Spilsbury

Heinemann
LIBRARY

www.heinemannlibrary.co.uk
Visit our website to find out more
information about Heinemann
Library books.

To order:
☎ Phone +44 (0) 1865 888066
▤ Fax +44 (0) 1865 314091
▣ Visit www.heinemannlibrary.co.uk

Text © Capstone Global Library Limited 2009
First published in hardback in 2009
The moral rights of the proprietor have been
asserted.

Edited by Harriet Milles and Adam Miller
Designed by Philippa Jenkins and Artistix
Picture research by Elizabeth Alexander and
    Maria Joannou
Production by Victoria Fitzgerald
Originated by Heinemann Library
Printed and bound in China by South China
    Printing Company Ltd.

ISBN 978 0 431112 68 8
13 12 11 10 09
10 9 8 7 6 5 4 3 2 1

**British Library Cataloguing in Publication
Data**
Spilsbury, Louise
  Be smart, stay safe! - (Life skills)
  1. Offenses against the person - Juvenile
literature
  2. Accidents - Prevention - Juvenile literature
  I. Title
  613.6
A full catalogue record for this book is available
from the British Library.

Acknowledgements

We would like to thank the following for
permission to reproduce photographs:
© Alamy pp. **23** (Andrew Paterson), **20** (Andry
A/Alamsyah), **16** (Blend Images/Dave & Les
Jacobs), **40** (Jupiterimages/ BananaStock), **30**
(Tony French), **11** (Zak Waters); © Barcroft
Media p. **35**; © Corbis pp. **14** (Flirt/Ariel
Skelley), **29** (Kevin Dodge), **5** (Thinkstock); ©
Getty Images/Taxi/Carl Schneider p. **7**; © Iofoto/
Dreamstime.com p. **33**; © iStockphoto pp. **13**
(Carsten Madsen), **26** (Paige Falk); © Masterfile
pp. **22** (Peter Griffith), **25** (Ron Fehling); ©
Photolibrary pp. **43** (Digital Vision), **45** (Index
Stock Imagery/Donald Higgs); © Rex Features/
Oliver Grove/PYMCA p. **39**; © Science Photo
Library pp. **49** (AJ Photo), **47** (Faye Norman); ©
Shutterstock pp. **19** (Arland Croquet), **9** (Andrija
Kovac), **36** (Jose AS Reyes).

Cover photograph of a teenage girl with a laptop
computer and cell phone reproduced with
permission of © Shutterstock/David Davis.

We would like to thank Robin Lomas for his
invaluable help in the preparation of this book.

Every effort has been made to contact copyright
holders of material reproduced in this book.
Any omissions will be rectified in subsequent
printings if notice is given to the publishers.

Contents

Some words are printed in bold, **like this**. You can find out
what they mean by looking in the glossary.

TAKING RISKS

News headlines often shout about the problems of risk-taking teenagers. They usually highlight the trouble teenagers cause for other people, such as **vandalism** or late-night noise. Sometimes they focus on the damage teenagers do to themselves, such as sustaining injuries from street jumping or missing out on an education because they play truant. But is it always bad to take risks?

POSITIVE RISK-TAKING

Taking risks is an inevitable and important part of teenage life. As a teenager you are much more independent – you're out on your own more, making your own friends, trying new things and new experiences. Increased independence means more choices and of course that means more risks. This isn't necessarily a bad thing. People need to take on new challenges to work out who they are and what they can and want to be.

Taking risks can be a good thing when it means trying a new challenge. This could be something you have wanted to do for a long time but didn't dare to do, such as playing a solo at a gig or running a race. Alternatively, it could be trying a totally new sport, or joining a club to make new friends. Healthy risk-taking is anything that puts you in a difficult or unfamiliar situation. It may involve the possibility of failure, but it also gives you the chance to have positive experiences and gain a new belief in yourself. Taking risks like this gives you a real buzz as that rush of adrenalin kicks in, whether you succeed or fail in your goals.

Negative risk-taking

Negative risk-taking is anything that puts you or someone else at risk of being hurt or damaged. Such damage could be emotional or physical. Negative risky behaviours range from going on a blind date with someone you met online or drinking at parties, to doing your own body-piercings, or carrying a knife.

Most of the time and for most people, even these risky behaviours won't result in disaster, but sometimes negative risk-taking has deadly consequences. The number of accidental deaths caused by fighting, driving too fast, or just fooling about dangerously peaks in males aged from 16 to 25 years old.

When people get up on stage to perform, they take a big risk. They face the fear that they might be laughed off or that people simply won't like what they do. It takes a lot of guts to take risks like these, far more so than a lot of the negative risks people take.

→

There are many ways you can take positive new risks, including:

Getting it Right

- Joining a band, club, or group
- Trying rollerblading, rock climbing, or sailing
- Taking an extra course in a school subject you find difficult
- Trying out for a sports team
- Auditioning for a school play
- Running for student council
- Volunteering to help out for a worthy cause, such as at an animal shelter, at a home for the elderly, or for an environmental organization.

Why take risks?

What motivates one person to take more risks than another depends on the individual. Some people have a stronger drive to feel different from their **peers**, and some are more susceptible to peer pressure than others.

For some people, just being around friends makes them more likely to take risks. Others end up taking more risks because they make decisions based purely on what's happening at that moment without thinking about how it might affect themselves, other people, or the world around them.

Which risks are real?

It can be tough deciding which risks are real and which are not. You may think that parents and caregivers over-exaggerate risks. It is true that this can sometimes happen, but it is usually because they love you and want to protect you.

In order to stop your parents' or caregivers' fears restricting the positive risks you take, talk things through with them first. Find out if their fears are based on facts, or whether they are based on media hype. They'll be impressed that you are mature enough to be willing to discuss it properly. Faced with the facts, they are more likely to give you more freedom.

There are some activities, such as white-water rafting or sky-diving, that carry a certain degree of real risk, but that doesn't necessarily mean you should never try them. The risks are greatly reduced if you choose to do these things with a company or organization that follow strict safety guidelines and have a great safety record. Taking steps to keep the real risks to a minimum will be reassuring for you and your family.

Get it in perspective

Thinking about risks is not about trying to scare yourself. In reality, the likelihood of something bad happening to you is pretty low. However, taking chances and making the wrong choices in a situation obviously puts you at greater risk, so it is best to think ahead and take precautions to keep yourself, your possessions, and your friends and others safe.

When you learn how to evaluate risks and anticipate the consequences of your choices, you will be safer and more able to cope with challenges in all parts of your adult life.

White-water rafting does involve some risk-taking – but very few people who have tried it have regretted the experience!

At the age of 14, UK **entrepreneur** Nick Bell set up an online teen magazine and sold it two years later for almost £1 million. He has since bought back the company and set up a number of other successful websites. Nick says: "I tell people who have an idea to go for it and follow their instincts. I suppose I am living proof that you can be successful. I have taken risks but if you have a dream I think you have to follow it."

Getting it Right

PLAY IT SAFE

It may be the last thing you want to think about when you're planning a weekend or a night out, but taking undue risks at gigs or parties, when playing sports, or at the beach is a surefire way to put a dampener on things. Taking a few simple precautions can make the difference between having a great weekend, or one that you'd rather forget!

PARTY TIME

At parties or discos, one of the greatest dangers you will face is alcohol. It is tempting to think that drinking alcohol will give you more confidence and help you feel relaxed. Some people see their parents or other adults drinking and believe that it is a "socially acceptable" drug. They feel confident that they know and can set their own limits. In fact, alcohol has a far stronger effect on a young person's body than it does on an adult's. This means that you will lose control far more quickly on far fewer drinks.

Studies have shown that the younger people start drinking, the more likely they are to develop problems with alcohol – with serious implications for health. Even moderate drinking can cause short-and long-term damage to a young, growing brain. Longer-term risks from alcohol include **cancer**, high blood pressure, and liver disease.

Drinking alcohol clouds your judgement and makes you do embarrassing, stupid, or dangerous things that you regret the next day. If you drink alcohol, you are far more likely to do something dangerous or violent, such as getting into a fight or driving when drunk. You may even be taken advantage of in a way that you can never undo; for instance, having underage and unprotected sex.

Getting it Right

If you're at a party where a lot of people are drinking alcohol, the safest thing to do would be to leave. If that's not possible, take care to pour your own drinks so you can be sure nobody has spiked them with alcohol. Never leave your drink unattended, in case someone spikes it when you're not looking. Stay among groups of people you know and trust.

Turn down the volume

Another serious risk for party-goers is – NOISE! Ever got back from a night out and felt that ringing in your ears or a dulled sense of hearing? Any sustained loud noise puts a person's hearing at risk, and the **decibel levels** in a club or at a gig can be as bad as standing near a high-powered drill. Hearing damage is caused by two factors: the volume at which you listen to it, and how long you listen to it.

Try the following tips and you'll be able to give your ears a break but still enjoy the music:

- If you're at a music festival or gig, take time out somewhere quiet to give your ears a rest.

- Never stand too close to loudspeakers.

- If you want to watch the main act at the front of the stage, watch the support from further back.

Avoid dancing or standing next to loudspeakers because your ears will suffer.

SPORT

Playing sports or doing some other form of regular exercise will keep you in good shape. However, there is some potential for injuries in sport. There are many things you can do to keep yourself injury-free. Start by learning the rules of the game; they are there to make games fair and to keep players safe. Knowing the rules means that you are prepared so you won't be caught off guard. For example, in football it is against the rules to kick a ball after the referee's whistle has blown because an unexpected tackle could cause serious injuries.

Be properly equipped

One of the main reasons why people get injured during sport is because they use the wrong or badly-fitting equipment. Save your smile by wearing mouth guards for fast-moving sports such as rugby and hockey. Wear elbow, wrist, and knee guards to prevent bone fractures when skating or skateboarding. Goggles will protect your eyes in a game of squash.

Wearing the right shoes can stop you falling and injuring yourself, and will also improve your play. If you want to try extreme sports, make sure you take all the right precautions, wear all the correct safety gear, and have a qualified instructor who can use his or her skills and experience to control the risks.

Warm up, cool down

Before you get out on the pitch and involved in the action, it's important to do a **warm-up** such as jogging on the spot or stretching. Warm-ups prepare your heart for an increase in activity and increase the blood flow to the muscles, making them warmer and more elastic (ready to move). Cold muscles do not absorb shock or impact as well, and are more easily **strained** or pulled. Doing some gentle walking or stretching exercises after sport also helps to relax your muscles and prevent soreness. This is known as a **cool-down**.

Getting it Right

If you feel the need to take on physically challenging risks, you should sign up for a class or join an organization where you can test your limits in a relatively safe environment. You could try rock climbing, surfing, white-water rafting, or join a group like the army cadets.

Controlling risks by using the proper equipment makes the difference between taking part in a real sport and plain dangerous behaviour.

Pain is the body's way of telling you something is wrong, so:

- Never play sport when you are injured or in pain.
- Never play when you have a cold or flu bug or are ill in some other way.
- Don't take pain relievers to get you through a game.
- Don't return to a sport before you are fully healed after an injury.

Getting it Wrong

HOLIDAY HIGHS AND LOWS

It's great to go on a summer trip with friends – mountain biking, camping in the woods, or visiting the beach to swim or surf – but be alert for risks. This is particularly important at the seaside. Unfortunately every year people are killed after being swept out to sea on inflatables, or surfing too far out to sea with no understanding of currents, or being trapped on a beach when the high tide comes in.

When camping, take warm clothing and sleeping bags because in most places the temperature drops dramatically at night. If you light a camp fire, build it in a shallow pit away from the tent and anything else that might catch alight, and surround it with stones. Keep a bucket of water nearby and use this to put out the fire. Embers can stay hot enough to reignite or burn skin for up to a day if a fire is only covered with sand.

Sun sense

Up to 80 percent of teenagers put themselves at risk by failing to use a sunscreen lotion. Sun damage to the skin in your youth can make your skin patchy and wrinkled in later life, and even lead to skin cancers. Doctors advise that sunscreens should be applied just before going out in the sun and reapplied frequently throughout the day, particularly after swimming. You should also cover up exposed areas such as the head, arms, and legs in hats and clothing made of light-coloured fabrics.

When you are camping or hiking:

TIP

- **Take first aid supplies and plenty of drinking water. Stream or river water may be unsafe.**

- **Carry a mobile phone, or find out where the nearest telephone is located.**

- **Check the weather forecast before you leave.**

- **Pack essentials, such as a torch, extra food, water, and rain gear, even if it looks sunny.**

- **Tell people where you are going, who is with you, and when you'll return.**

- **Follow well-marked trails and do not stray from the route.**

Getting it
Wrong

Tombstoning is a craze where people jump into water from high cliffs, walls, and piers. Several people have died tombstoning, either drowning or crashing into rocks. In 2008 Steven Andrews, 25, was paralysed from the neck down after jumping 8 metres (26 feet) into just 1 metre (3 feet) of water. He said: "I want to warn people that you should never mess around on rocks or cliffs or anywhere dangerous near water. It can happen so quickly – in a matter of seconds my life changed forever. I wish I could turn back the clock but now I'm just going to have to try and deal with it."

WORKWISE

Having a part-time job is great because it gives you cash of your own to spend. It also gives you the chance to try a few different jobs before you get out into the world of full-time work. However, every year tens of thousands of teenage employees end up in the Accident and Emergency room with injuries sustained through unsafe equipment or conditions at their workplace (for instance, slippery floors). These accidents tend to happen when young people are working too fast or for too long, or when they have not been given proper safety training or **supervision**.

Keep it legal

Most countries have laws to protect young people at work. These laws should prevent you taking on dangerous jobs, or jobs for which you have not been properly trained. The laws also restrict the number of hours that under-18s can work. This is mainly to ensure that, at this important age, you have time for your studies, and to relax and get the sleep that you need.

Check out how the law affects you before you agree to start any new job. Always discuss a job with your parents or caregivers first to make sure they are happy for you to do it.

To be safe at work:

- **Follow all the safety rules.**

- **Use safety equipment and wear protective clothing when needed.**

- **Keep work areas clean and in a tidy order.**

- **Know what to do in an emergency.**

- **Report any health and safety hazards to your supervisor.**

One of the most important things you can do to reduce the risks at work is to have the confidence to speak up if you are unhappy about something you are being asked to do.

 **HOW SAFETY SAVVY ARE YOU?**

Are you in the know, or too dozy to be let out alone? Find out in this true or false quiz. The answers are on page 50.

The answers are on page 50.

1) Some music just has to be listened to at maximum volume.
2) You only need safety gear for a sport if you're a professional.
3) During term time 14–16-year-olds are allowed to do a maximum of two hours work on school days and on Sundays.
4) From the age of 15 you can work up to eight hours a day on Saturdays and during the holidays.
5) Red and yellow flags mean it is safe to swim on a beach.
6) It is safe to swim in polluted water, so long as you don't swallow any of it.
7) You should stay out of the sun in the afternoon.
8) It's okay to swim alone so long as you are a strong swimmer.
9) In sport, a warm-up is a drink of hot chocolate after a winter game.

Be Streetwise

The risks of having an accident or being mugged or attacked while you are out in the streets are low, but it is wise to think ahead and avoid potential dangers. When you go out at night it is especially important to know how you can get home safely at the end of the evening.

PLAN AHEAD

You never want to end up hitchhiking or taking lifts from strangers as these options are far too risky. Always arrange to get a lift from a responsible person, catch a bus or train, take a taxi, or stay at a friend's house. Another important thing to remember is to tell your family where you are going, when you plan to be back, and the route you intend to take.

If a stranger stops to ask for your help, or offers you a lift, keep your distance and never get into a car with them – whatever their sex, and however friendly they seem. If they harass or scare you, shout clearly "Help me!" or "Call the police".

TIP

Public transport is usually a safe option, but it is worth remembering these tips:

- Choose a bus stop or station that is well lit and used by lots of people, if possible.

- Be aware of where the emergency alarms are and sit or stand near them.

- Check the departure times of the last buses, tubes, or trains and don't miss them.

- Take extra money so that you can take another bus or train or ring for a lift if you get stranded.

Alternatively, agree to text or phone parents or caregivers before you set off, so that they know when to expect you. If you don't have a safe ride home, call your parents. Even if it is late, they would rather you called so that they can make sure you get home safely, rather than let you take risks.

Road safety

Car crashes are the biggest single cause of accidental death for 12–16- year-olds in the UK and the United States. Teenagers have the lowest rate of safety-belt use and the highest crash rate compared to other age groups. They are more likely to be in a car accident and less likely to be using a seat belt when it happens. Teenagers are involved with more accidents because they or their friends are inexperienced drivers and because teen drivers are more likely to speed and drive dangerously when they are with friends. (Drivers aged 17 are 39 percent more likely be killed with one passenger and 86 percent more at risk with two passengers.) To keep safe, simply belt up and choose who you take a lift with carefully.

"One fact quoted to me quite often is that the single biggest killer now of teenage girls is their teenage boyfriends driving their cars."

Meredydd Hughes, Chief Constable of South Yorkshire Police

17

CYCLE SAFETY

Cycling is a great way to travel independently. It's also a cheap form of transport, it keeps you fit, gets you out in the fresh air, and it is environmentally friendly because it reduces the amount of fuel-driven traffic on the road. The benefits of cycling far outweigh the risks, but it pays to be clued up.

Get the gear

One of the simplest things you can do to keep safe on your bike is wear a helmet. OK, so no one likes helmet hair but the alternative could be far more depressing: around three-quarters of people killed in cycling accidents die from major head injuries. You might want to invest in a pair of cycling gloves as these help you to grip the handlebars and protect your knuckles if you fall. However, what is even more important is making sure that you can be seen. Wear high-visibility clothing such as an over-the-shoulder style **reflective** belt.

Rules of the road

Many accidents involving bikes and cars happen at road junctions or roundabouts, where cyclists may not be sure of the rules of the road or take unnecessary risks. It's a good idea to take a course in cycle safety, as this will improve your safety awareness and your confidence. Buy yourself a copy of the Highway Code and make sure you know the rules of the road.

When you cycle, especially in a city, be smart:

- Never cycle in places that are too dangerous to walk in.

- Use a cycle lane when you can; otherwise keep on the inside of traffic without getting too close to the kerb or road edge.

- Keep well behind lorries or large vehicles so that drivers can see you clearly in their wing mirrors.

- Watch the road. Drain covers, potholes, and litter can send you off-course. On busy streets, watch for people in parked cars opening their doors.

- Lock your bike securely whenever you leave it.

By checking your bike regularly for faults and keeping it in good condition you can reduce the chances of having an accident or break-down.
For example, you should keep the chain clean and oiled, check the brakes and brake cables, and make sure your tyres are pumped up and that the wheels run smoothly when they spin.
Caring for your bike will make it last longer, and it should only take you about an hour or two a month.

*In dim light or rain, cyclists are almost invisible to drivers. The only way to be seen clearly is to wear **fluorescent** reflector bands and use both front and rear lights.*

DON'T BE A MUG!

The risk of being mugged or attacked is pretty low, but there are a number of things you can do to keep yourself safe on the streets. Simple precautions include travelling with a friend and keeping to well-lit main roads when you have to walk somewhere. It is also best to avoid deserted and wooded or bushy areas if you can, and to resist the temptation of taking short cuts through alleyways or across waste ground, where people can lurk unseen.

Protect your possessions

It is also important to protect your possessions when you are out and about. One simple option is to only take a small amount of cash with you and reduce the number of valuable goods that you carry. Try not to have items such as mobile phones or MP3 players on show. Keep them in a pocket. Cover any valuable jewellery with a scarf.

If someone does grab your bag or demand your valuables, give them up rather than fight to keep them. Your things can be replaced and it is not worth taking the risk of being hurt, or worse. If you are scared or attacked, shout about it. Don't be shy – screaming can scare off an attacker and get help fast.

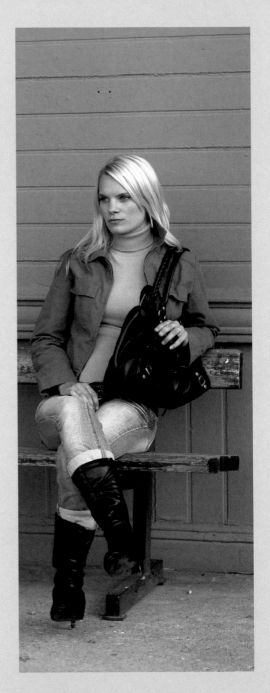

Protect your possessions by carrying your bag close to your body, with the fastenings done up, and facing towards you.

To keep safe on the streets:

- Stay alert. Be aware of what's going on around you and keep your eyes and ears open. Talking on the phone or listening to an MP3 player as you walk is not a good idea.

- Trust your instincts. If you feel that something isn't safe, you are probably right.

- If you think someone is following you, go straight into a shop and tell the shopkeeper.

TIP

 **HOW STREETWISE ARE YOU?**

Try this quiz then turn to page 50 to see if you're streetwise or street-simple!

1) **When walking down a street alone do you:**
   a) Keep to well lit roads and avoid quiet streets, alleys, or shortcuts and set your mobile to silent or vibrating so you don't attract attention if it goes off.
   b) Try to look confident and walk quickly with your head up.
   c) Pop in your headphones and listen to music to make the walk more interesting?

2) **What colour traffic light can you legally cycle through?**
   a) Red   b) Amber   c) Green

3) **At a party you meet some people who you get on really well with, so when one of them offers you a lift home do you:**
   a) Say thanks but explain that you have already got a lift.
   b) Say yes but tell one of your friends who you have gone with.
   c) Say yes because it will save you money?

4) **When you're cycling along a road and want to take a left turn, what is the first thing you do?**
   a) Look behind you at the traffic.
   b) Put your arm out to indicate you plan to turn.
   c) Brake to slow down.

Safe Surfing

Going online can be both useful and fun. It's a great way to find information quickly, chat to people around the world, download music and films, and much more. But the Internet can have a downside. For example, you can be duped by **chatroom** liars, have your personal details stolen and abused, or receive unwanted and nasty emails or texts. Reduce the risk of Internet abuse by getting cyber-savvy.

PICK AND CHOOSE

There are some great websites out there, but there is also a lot of rubbish. When you search for homework help just remember that not all sites are reliable and that any facts you find should be checked against a reliable source before you use them. When you use a search engine you also risk opening up sites with offensive or pornographic material. You can configure your computer to filter out these types of sites and report any you find to your **Internet service provider (ISP)**.

Catching a virus

Viruses are computer programs that are deliberately designed to cause problems for computer users. At worst, they can wreck your computer. **Spyware** programs are not viruses but they can be a nuisance when they get into your system. They may cause you to be inundated by annoying pop-up ads, or even allow someone else to take control of your PC.

These problem programs can arrive via email, **instant messenger (IM)**, your Internet connection, or even your web browser if you visit the wrong website. Protect your computer from unwanted invaders by buying or downloading good anti-virus and anti-spyware software, and be sure to update it regularly.

Getting it Wrong

There are **copyright** laws that protect images, song files, and other information so make sure that you do not illegally use, post, share, or distribute stuff you find or download on the Internet. This goes for schoolwork, too. You can get into serious trouble for **plagiarism**, which is copying and pasting large blocks of text from the Internet and try to pass it off as your own work!

Getting it Right

Setting up a **blog** site is a great way to share your thoughts and opinions with your friends. However, make sure that is all you share by following these tips:

- Protect the blog with a password, so that only the people you invite can access the site.

- On a public blog, never publish photos of yourself or your friends.

- Never give out personal information about yourself or your friends – for instance your home address, the name of your school, or your mobile phone number.

Most of us can't imagine life without the Internet. But be aware that it can also open the door to offensive, threatening, or unwanted sites or people.

In the chatroom

Chatting to people online can be a great way to spend time, but talking to people you cannot see also has real risks because it is easy for people to lie. Sometimes this is a white lie, for example when someone boasts that they have a better job than they do in real life. However, sometimes it is more serious, for example when a 40-year-old creep passes himself off as an attractive 15-year-old boy to a lonely girl.

Simple systems

There are a number of basic things you can do to weed out the creeps in a chatroom. Find out about the privacy settings on Facebook, Bebo, and other social networking sites before signing up. Once you're in a chatroom, keep your messages public. Only join a private chatroom with people you already know because if you join with a stranger it is easier for them to hassle you.

Finally, never give out photos or any personal details to anyone you do not already know in real life in case they try to trace you. Whatever online contacts might say to you, or however friendly they may seem, in reality you don't know anything for certain about them, so keep your distance. It is also a good idea to use a chatroom nickname that is different from your screen name so that cyber predators cannot track you down easily.

Take control

One of the great things about online chatting is that you are totally in control. It might be hard to escape an annoying person in the classroom, but if you don't like what someone is saying online you can simply log off. If someone says something you think is really dodgy or makes you feel uncomfortable, then you should also tell your parents or the chatroom moderator. You could be saving not only yourself but also someone else a lot of trouble in the future.

Getting it Right

Never arrange to meet anyone that you chat to on the Internet in person. Meeting someone you have only been in touch with online can be very dangerous. If you really feel you want to risk a meeting, then for your own safety you must tell a parent or caregiver – and take them or a couple of friends with you to the meeting. Always insist that you meet up in the daytime in a busy public place, such as a shopping centre. If your online contact tries to persuade you not to do this, cancel the meeting – fast!

 Anyone can become a victim of online deception. It has nothing to do with being easy to fool – and neither are girls the only targets. Online fraudsters can be very clever, so take the greatest care.

Getting it Wrong

In 2008 a 31-year-old Belgian man called Duval struck up a conversation with a 13-year-old teenage girl in a chatroom. After more than 3,000 emails and many mobile phone calls, Duval flew to Montreal, Canada and invited his victim to meet with him in his hotel room. When the girl went missing, her parents called the police. After checking her computer and reading her emails, the police tracked the pair down at a hotel room. She had a lucky escape, but many girls and boys have not been so lucky.

Cyber bullying

Cyber bullying is when someone uses email, instant messaging, chat rooms, or blogs to insult or threaten someone, spread rumours about them, or otherwise deliberately upset them. This type of bullying can affect someone not just at school, but anywhere and any time.

Some cyber bullies may not realise what harm they are doing. They may think that sending stupid messages, or posting gossip, facts, or photos of people without asking them is just a big joke.

The fact is that uploaded information is out there for everyone to see, and the victim of the "joke" may find it anything but funny. And remember that giving out information about someone's private identity, thus making it available to strangers, is not only wrong but dangerous.

Don't bottle things up. If you are being bullied, the first thing to do is talk to someone – a parent or carer, a teacher at your school, an aunt or uncle. Other people will be able to help you make it stop.

Bullies are usually cowards. By blocking their number or posting things on a website anonymously or from an unknown location, they think they can hide who they are. However, there are a number of ways that you can use technology to fight cyber bullies.

- If you are getting problem text messages, tell your mobile phone company or your Internet service provider about the bullying. They may be able to track the bully down.

- Use blocking software. You can block instant messages from certain people or use mail filters to block emails from specific email addresses. (See the TIP box below.)

- Log into a chatroom with a different user ID or nickname so the bully won't know who you are.

- Change your mobile phone number and only give it out to friends you trust.

What to do about cyber bullying

If you are suffering from cyber bullying, one thing you should *not* do is reply to bullying text messages or emails because this could make matters worse. If you don't respond, the bully is likely to get bored and move on.

If the bullying continues, save or copy and paste into a Word file any nasty emails, voicemails, or things posted on your profile, so you can use them as proof. This evidence can be used to catch the bully and stop them. If the bullying persists for too long or escalates to physical threats, you should also notify the police.

To block messages from a particular person on your computer:

1. Click on the person's name in the contact list to open a range of options: one of these is "Block".

2. Click on "Block" and you should not receive messages from this person anymore.

(Block is sometimes called "Ignore", and if just clicking on it doesn't work, have a look in your Preferences, or see if there is a Block/Ignore button in the chatroom you use.)

Privacy issues

Nothing is really ever private or temporary when you are online. The things you do online can be sent all over the world, time and again, and the information you reveal online can be used to trace you or commit acts of cyber bullying. There are a number of ways of protecting your online identity and limiting the risks involved.

Spam alert

"**Spam**" is unwanted emails from people you do not know. These can include chain email letters that you are supposed to send on to people in your address list. Sometimes these can be very nasty. One 13-year-old girl was terrified when she received an email that included a picture of a dead child with the threat that this would be her if she did not forward the email to 15 of her friends. The simple solution to these kinds of spam or threats is to delete them immediately.

Gone phishing

Phishing is when fraudsters try to fool you into revealing personal information for criminal gain. They send out a number of official-looking emails or pop-ups asking you to visit a (fake) website and enter personal or private information, such as passwords and bank account numbers. Sometimes they pretend to be well-known high street banks. If some poor person takes the bait, the identity thieves use their information to remove money from their bank accounts. It is quite hard to tell phishing emails or web pages from real ones. But remember that no reputable organization would ask for all that information in an email or open web page, so NEVER provide it.

Here are some tips to help you avoid email scams:

- Never open email attachments from people you do not know.
- Ask your ISP about spam and junk mail filters to block nuisance mails.
- Do not click on any links in spam emails you receive. You do not know where you will end up, and it could make your computer vulnerable to viruses.
- Never forward spam on to your friends, even if chain emails promise great money rewards, or contain threats.

TIP

 Think carefully before you let someone take photos of you with a mobile phone. They can be changed and shared around very easily. Once it's out there, anyone can see it!

Getting it Right

If you are going into a new chatroom or blog site, make sure you choose nicknames and screen names carefully. Web experts recommend that you create a unique password or screen name that has a mixture of letters and numbers, and which doesn't give any important information away. For example, never use your birth date or street name as a password, and try not to indicate whether you are male or female.

Online gaming

Online gaming allows you to create new identities in a virtual world, or take part in adventures with people on the other side of the world. Online gaming risks include meeting strangers who may trick you into revealing your personal or financial details.

Another hazard can be viruses and other nuisance programs hidden in game files that you can download. However, using a computer security system such as a **firewall** should guard against these viruses.

Online gambling is big business worldwide. But don't be tempted by the lure of fast money. For most people, the only pockets they manage to line belong to the owners of the gaming sites.

Gambling

Gambling on the Internet has become increasingly popular. Although teenagers can only legally play for free and without any risk of losing real money, there are other risks.

Think about why gambling sites would offer you free games in the first place. Free sites can be good fun, but they can also encourage you to develop an **addiction** to gambling. After a while, you may be tempted to start gambling for real money as soon as (or even before) you are legally old enough to do so.

The problem with this is twofold: first, under-age gambling is against the law; second, you could become addicted to gambling for life. Not only would this put you at risk of being cheated by fraudsters, but it could lead to serious debt and untold misery in the future.

Getting it Wrong

It is possible to become addicted to being online. As a result, people may find themselves isolated from friends and family, and this can lead to depression. To stop this happening to you, make sure you develop other interests, and spend time doing other things with friends. If you play online games too often and for too long, without taking regular breaks, you also risk repetitive strain injury to your hands and wrists. In South Korea the average high school student spends 23 hours per week gaming online, and the country considers Internet addiction a major public health issue!

QUIZ
ARE YOU AN ONLINE ADDICT?

Answer this quiz to find out if you are addicted to the Internet. Then turn to page 50 for the verdict.

Then turn to page 50 for the verdict.

- Do you think about your online games or conversations during the rest of the day and plan your next online session?

- Do you find you have to spend more and more time online before you have had enough?

- Have you tried before to control or cut back on your Internet time but failed?

- Do you feel restless, moody, or irritable when you miss a couple of days or more of Internet use?

- Do you frequently stay online longer than you planned or than you know you should?

- Have you missed out on something important, like a great day out or failing to hand in important coursework, because of the Internet?

- Have you lied to people about how much time you spend online?

- Do you often go online to escape from problems, such as feelings of anxiety?

UNDER PRESSURE

At certain times of your life you face a lot of pressure – pressure to fit in, to please other people, to do or try things you feel unhappy about. Some pressures are normal and possibly useful, like the stress you feel before taking an exam, or rehearsing your lines for a show. Other pressures – such as the pressure to look right, to try drugs, or join a gang – can be more risky.

UNHEALTHY EATING

Some people try to alter the way they look by dieting. This is fine if the diet is for health reasons, and followed sensibly. However, strict dieting can sometimes result in an eating disorder. **Anorexia** is a condition where people eat so little that they may end up starving themselves. It is a serious illness, and, in the worst cases, can result in death. **Bulimia** is an equally serious condition where people "binge eat" huge quantities of food, and then get rid of the food by vomiting or taking laxatives. Anorexics and bulimics risk serious, long-term damage to their health. If you think you or someone you know has an eating disorder, get help as fast as you can (check out the websites and helplines at the end of this book).

Smoking is a risk that your body can do without. One in ten of the chemicals in cigarettes are carcinogenic (cause cancer), which is why long-term smoking can kill you. Some people seem to think smoking is cool, but they are seriously mistaken. Smoking will leave you with smelly clothes and hair, stained teeth, bad breath, a hacking cough, and dry, wrinkled skin. It is also so expensive that you won't have much money left for anything else. So, no – not cool at all!

Getting it **Wrong**

Bodywise

You may be sick of hearing about the importance of a healthy diet and getting a good night's sleep, but these things make a real difference. It's worth remembering that regularly getting enough sleep and eating a decent diet makes you look good, feel good, and ensures you have enough energy to fit in all the things you want to do in your day. Without nine or ten hours of sleep every night, teenagers might find they have problems concentrating, which can affect schoolwork. They may also find themselves less able to deal with emotional problems and become easily depressed.

Body art

Tattoos and body piercing have become very popular, but before you rush out to get some, be aware of the risks. Both tattooing and piercing involve breaking the skin. If unsterile needles have been used, you risk infection with some serious diseases, including **HIV**. Also, think about how much your style or tastes have changed in the past few years. Will you still want to be covered in serpents and skulls when you're older?

We all know it's unfair, but appearances do count. You may risk not getting the job you want if a future employer is put off by your body piercing and tattoos.

THE DEAL WITH DRUGS

Drugs change the way your body works. Whether injected, snorted, or swallowed, once drugs are in your bloodstream they travel around your body and reach your brain, where they basically intensify or dull your senses and make you feel high or relaxed. The problem is they can also create **hallucinations**, affect your sight, coordination, and speech, can make you unconscious or unable to move, or in the worst case, even kill you.

The risks

When you're a teenager your body is growing and going through massive changes as you develop into an adult. Taking drugs can have long-lasting consequences. It may be true that one hit won't usually kill you, but using drugs (and alcohol and tobacco) when you are young increases the risk of becoming addicted. As well as the serious health problems addiction brings, addicts also end up detached from the world by dropping out of activities they used to love, often becoming angry and aggressive over

In an ideal world it should be easy for you to say "no" to drugs or alcohol — and have that totally accepted, without being made to feel uncool, or "chicken". However, in the real world it is often not so easy. If you feel the need to back up your refusal to take drugs or alcohol with a good reason, try one of these:

- Say you have coursework, an important sports match, or an exam to do the next day and you can't risk messing it up.

- Say you're unwell and don't want to get even worse and ruin everyone else's evening.

- Lie, and say you've tried it before and became really ill. Your doctor suspects that you have a dangerous allergy to the stuff.

- Say that your parents have threatened to stop your allowance and ground you for a month if you go home high or drunk.

- Say you recently met someone with a drug or drink problem and there is no way you want to go down that road.

TIP

nothing. Drug users can lose friends and confidence, and when they start to miss school and fail exams, they risk their chances of making a great future for themselves.

So why do it?

It may seem that lots of people are doing drugs, but they are not and you are not unusual or weird if you choose not to! Some people do drugs because they think that it will help them escape the stresses of the real world. In reality, drugs may temporarily alter your sense of reality, but afterwards most people feel far worse and more stressed. Taking substances like drugs or alcohol makes you take more dangerous risks and may make you do something you will deeply regret later.

The simplest answer to give people who try to press you into trying alcohol or drugs is NO. You should be able to say "no" firmly and confidently and without giving any explanation. But it isn't always as easy as that because some people can be really pushy. (See the Tip box on page 34 for some advice on how to deal with this.)

These two photos of the same young crystal meth addict were taken 18 months apart. It is easy to see how badly her health and looks have been damaged by the drug.

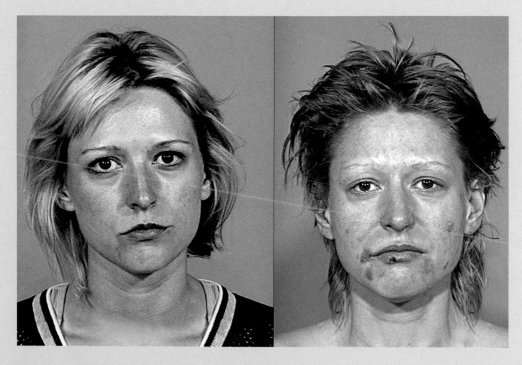

You should never keep quiet about abuse. If you are the victim of neglect, or physical or sexual abuse, it is important that you tell someone you trust as soon as you can.

If someone touches you in places that make you feel uncomfortable or hurts you, or tells you to take your clothes off when you don't want to, this is sexual abuse and you need to tell someone you trust immediately. Remember, it is never *your* fault – however friendly you have been to this person before it happened, or whoever they are. Their behaviour is unacceptable and it must be stopped.

Getting it
Right

WHAT IS ABUSE?

The temptation to abuse their own bodies with drugs, alcohol, or tobacco is not the only risk some people face. They may also suffer abuse from other people.

Physical abuse is when someone hits, punches, or otherwise hurts someone else. Sexual abuse is when someone forces sexual contact upon someone else without their consent. Physical and sexual abuse is always unacceptable, and particularly so when the abuser is an adult and the victim is a child or young person.

Neglect is a type of abuse, too. Neglect is when parents or caregivers either do not provide children with their physical needs, such as adequate food, or medical care, or when they don't fulfil a child's emotional needs and constantly criticize, threaten, or shout at them.

The impact of abuse

As well as the immediate effects of any physical abuse, people who are or who have been abused often have trouble eating and sleeping. They may feel scared, depressed, or angry a lot of the time. They also feel cut off from friends and school life and lose all **self-esteem**.

The most important thing to recognise about abuse is that if it happens to you it is not, in any way, shape, or form, your fault or the result of anything you may or may not have done. Whatever anybody says to you or threatens you with, you are not to blame and must not risk letting the abuse continue.

Dealing with it

Never listen if an abuser threatens you with trouble if you tell anyone what they have been doing. They are only saying this because they know that what they've done is terribly wrong, and they are scared of being found out. The more usual outcome of letting people know what has happened is that the abuser is never allowed to behave like that again – which can only be a good thing. If you or someone you know has been or is being abused you must report it immediately to someone you trust – a parent, caregiver, teacher, doctor, or the police.

This is more straightforward when the abuser is a stranger, but it may be harder to do if the abuser is someone you know – especially if they are a member of your family who treats you kindly most of the time. However you have to go through with it – to reduce the risk to yourself, to other people who might also be harmed by the abuser, and also to the abuser themselves, so that they can get the help they need to sort out their problem.

You can get free, confidential help from a variety of different organizations (see page 53 for some suggestions). They can advise you on what you should do if you think someone you know is being abused.

BAD BEHAVIOUR

Anti-social behaviour is any activity that impacts on other people in the community in a negative way. It includes letting off fireworks late at night in a quiet street, getting into fights, shoplifting, or vandalising property. Anti-social behaviour puts teens at risk because they may get hurt or get into trouble with the law. For instance, more than half of the people injured and burnt by fireworks each year are under 16 years old.

When you hang about with a bad crowd, there is increased pressure to try drugs and drink. This makes it more likely that you will get injured in fights because statistically alcohol and substance abuse increases the likelihood and severity of violence.

Find alternatives

Some young people end up committing petty crimes, such as vandalism, graffiti, or shoplifting, because their friends do it or because they like the buzz they get from trying something risky. Some people think these activities are not that serious but they are all criminal offences for which you could be arrested and end up with a criminal record.

The best way of avoiding risks like these is to stay away from friends who make these mistakes, and keep busy! Find healthier and low-risk activities, such as sports, a part-time job, or a craft project.

A good example is an alternative to graffiti vandalism. A great many of the kids who spray graffiti have a lot of artistic skill and talent. If they transferred those talents to canvas or wood they would have a great piece of art to hang, give to friends, or even sell for extra spending money. And they wouldn't run the risk of having their hard work spoiled or painted over by other "graffiti artists"!

What does it give you?

If you sit down and think about it, finding something else to do that actually improves your life (such as sport, or earning extra cash), or that teaches you something valuable for later life (such as a mechanics' course, or classes to improve your computer or craft skills), has got to be better than spending your spare time on a mindless course of destruction.

Anti-social behaviour gives you precisely *nothing*. It does nothing for your self-esteem, results in nothing but upset and anger from everyone around you, puts you in danger, and may possibly leave you with a criminal record, and a bad reputation that could stick with you for the rest of your life.

Knife crime is becoming increasingly common. In 2007 26 teenagers were shot or stabbed in London alone.

Some young people carry knives or guns for "protection", but carrying a weapon actually increases the likelihood that you'll become a victim of crime. If you get into an argument while carrying a weapon, you are more likely to use it. You could end up hurting or killing someone, or the weapon could be taken from you and used on you instead. You risk a heavy fine or prison just for carrying a weapon, and a heavier prison sentence if you hurt someone.

Getting it Wrong

If someone is so angry you think they are going to turn violent, just walk away.

SELF-DEFENCE

When someone is angry or threatening you, the best response is not to shout or fight back as this is only likely to make matters worse. Instead, try to defuse the situation.

For instance, if someone is bullying you or trying to lure you into a fight, you can simply walk away – ideally towards a crowded place where they won't dare continue their taunts. Alternatively, you could make it appear that you agree with them until you get a chance to escape. It is also best to quietly hand over your bag to a mugger rather than struggle with them and risk getting hurt.

Getting it Right

When faced with a difficult situation don't just follow along because you don't want to look uncool in front of your friends. Take a moment to think about what you really feel and think about and judge the options for yourself. Trust your instincts and get out of a situation you feel uncomfortable with before anything bad can happen.

Resisting pressure

Have you ever been faced with another teenager wanting you to do something dangerous, harmful, or illegal? The first thing to remember is that you have an absolute right to be treated with respect – which means the right to refuse to do something you don't want to do without being bullied or taunted.

The best weapon to use against people who confront you or try to push you into doing something you don't want to do is assertiveness. Being assertive simply means being firm without being aggressive.

To become more assertive, the first step is to recognise that everyone has the right to say "no" and to refuse a request to do something they don't want to do without feeling guilty. So, if someone is trying to persuade you to do something you feel uncomfortable with, look them right in the eye and with a serious face say simply, "No, I don't want to do that".

CAN YOU DEAL WITH PEER PRESSURE?

Does peer pressure control you or do you know your own mind? Answer "yes" or "no" to these questions and then turn to page 50 to find out what your answers mean.

1) Have you ever bought clothes or had your hair cut to look like your friends?

2) Do you pick on people just because everyone else in your group is doing it?

3) Have you ever helped a friend cheat with schoolwork or during a test?

4) Have you ever tried cigarettes or alcohol at a party or with friends because everyone else was doing it?

5) Have you ever joined a club or team you weren't particularly interested in, to be with a friend?

6) Have you ever lied to your parents to be with friends or because friends told you to?

7) Have you ever done anything you later regretted just to make somebody like you?

8) Have you ever done something physically risky or illegal because others were doing it?

9) Do you sometimes get talked into doing things that you regret later?

10) Have your friends ever talked you into doing something illegal or harmful?

If The Worst Happens . . .

An emergency is a sudden and unexpected crisis that threatens people or property and requires immediate attention. By its very nature an emergency is something you cannot really plan for, but there are precautions you can take. You should also know some of the safety procedures used in an emergency, just in case you ever need to use them.

Be Prepared

When you are in charge of a house, either at home or babysitting at someone else's home, you should be prepared. To start with, your parents should know where you are and you should know how to get hold of them at all times. You should also have a list of local emergency services and telephone numbers of adults you can call if anything goes wrong. It is also important to make sure the house is secure, so lock all the doors and windows.

Never open the door to someone you don't know. If the phone rings, never let a caller know that no one is home. Simply say that your parents are busy and take a message.

In case of fire

The best preparation for fire is to reduce the risk of having one in the first place. Take great care when using candles, lighters, or matches and never leave them unattended. When you are cooking, remember to

Getting it Right

To reduce the risk of being trapped or injured by fire, every home should be fitted with smoke alarms that make a loud beeping noise when they sense smoke.

- There should be smoke alarms on every floor of a house, especially by bedrooms.

- Test smoke alarms monthly to make sure they are working.

- Replace old batteries with new ones at least once a year.

Never throw water directly on to a chip pan fire. It will explode. Instead, cover the pan with a damp towel.

use a timer so you don't forget what is cooking. Remember to switch off appliances after using them.

Get your family to discuss and plan an escape route that you can all use in case of fire. Fires can burn fast and smoke can make a home very dark, so you should all know where the fire escapes or exits are located in case you need to use them. This is especially important in a house with two storeys or more.

The kitchen can be a dangerous place so follow these tips to keep safe.

TIP

- Turn pot handles so that they're not sticking out over the edge of the hob
- Use a heatproof stand for putting hot pans and pots on
- Use a thick, dry cloth or oven gloves to handle hot pans
- Keep cloths away from cookers so they do not catch fire
- Take great care with sharp knives.

Who to call in an emergency

If you find yourself or someone else in danger you should dial 999 immediately. You can call from any phone at no charge – calls to emergency numbers are free. The number gets you through to an operator who will link you up with whichever of the different emergency services you need – the fire brigade, ambulance service, police, or the coastguards.

If you are not sure which service you need, the 999 operator will help you decide before putting you through to the right emergency service. Their operator will then ask for more details.

Getting it
Wrong

While it is absolutely right to call emergency numbers in a real emergency, in many countries it is considered a crime to dial 999 as a joke or to ask about something minor like getting a cat out of a tree. If you take up an emergency operator's time, it could cause a delay getting help to people involved in a real emergency, and you could be responsible for a tragedy.

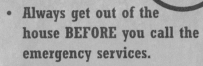

If you are involved in a fire:

- Always get out of the house BEFORE you call the emergency services.

- Never stop to collect belongings, just get yourself and people you are with outside fast!

- Shout "Fire" as you run to make sure everyone else in a big building is alerted.

- Feel a closed door before opening it. If it is hot, there may be fire on the other side so get out another way.

- When escaping, stay low to the floor. Smoke rises so the safest air to breathe is down low.

- If your clothes catch on fire, drop to the floor and roll over to put them out.

When phoning the emergency services try to stay as calm as possible. The more information you can give the operator about where you are and what has happened, the better.

What to do after a collision

If you are involved in a minor road accident, the first thing to do is to check that no one (including you) is injured. You should then note down the other person's name, address, and, if necessary, car registration number. You should also write down the contact details of at least two witnesses, if possible. One of the people involved in the accident should report the incident to the police, if possible, from the scene of the accident. If you have a mobile with a camera, it is also a good idea to take pictures of the scene and jot down what happened, in case you need to explain it to the police.

You might also think about booking a visit to the doctor. Even if you don't think you are hurt, injuries sometimes show up later.

✚ FIRST AID

First aid is giving basic assistance to someone who has just been injured, or become suddenly unwell, until proper medical assistance arrives. Ideally, we should all get first aid training so we know exactly what to do when someone is hurt. But having even a small amount of knowledge of first aid could make the difference between life and death.

BURNS AND SCALDS

To deal with burns and scalds: put the injury under cold running water for at least 10 minutes (as long as the skin is not cut), or cover it with clean, wet towels. Take off or cut away clothing or jewellery near the affected area, unless it is stuck to the burn. Do not use ice, ointments, or anything else on the wound, but just put some cling film or a clean pad over it.

CHOKING

If someone is choking: hit them firmly between the shoulder blades up to five times with the base of your hand. If this doesn't work, stand behind them, clasp your hands together tightly just above their navel (belly button), and pull inwards and upwards. If this doesn't work, call an ambulance immediately.

BLEEDING

To deal with someone who is bleeding: wear clean rubber gloves or put a clean plastic bag over your hand if you can. Try to stop the bleeding by putting pressure on the wound, for example, by holding your finger over the wound. Alternatively, put a clean cloth or bandage over the wound and hold it in place with a cloth strip, a belt, or even a tie.

POISONING

If someone has taken a poisonous substance: regardless of whether they just have a stomach ache or are throwing up, call a doctor or ambulance immediately. While you are waiting for help, stay with them and find out as much as you can about what the person took, and how much. Keep the bottle or container with you to help the medics.

• C H E C K L I S T •

THE RECOVERY POSITION

If you are present when someone has had an accident, or has been pulled out of water, and seems to be unconscious, you can help by putting them in the recovery position.

- First check that airways (breathing tubes) are clear, and there is nothing in the mouth to stop them breathing. Place the person on their back, tilt the head back, and lift the chin. To check breathing, watch, listen, and feel their chest.

- The person's arm nearest to you should be positioned at a right angle to the body, with the elbow bent, and palm facing upwards.

- Lift their other arm towards you, over the body, and gently roll the person towards you on to their side. Position this arm across the body, with the hand tucked under the cheek.

- Adjust the person's uppermost leg, so that the knee is bent at a right angle and touching the ground in front of their body, with the foot flat on the ground.

- Tilt the person's head back to ensure that the airway is open.

- Call the emergency services for immediate help.

IMPORTANT NOTE: You should NEVER move someone if you suspect they may have a back or neck injury.

AFTERCARE

When you have been through a crisis, accident, or trauma of any kind, you may find that the emotional upset takes longer to get over than any physical damage. In most cases, it is wrong to ignore the incident or to try to pretend that it never happened to you; instead it is better to talk about it. You could either talk to friends or family, or you could consider seeing a **counsellor** or **therapist**. These are trained, qualified professionals who help others work through their problems or issues.

Seeking help from professionals for stress, addiction, or emotional difficulties is not a sign of weakness. There is no difference between seeing a counsellor and seeing a doctor for a physical illness. The degree of importance is the same – you need help as soon as possible to sort out a problem that is affecting your life.

Change your ways

Counsellors and therapists can also help you deal with addictions to cigarettes, alcohol, or drugs – or to control and stop other risky kinds of behaviour. A counsellor or adviser will not tell you what to do or judge you. They will ask you how you would like things to be different, and encourage you to suggest ideas of how you could change your behaviour. Then they will help you find ways to make those changes a reality.

How counselling works

Most people have a meeting with their counsellor or therapist once a week or fortnightly, either alone or with parents. During the sessions the counsellor may ask you questions about the main problem in your life, but you can also feel free to talk about anything that is on your mind. You can continue going to sessions with your counsellor for however long you feel you need to work through your problems.

TIP

If you think you would like to talk to a counsellor or therapist you can ask your parent or carer to help you find one. Your doctor can recommend one, or you can ask a teacher, school nurse, youth advisor, or religious leader.

Sometimes it is easier to discuss all your feelings honestly with someone who does not know your friends and family, but who can still understand and is experienced in helping people with similar difficulties.

Alongside talking things through with your counsellor, there are a number of things you can do to help yourself through tough times. You might try writing down your feelings in a journal or diary; or try relaxation exercises, listening to music, or exercising. When you are finding life tough, it's important to carry on doing the things that you enjoy. So, play football, watch a film, read a book, and spend time with your friends – anything that makes you smile.

Getting it Right

QUIZ RESULTS

ANSWERS FOR QUIZ ON PAGE 15

1) False — there is no band on Earth worth losing your hearing for.
2) False — in some ways you are more likely to get injured when you are inexperienced, so everyone who plays a sport should wear the recommended safety gear.
3) True
4) True
5) True
6) False — polluted water contains disease-causing micro-organisms, which can enter the body through the ears, eyes, nose, mouth, or through broken skin.
7) False — avoid the sun at the peak of the day, between 11am–3pm.
8) False — always swim with a friend so they can call for help if you get into unexpected difficulties.
9) Obviously false! Warming up means stretching and loosening your muscles to prepare them for a serious workout!

ANSWERS FOR QUIZ ON PAGE 21

All As: Congratulations! You know what you are doing — just make sure that you always put into practice what you know.
All Bs: You're not totally lacking in street sense but you need to read some safety advice more carefully.
All Cs: You shouldn't be allowed out of the house without a minder!

ANSWERS FOR QUIZ ON PAGE 31

If you answered "yes" to five or more of the questions in this quiz, you are probably spending too much time glued to your screen and may even have an addiction to the Internet or online gaming. Try to gradually cut down on the number of hours you spend at the screen — perhaps even setting an alarm clock to remind you when your time is up. Make a promise to yourself that you will go out with friends regularly, exercise more, and that you will rejoin that sports team or band you left. As you gradually regain a social life, you will start to enjoy being part of the real world more and more and will not be so reliant on the virtual world.

ANSWERS FOR QUIZ ON PAGE 41

Mostly "yes": You tend to do what your friends do and rarely stand up for yourself. The problem is that this probably leaves you feeling bad, which makes you less self-confident and even more likely to follow other people. Now is the time to change. You know when something feels wrong, so speak up for yourself and do what you think is best. It will feel good and give you new confidence and self-respect.
Mostly "no": You are likely to keep safe because you are smart! You are confident enough to stand your ground against peer pressure and do not follow the crowd. You have a strong sense of what is right and wrong and you are unlikely to let anyone pull you in the wrong direction.
About half "yes" and half "no": You manage to think for yourself and do the right thing most of the time. When you don't, it is probably because you don't really know where you stand on an issue, so you just go with the flow. The best thing to do is trust your instincts. If something inside you says no, go with that — you don't have to explain your decision; you just have to go with it.

20 THINGS TO REMEMBER

1 Take positive risks! It's important to be safe, but so long as you take precautions and make sensible choices, no one is saying you should never try sky-diving or white-water rafting!

2 Think about the potential dangers in a situation, but don't make yourself scared. The chances of something bad happening to you are low, but it pays to be aware of the risks involved.

3 Take your time. Don't rush into making a decision. Assess the risks and think about why you might do something.

4 Be assertive. Learn how to stand your ground firmly and convincingly – and without anger.

5 Kit yourself out. Make sure you have and wear the right gear for any sports you do.

6 Get organized. Being safe is about thinking ahead. How will you get back from that party? If you are cycling, do you need bike lights?

7 Trust your instincts. If it feels wrong, say "no" right away.

8 Be streetwise. Avoid travelling alone if you can. Don't let pride prevent you calling out for help if you need it.

9 If you get a part-time job, check out what permits you need and what hours you can work.

10 If in doubt, talk it out. Learn from other people's experiences.

11 If someone bothers you online, log off. Create a new screen name and start over.

12 Keep parents and caregivers informed about where you are and who you are with.

13 Don't take chances on the road. Belt up and only take lifts with responsible drivers. Anything else just isn't worth the risk.

14 Take care of your body. You've only got one to last you a lifetime.

15 Avoid cigarettes, drugs, and alcohol. There are far better ways of spending your cash.

16 Walk away from trouble. The best thing to do when someone is being aggressive or trying to fight with you is to leave the situation.

17 Learn some basic first aid skills. They could save someone's life – or even your own.

18 Try not to flash cash or belongings around. Keep valuables and purses covered and stowed away safely when you are out.

19 Keep emergency phone numbers on you at all times and, if you can, carry a mobile phone. Check it is fully charged and has credit before you go out so that you can always get help if you need it.

20 Shout about it! If something happens to you that harms you or makes you unhappy, tell someone about it and get help. That is the only way that things will change.

Further Information

BOOKS

Cyber-safe Kids, Cyber-savvy Teens: Helping Young People Learn to Use the Internet Safely and Responsibly, Nancy E. Willard (Jossey Bass, 2007)

Issues That Concern You: Internet Safety, Hayley Mitchell Haugen and Susan Musser (Editors) (Greenhaven Press, 2008)

Perspectives on Violence: Travel Safety, Gus Gedatus (LifeMatters, 2000)

What's the Deal? (10-book series on all aspects of drug abuse and addiction), Karla Fitzhugh, Jane Bingham, and Suzanna Drew-Edwards (Heinemann Library, 2006)

WEBSITES

http://kidshealth.org/teen/safety/safebasics/internet_safety.html
A website that offers tips for safe surfing on the Internet for young people.

http://www.bbc.co.uk/chatguide/teens/
This BBC website has tips for keeping safe in chatrooms.

http://endabuse.org/section/programs/teens
A safety plan that abused teenagers can follow.

http://vulpeculox.net/cycling/quiz/qstart.php
Take a cycling quiz to see if you really know what you're doing on your bike.

ORGANIZATIONS

Childline
http://www.childline.org.uk
A free 24-hour helpline for young people in the UK. Young people can call the helpline on 0800 1111 about any problem, at any time – day or night. ChildLine's counsellors are there to help you find ways to sort things out. ChildLine is also confidential, which means they won't tell anyone about your call unless you want them to talk to somebody for you, or you are in danger. Find out more on their website.

Crimestoppers
http://www.crimestoppers-uk.org
Crimestoppers is a UK charity aimed at putting criminals behind bars through an anonymous Freephone number: 0800 555 111.

National Society for the Prevention of Cruelty to Children (NSPCC)
http://www.nspcc.org.uk
The NSPCC offers a free 24-hour helpline on 0808 800 5000.

Victim Support
http://www.victimsupport.org.uk
An organization that gives free and confidential help to anyone who has been affected by crime. They provide practical information and they will also help you get counselling if you feel you need it. Look online for your local Victim Support branch.

St John's Ambulance
http://www.sja.org.uk/sja/training-courses/courses-for-young-people.aspx
SJA offers first aid training courses for young people from aged 7 to 18 years. Visit their website to find out more.

GLOSSARY

addiction physical dependence on something

anorexia eating disorder involving loss of appetite for food, severe weight loss, and muscle wasting

anti-social behaviour acting in a way that causes harassment, alarm, or distress to other people

blog online diary or journal where people can post messages for others to see and respond to

bulimia eating disorder in which a person binges (eats large amounts of food) and then vomits or uses laxatives to get rid of it in order to prevent weight gain

cancer abnormal, uncontrolled growth of cells in any part of the body, which can spread to surrounding or distant organs and can cause death

chatroom site on the Internet where a number of users can have an online conversation

cool-down short period of gentle exercise such as slow running or jogging done after a workout or competition to loosen muscles

copyright law that protects an original artistic or literary work

counsellor someone who gives advice about problems

decibel level measure of the intensity or loudness of a sound

entrepreneur person who takes the risk of organizing and operating a new business venture

firewall computer system that prevents unauthorised access to or from a private network

fluorescent bright vivid colour that glows in the dark

hallucination when a person sees, hears, smells, tastes, or feels something that is not really there

HIV stands for human immunodeficiency virus. It is the virus that causes AIDS. It is passed from one person to the other through infected blood and body fluids.

instant messenger (IM) service that allows users to send and receive short messages instantly via the Internet

Internet service provider (ISP) company that provides Internet access for a fee

peer someone who is your equal, for example is the same age as you